AMC Guide to Mount Washington and the Presidential Range

AMC Guide to Mount Washington and the Presidential Range

Fourth Edition

Appalachian Mountain Club
BOSTON, MASSACHUSETTS

The trail descriptions in this book are taken from the *AMC White Mountain Guide*, 1987 edition, edited by Eugene S. Daniell III.

AMC GUIDE TO MOUNT WASHINGTON AND THE PRESIDENTIAL RANGE

Printed in the United States of America
Paperbound International Standard Book Number: 0-910146-67-5

Due to changes in conditions, use of the information in this book is at the sole risk of the user.

Cover photograph by Ron Paula
Cover design by Outside Designs
Composition by Shepard Poorman Communications Corp.

5 4 3   89 90 91

CONTENTS

To the Owner of This Book

The White Mtns. are an ever-changing area, and a guidebook to this region can never be more than a record of the way things were at a given moment in time. While every care has been taken to make this book as accurate as possible, changing conditions may render almost any trail difficult to follow, and use of the information in this book is at the sole risk of the user. The various maintaining organizations, including the AMC, reserve the right to discontinue any trail without notice, and expressly disclaim any legal responsibility for the condition of any trail. Trails can be rerouted or abandoned or closed by landowners. Signs are stolen or fall from their posts. Storms may cause blowdowns or landslides, which can obliterate a trail for an entire climbing season or longer. Trails may not be cleared of fallen trees and brush until late summer, and not all trails are cleared every year. Logging operations can cover trails with slash and add a bewildering network of new roads. Momentary inattention to trail markers, particularly arrows at sharp turns, or misinterpretation of signs or guidebook descriptions, can cause one to become separated from all but the most heavily traveled paths. So please remember that a guidebook is an aid to planning, not a substitute for observation and judgment. We request your help in keeping this book accurate; new editions are published at intervals of about four years. If you encounter a problem with a trail, or with a map or description in this book, please let us know. Any comments or corrections can be sent to the Presidential Range Guide, AMC, 5 Joy St., Boston MA 02108. The comments of a person who is inexperienced or unfamiliar with a trail are often particularly useful. This book belongs to the entire hiking community not just to the AMC and the people who produce it.

TRIP PLANNING

The descriptions in this book are intended to apply approximately from Memorial Day to Columbus Day. In some years snowdrifts may remain into late May—and much later in some ravines—and there will certainly be some severe weather in the early fall. Many trails are far more difficult to follow (or even dangerous) when snow or ice is present. Spring and fall are particularly dangerous seasons in the mountains, since the weather may be pleasant in the valleys and brutal on the summits and ridges. A great portion of the serious incidents in the mountains occur in the spring and fall. Wintry conditions can occur above treeline in any month of the year. Even in midsummer, hikers above treeline should be prepared for cold weather with a wool sweater, hat, mittens, and a wind parka, which will give comfort on sunny but cool days and protection against sudden storms.

Plan your trip schedule with safety in mind. Consider the general strenuousness of the trip: the overall distance, the amount of climbing, and the roughness of the terrain. Get a weather report. Be aware of the fact that most forecasts are not intended to apply to the mountain region, and a day that is sunny in the lowlands may well be inclement in the mountains. The National Weather Service in Concord NH (603-225-5191) issues a recreational forecast for the White Mtn. region and broadcasts it each morning; this forecast is posted at Pinkham Notch Camp at about 8 AM. Plan to finish your hike with daylight to spare (remember that days are shorter in late summer and fall). Hiking after dark, even with flashlights (which frequently fail), makes finding trails more difficult and crossing streams hazardous. Let someone else know where you will be hiking, and do not let inexperienced people get separated from the group. Many dirt roads are not passable until about Me-

morial Day, and the WMNF closes many of its roads with
locked gates from November to May; many trips are much
longer when the roads are not open.

FOLLOWING TRAILS

Hikers should always carry a compass and carefully keep
track of their approximate location on the map. The best
compass for hiking is the protractor type: a circular compass that turns on a rectangular clear plastic base. Excellent compasses of this type, with leaflets which give ample
instructions in their use, are available for less than $10.
Such a compass is easily set to the bearing that you wish to
follow, and then it is a simple matter of keeping the compass needle aligned to north and following the arrow on the
base. More sophisticated and expensive compasses have
features designed for special applications which are not
useful in the woods; they are normally harder to use and
apt to cause confusion in an emergency situation. Directions of the compass given in the text are based on true
north instead of magnetic north, unless otherwise specified. There is a deviation of 16 to 17 degrees between true
north and magnetic north in the White Mtns. This means
that true north will be about 17 degrees to the right of
(clockwise from) the compass's north needle. If you take a
bearing from a map, you should add 17 degrees to the
bearing when you set your compass. On the map included
with this Guide, the black lines that run from bottom to
top are aligned with true north and south. Diagonal light-
brown lines point to magnetic north.

In general, trails are maintained to provide a clear path-
way while protecting and minimizing damage to the environment. Some may offer rough and difficult passage. Most
hiking trails are marked with paint on trees or rocks, or
with axe blazes cut into trees. The trails that compose the

Appalachian Trail through the White Mtns. are marked with vertical rectangular white paint blazes throughout. Side trails off the Appalachian Trail are usually marked with blue paint. Other trails are marked in other colors, the most popular being yellow. Except for the Appalachian Trail and its side trails, the color of blazing has no significance and may change without notice. Above timberline, cairns (piles of rocks) mark the trails. Where hikers have trodden out the vegetation, the footway is usually visible except when it is covered by snow or by fallen leaves. In winter, signs at trailheads and intersections and blazes also are often covered by snow.

If a trail is lost and is not visible to either side, it is usually best to backtrack right away to the last mark seen and look again from there. Trails following or crossing logging roads require special care at intersections in order to distinguish the trail from diverging roads, particularly since blazing is usually very sparse while the trail follows the road. Around shelters or campsites, trodden paths may lead in all directions, so look for signs and paint blazes.

If you become separated from a trail in the Presidentials, it is not necessarily a serious matter. Few people become truly lost; a moment's reflection and five minutes with the map will show that you probably know at least your approximate location and the direction to the nearest road, if nothing else. Most cases in which a person has become lost for any length of time involve panic and aimless wandering, so the most important first step is to take a break, make an inventory of useful information, decide on a course of action and stick to it. (The caution against allowing inexperienced persons to become separated from a group should be repeated here, since they are most likely to panic and wander aimlessly. Make sure also that all party members are familiar with the route of the trip and the names of the trails to be used.) In many instances, retracing your steps will lead you back to the point of departure from the trail. If you have carefully kept track of your location on the map, it will usually be possible to find a nearby stream, trail, or road to which a compass course may be followed. Most distances are short enough that it is possible, in the absence of alternatives, to reach a highway in half a day, or at most in a whole day, simply by going downhill, skirting the tops of any dangerous cliffs, until you come upon a river or brook. The stream should then be followed downward.

WHAT TO CARRY

Good things to have in your pack for a summer day hike in the White Mountains include maps, guidebook, water bottle (plastic soft-drink bottles work well), compass, knife, rain gear, windbreaker, wool sweater(s), hat, waterproof matches, enough food plus extra high-energy foods in reserve (such as chocolate or candy), first-aid supplies (including personal medicines, aspirin, adhesive bandages, gauze, and antiseptic), needle and thread, safety pins, nylon cord, trash bag, toilet paper, and a (small) flashlight with extra batteries. Wear comfortable hiking boots. Blue jeans are popular but, once wet, dry out very slowly. Most fabrics dry faster than cotton, and wool keeps much of its insulation value even when wet.

EMERGENCIES

For emergencies call the toll-free New Hampshire State Police number (1-800-852-3411) or Pinkham Notch Camp (603-466-2727).

Hypothermia, the most serious danger to hikers, is the loss of ability to preserve body heat because of injury, exhaustion, lack of sufficient food, and inadequate or wet clothing. Most of the dozens of deaths on Mt. Washington have resulted from hypothermia. The symptoms are uncontrolled shivering, impaired speech and movement, lowered body temperature, and drowsiness. The result is death, unless the victim (who will not understand the situation, due to impaired mental function) is rewarmed. In mild cases the victim should be given dry clothing and placed in a sleeping bag, perhaps with someone else in it to provide body heat, then quick-energy food, and, when full consciousness is regained, something warm (not hot) to drink. In severe cases only hospitalization offers hope for recovery. It is not unusual for a victim to resist treatment and even combat rescuers. It should be obvious that prevention of hypothermia is the only truly practical course. Most cases occur in temperatures above freezing; the most dangerous conditions involve rain, with wind, with temperatures below 50° F. Uncontrollable shivering should be regarded as an absolute evidence of hypothermia; this shivering will eventually cease on its own, but that is merely the sign that the body has given up the struggle and is sinking toward death.

Other Hazards

Mosquitoes and black flies are frequently encountered by hikers. Mosquitoes are worst in low, wet areas, and black flies make their most aggressive attacks in June and early July. There are no poisonous snakes or other dangerous animals in the mountains. Deer-hunting season is in November, when you'll see many more hunters than deer. Bears tend to keep well out of sight, but are a nuisance at some popular campsites.

BROOK CROSSINGS

Rivers and brooks are often crossed without bridges, and it is usually possible to jump from rock to rock; a hiking staff or stick is a great aid to balance. Use caution; several fatalities have resulted from hikers (particularly solo hikers) falling on slippery rocks and drowning in relatively small streams. If you need to wade across (which is often the safer course), wearing boots, but not necessarily socks, is recommended. Note that many crossings, which may only be a nuisance in summer, may be a serious hazard in cold weather when one's feet and boots must be kept dry. Higher waters, which can turn innocuous brooks into virtually uncrossable torrents, come in the spring as snow melts, or after heavy rainstorms, particularly in the fall when trees drop their leaves and take up less water. Do not plan hikes with potentially hazardous stream crossings during these high-water periods. Rushing current can make wading extremely hazardous, and several deaths have resulted. If you are cut off from roads by swollen streams, it is better to make a long detour, even if you need to wait and spend a night in the woods. Flood waters may subside within a few hours, especially in small brooks. It is particularly important not to camp on the far side of a brook from your exit point if the crossing is difficult and heavy rain is predicted.

DRINKING WATER

The pleasure of quaffing a cup of water fresh from a pure mountain spring is one of the traditional attractions of the mountains. Unfortunately, in many mountain regions, including the White Mtns., the presence of cysts of the intestinal parasite *Giardia lamblia* is becoming more and more common. It is impossible to be completely sure whether a given source is safe, no matter how clear the water or remote the location. The safest course is for day hikers to carry their own water, and for those who use sources in the woods to treat the water before drinking it. A conservative practice is to boil water for 20 minutes or to use an iodine-based disinfectant. Chlorine-based products, such as Halazone, are ineffective in water that contains organic impurities and they deteriorate quickly in the pack. Remember to allow extra contact time (and use twice as many tablets) if the water is very cold. The symptoms of giardiasis are severe intestinal distress and diarrhea. The principal cause of the spread of this noxious ailment is careless disposal of human waste. Keep it at least 200 ft. away from water sources. If there are no toilets nearby, dig a trench 6 to 8 in. deep (but not below the organic layer of the soil) for a latrine and cover it completely after use. The bacteria in the organic layer of the soil will then decompose the waste naturally.

DISTANCES AND TIMES

The distances and times that appear in the tables at the end of trail descriptions are cumulative from the starting point at the head of each table. Estimated distances are denoted by est. Small disagreements due to rounding will occasionally be observed in measured distances. The distances given will sometimes be found to differ from those on trails signs; we provide the most accurate distances available to us. There is no reliable method for estimating hiking times; in order to give inexperienced hikers some basis for planning, the times given in this book have been calculated by allowing a half hour for each mile or 1000 ft. of climbing. These times may be very inadequate for steep or rough trails, for hikers with heavy packs, or for large groups, particularly with inexperienced hikers. In winter, times are even less predictable: on a packed trail, times may be faster than in summer, but with heavy packs or in deep snow it may take two or three times the summer estimate.

FIRE REGULATIONS

Campfire permits are no longer required in the WMNF, but hikers who build fires are still legally responsible for any damage they may cause. During periods when there is a high risk of forest fires, the Forest Supervisor may temporarily close the entire WMNF against public entry. Such general closures apply only as long as the dangerous conditions prevail. Other forest lands throughout NH or ME may be closed during similar periods through proclamation by the respective governors. These special closures are given wide publicity so that local residents and visitors alike may realize the danger of fires in the woods.

PROTECTING THE BEAUTY OF THE MOUNTAINS

Please use special care above timberline. Extreme weather and a short growing season make these areas especially fragile. Just footsteps can destroy the toughest natural cover, so please try to stay on the trail or walk on rocks. And, of course, don't camp above timberline.

Once every campsite had a dump, and many trails became unsightly with litter. Now visitors are asked to bring trash bags and carry out everything—food, paper, glass, cans—they carry in. Cooperation with the "carry in/carry out" program has been outstanding, resulting in a great decrease in trailside litter over the past few years, and the concept has grown to "carry out more than you carried in." We hope you will join in the effort. Your fellow backcountry users will appreciate it.

A FINAL NOTE

Hiking is a sport of self-reliance. Its high potential for adventure and relatively low level of regulation have been made possible by the dedication of most hikers to the values of prudence and independence. This tradition of self-reliance imposes an obligation on each of us: at any time we may have to rely on our own ingenuity and judgment, aided by map and compass, to reach our goals or even make a timely exit from the woods. While the penalty for failure rarely exceeds an unplanned and uncomfortable night in the woods, more serious outcomes are possible. Most hikers find a high degree of satisfaction in obtaining the knowledge and skills that free them from blind dependence on the next blaze or trail sign, and enable them to walk in the woods with confidence and assurance. Those who learn the skills of getting about in the woods, the habits of studious acquisition of information before the trip and careful observation while in the woods, soon find that they have surely earned "the Freedom of the Hills".

The AMC earnestly requests that those who use the trails, shelters, and campsites heed the rules (especially those having to do with camping) of the WMNF, NHDP, and SPNHF. The same consideration should be shown to private owners. In many cases the privileges enjoyed by hikers today could be withdrawn if rules and conditions are not observed.

The trails that we use and enjoy are only in part the product of government agencies. Many trails are maintained by one dedicated person, or a small group. Funds for trail work are scarce, and unless hikers contribute both time and money to the maintenance of trails, the variety of trails available to the public is almost certain to experience a sad decline. Every hiker can make some contribution to the improvement of the trails. (For information, write to

AMC Trails, Pinkham Notch Camp, Box 298 Gorham, NH 03581. Trails must not be cut in the WMNF without the approval of the Forest Supervisor, nor elsewhere without consent of the owners and without definite provision for maintenance.

Introduction

According to Ticknor's *White Mountains*, published in 1887, the higher peaks "seem to have received the name of White Mountains from the sailors off the coast, to whom they were a landmark and a mystery lifting their crowns of brilliant snow against the blue sky from October until June."

This book aims for reasonably complete coverage of hiking trails located on the Presidential Range and its subsidiary ridges. No attempt is made to cover any kind of skiing (alpine, downhill, or cross-country), although several cross-country (ski-touring) trails are mentioned where they happen to cross hiking trails. Because of extreme hazards to inexperienced or insufficiently equipped climbers or groups, rock climbs are not described in this book. Rock climbing requires special techniques and equipment, and should not be undertaken except by roped parties under qualified leaders.

CLIMATE AND VEGETATION

The climate gets much cooler, windier, and wetter at higher elevations. The summit of Mt. Washington is under cloud cover about 55% of the time. On an average summer afternoon, the high temperature on the summit is only about 52° F (11° C); in the winter, about 15° F (-9° C). The record low temperature is -46°. Average winds throughout the day and night are 26 mph in summer and 44 mph in winter. Winds have gusted over 100 mph in every month of the year, and set the world record of 231 mph on April 12, 1934. During the storm of February 24–26, 1969, the observatory recorded a snowfall of 97.8 in. Within a 24-hour period during that storm, a total of 49.3 in. was recorded, a record for the mountain and for all weather observation stations in the United States. Other mountains also have severe conditions, in proportion to their height and exposure.

The forest on the White Mtns. is of two major types: the northern hardwoods (birch, beech, and maple), which are found at elevations of less than about 3000 ft., and the boreal forest (spruce, fir, and birch), which is found from about 3000 ft. to the timberline. At lower elevations oaks and white pines may be seen; red pines and (rarely) jack pines may be seen at up to about 2000 ft. in ledgy areas. Above the timberline is the "krummholz," the gnarled and stunted trees that manage to survive wherever there is a bit of shelter from the violent winds, and the tiny wildflowers, some of which are extremely rare. Hikers are encouraged to be particularly careful in their activities above treeline, as the plants that grow there already have to cope with the severity of the environment. For information about these trees and plants, consult *Trees and Shrubs of Northern New England*, published by the SPNHF, and the *Field Guide to Mountain Flowers of New England* and *At Timberline*, both published by the AMC.

MAPS

The published topographic quadrangles of the USGS cover all of NH and ME. Many areas are covered by the more recent and detailed 7.5 min. quads. New metric maps are being produced; they are now available only for the Presidential Range and nearby areas, but more should be released in the next few years. Although topography on the newer maps is excellent, some recent maps have been inaccurate in showing the locations of trails. Index maps to USGS quads in any state (specify states) and pamphlets concerning USGS maps are available free from the Branch of Distribution, USGS, 1200 South Eads St., Arlington VA 22202.

Extra copies of AMC maps may be purchased at the AMC's Boston and Pinkham Notch offices and at some book and outdoor equipment stores.

The RMC map of the Northern Peaks is useful for the dense trail network on the Northern Peaks; see page 74 for details.

CAMPING

Those who camp overnight in the backcountry tend to have more of an impact on the land than day hikers do. In the past some popular sites suffered misuse and began to resemble disaster areas, with piles of trash and surrounding trees devastated by campers gathering firewood. For this reason backpacking hikers should take great care to minimize their effect on the mountains by practicing low-impact camping and making conscious efforts to preserve the natural forest. One alternative is to camp in well-prepared, designated sites; the popular ones are supervised by caretakers. The other alternative has come to be called "clean camping": to disperse camping over a wide area, out of sight of trails and roads, and to camp with full respect for wilderness values. The objective of clean camping is to leave no trace of one's presence, so that the site will not be reused before it has a chance to recover. Repeated camping on one site compacts the soil and makes it difficult for vegetation to survive.

There are more than fifty backcountry shelters and tent sites in the White Mountain area, open on a first-come, first-served basis. Some sites have summer caretakers who collect an overnight fee to help defray expenses. Most sites have shelters, a few have only tent platforms, and some have both. Shelters are overnight accommodations for persons carrying their own bedding and cooking supplies. The more popular shelters are often full, so be prepared to camp off trail with tents or tarps at a legal site. Make yourself aware of regulations and restrictions prior to your trip.

If you camp away from established sites, look for a spot more than 200 ft. from the trail and from any surface water, and observe local Restricted Use Area rules. Bring all needed shelter, including whatever poles, stakes, ground insulation, and cord are required. Try to choose a clear, level site on which to pitch your tent. Use a compass, and check landmarks carefully to find your way to and from your campsite. Do not cut boughs or branches for bedding. Avoid clearing vegetation and never make a ditch around the tent. Wash your dishes and yourself well away from streams, ponds, and springs. Heed the rules of neatness, sanitation, and fire prevention, and carry out everything—food, paper, glass, cans, etc.—that you carry in (and whatever trash less-thoughtful campers may have left). In some areas you may have to hang your food from a tree to protect it from raccoons and bears.

In some camping areas, a "human browse line" where people have gathered firewood over the years is quite evident: limbs are gone from trees, the ground is devoid of dead wood, and vegetation has been trampled as people scoured the area. The use of portable stoves is practically mandatory in popular areas, and is encouraged elsewhere to prevent damage to vegetation. Operate stoves with reasonable caution. Campfire permits are no longer required in the WMNF but campers are legally responsible for damages caused by any fire that they build. On private land, you need the owner's permission to build a fire, and fires are generally not permitted on state land except at campgrounds. Wood campfires should not be made unless there is ample dead and down wood available near your site; never cut green trees. Such fires must be made in safe, sheltered places and not in leaves or rotten wood, or against logs, trees, or stumps. Before you build a fire, clear a space at least 5 ft. in radius of all flammable material down to the mineral soil. Under no circumstances should a fire be left unattended. All fires must be completely extinguished with earth or water before you leave a campsite, even temporarily. Campers should restore the campfire site to as natural an appearance as possible before leaving the campsite.

Roadside Campgrounds

The WMNF operates a number of roadside campgrounds with limited facilities; fees are charged. No reservations can be made, and many of these campgrounds are full on summer weekends. Consult the WMNF offices for details. Several NH state parks also have campgrounds conveniently located for hikers in the White Mtns. and other parts of the state. At these also no reservations can be made. For details on state parks, contact the Office of Vacation Travel, Box 856, Concord NH 03301 (603-271-2665).

Camping Regulations

Trailside camping is practical only within the WMNF, with a few limited exceptions, such as the campsites on the Appalachian Trail. The laws of the states of ME and NH require that permission be obtained from the owner to camp on private land, and that permits be obtained to build campfires anywhere outside the WMNF, except at officially designated campsites. Camping and campfires are not permitted in NH state parks except in campgrounds.

Overnight camping is permitted in almost all of the WMNF. To limit or prevent some of the adverse impacts of concentrated, uncontrolled camping, the USFS has adopted regulations for a number of areas in the WMNF that are threatened by overuse and misuse. The objective of the Restricted Use Area (RUA) program is not to hinder backpackers and campers, but to disperse their use of the land so that people can enjoy themselves in a clean and attractive environment without causing deterioration of natural resources. By protecting the plants, water, soil, and wildlife of the White Mountains, these areas should help to provide a higher quality experience for the visitor. Because hikers and backpackers have cooperated with RUA rules, many trails once designated as RUAs are no longer under formal restrictions. However, common sense and self-imposed restrictions are still necessary to prevent damage.

In summary, the 1986 RUA rules prohibit camping and wood or charcoal fires above timberline (where trees are less than 8 ft. in height); or within a specified distance of certain roads, trails, streams, and other locations, except at designated sites. Stoves are permitted, even for day use. Contact the USFS in Laconia NH (603-524-6450), or any Ranger District office for up-to-date information, including a current RUA map.

WINTER CLIMBING

Snowshoeing and cross-country skiing on White Mtn. trails and peaks have steadily become more popular in the last decade. Increasing numbers of hikers have discovered the beauty of the woods in winter, and advances in clothing and equipment have made it possible for experienced winter travelers to enjoy great comfort and safety. The greatest danger is that it begins to look too easy and too safe, while snow, ice, and weather conditions are constantly changing, and a relatively trivial error of judgment may have grave, even fatal, consequences. Conditions can vary greatly from day to day, and from trail to trail, thus much more experience is required to forsee and avoid dangerous situations in winter than in summer. Trails are frequently difficult or impossible to follow, and navigation skills are hard to learn in adverse weather conditions (as anyone who has tried to read a map in a blizzard can attest). "Breaking trail" on snowshoes through new snow can be strenuous and exhausting work. Some trails go through areas which may pose a severe avalanche hazard. In a "white-out" above treeline, it may be almost impossible to tell the ground from the sky, and hikers frequently become disoriented.

Winter on the lower trails in the White Mtns. may require only snowshoes or skis and some warm clothing. Even so, summer hiking boots are usually inadequate, flashlight batteries fail quickly (a headlamp with battery pack works better), and water in canteens freezes unless wrapped in a sock or sweater. The winter hiker needs good physical conditioning from regular exercise, and must dress carefully in order to avoid overheating and excessive perspiration, which soaks clothing and soon leads to chilling. Cotton clothes are useful only as long as they can be kept perfectly dry (an impossible task, thus the winter climbers' saying, "cotton kills"); only wool and some of the newer synthetics retain their insulating values when wet. Fluid intake must increase, as dehydration can be a serious problem in the dry winter air.

Above timberline, conditions often require specialized equipment, and skills and experience of a different magnitude. The conditions on the Presidential Range in winter are as severe as any in North America south of the great mountains of Alaska and the Yukon Territory. On the summit of Mt. Washington in winter, winds average 44 mph, and daily high temperatures average 15°F. There are few calm days, and even on an average day conditions will be too severe for any but the most experienced and well-equipped climbers. The Mt. Washington Observatory has often reported wind velocities in excess of 100 mph, and temperatures are often below zero. The combination of high wind and low temperature has such a cooling effect that the worst conditions on Mt. Washington are approximately equal to the worst reported from Antarctica, despite the much greater cold in the latter region. Extremely severe storms can develop suddenly and unexpectedly. But the most dangerous aspect of winter in the White Mtns. is the extreme variability of the weather: it is not unusual for a cold, penetrating, wind-driven rain to be followed within a few hours by a cold front bringing below-zero temperatures and high winds.

No book can begin to impart all the knowledge necessary to cope safely with the potential for such brutal conditions, but helpful information can be found in *Don't Die on the Mountain*, a booklet by Dan H. Allen ($1, available from the AMC), and *Winter Hiking and Camping* by John A. Danielson (1982, Adirondack Mountain Club). Hikers who are interested in extending their activities into the winter season are strongly advised to seek out organized parties with leaders who have extensive winter experience. Each year the AMC and Adirondack Mountain Club operate a week-long winter school which exposes participants to the techniques and equipment of safe winter travel. The AMC and several of its chapters also sponsor numerous workshops on evenings and weekends, in addition to introductory winter hikes and regular winter schedules through which participants can gain experience. Information on such activities can be obtained from the AMC information center at the Boston headquarters.

WHITE MOUNTAIN NATIONAL FOREST

Most of the higher White Mtns. are within the White Mountain National Forest (WMNF), which was established under the Weeks Act and now comprises about 750,000 acres, of which about 47,000 acres are in ME and the rest in NH. It is important to remember that this is not a national park, but a national forest; parks are established primarily for preservation and recreation, while national forests are managed for multiple use. In the administration of national forests the following objectives are considered: recreation development, timber production, watershed protection, and wildlife propagation. It is the policy of the USFS to manage logging operations so that trails, streams, camping places, and other spots of public interest are protected. Mountain recreation has been identified as the most important resource in the WMNF. The boundaries of the WMNF are usually marked wherever they cross roads or trails, usually by red-painted corner posts and blazes. Hunting and fishing are permitted in the WMNF under the state laws; state licenses are required. Much informational literature has been published by the WMNF and is available free of charge at the Forest Supervisor's Office in Laconia, the Ranger District offices (list below), and other information centers.

The national Wilderness Preservation system, which included the Great Gulf, was established in 1964 with passage of the Wilderness Act. The Presidential Range–Dry River Wilderness, the Pemigewasset Wilderness, and the Sandwich Range Wilderness have since been added to the system. It should be noted that wilderness areas are established by an act of Congress, and not merely by WMNF administrative action. The USFS has established nine scenic areas in the WMNF to preserve lands of outstanding or unique natural beauty: Gibbs Brook, Nancy Brook, Greeley Ponds, Pinkham Notch, Lafayette Brook, Rocky Gorge, Lincoln Woods, Sawyer Pond, and Snyder Brook. Camping is restricted in many areas under the Restricted Use Area (RUA) program to protect vulnerable areas from damage. To preserve the rare alpine flora of the Mt. Washington Range and to assure that the natural conditions on the upper slopes of the WMNF are maintained, removal of any tree, shrub, or plant without written permission is prohibited.

WMNF Offices and Ranger Districts (R.D.'s)

The Androscoggin and Saco Ranger District offices have been open seven days a week in the summer, sometimes with evening hours. Otherwise, the offices are open during normal business hours.

Forest Supervisor, PO Box 638, Laconia NH 03247 (on North Main St., across railroad tracks from downtown section).
Tel. 603-524-6450.

Ammonoosuc R.D., Trudeau Rd., Bethlehem NH 03574 (just north of US 3 opposite Gale River Rd.).
Tel. 603-869-2626.

Androscoggin R. D., 80 Glen Rd., Gorham NH 03581 (at south end of town along NH 16).
Tel. 603-466-2713.

Evans Notch R. D., RD #2, Box 2270, Bethel ME 04217 (on US 2).
Tel. 207-834-2134.

Pemigewasset R. D., 127 Highland St., Plymouth NH 03264 (to west of town, between Hatch Plaza on NH 25 and hospital).
Tel. 603-536-1310.

Saco R. D., RFD 1, Box 94, Conway NH 03818 (on Kancamagus Highway just west of NH 16).
Tel. 603-447-5448.

THE APPALACHIAN TRAIL (AT)

This footpath runs over 2000 mi. from Springer Mtn. in Georgia to Katahdin in Maine, and traverses the White Mtns. for about 170 mi. in a southwest to northeast direction, from Hanover New Hampshire to Grafton Notch in Maine. Its route traverses many of the major peaks and ranges of the White Mtns., following many historic and scenic trails. All of the AT through the Presidentials is described in this guide; a paragraph near the beginning of Sections 1 and 2 gives the route of the AT through each section. Persons interested in following the AT as a continuous path may also consult the Appalachian Trail Conference's *Guide to the Appalachian Trail in New Hampshire and Vermont*. Information on the Appalachian Trail and the several guidebooks which cover its entire length is available from the Appalachian Trail Conference, PO Box 236, Harpers Ferry WV 25425.

With the passage of the National Trails System Act by Congress on October 2, 1968, the Appalachian Trail became the first federally protected footpath in this country and was officially designated the Appalachian National Scenic Trail. Under this act the Appalachian Trail is administered primarily as a footpath by the Secretary of Interior in consultation with the Secretary of Agriculture and representatives of the several states through which it passes. In addition, an Advisory Council for the Appalachian National Scenic Trail was appointed by the Secretary of Interior. It includes representatives of each of the states and the several hiking clubs recommended by the Appalachian Trail Conference.

SOCIETY FOR THE PROTECTION OF NEW HAMPSHIRE FORESTS

This organization has worked since 1901 to protect the mountains, forests, wetlands, and farm lands of NH, and to encourage wise forestry practices. It owns Lost River in Kinsman Notch, a substantial reservation on Monadnock, and a number of other lands. In cooperation with the AMC, it protects and maintains the Monadnock–Sunapee Greenway. Its headquarters building in Concord NH was designed as a showcase in the latest techniques of energy conservation. For membership information, contact the SPNHF, 54 Portsmouth St., Concord NH 03301 (603-224-9945).

NEW ENGLAND TRAIL CONFERENCE

The New England Trail Conference was organized in 1917 to develop the hiking possibilities of New England and to coordinate the work of local organizations. The Conference serves as a clearinghouse for information about trail maintenance and trail use both for organized groups and for individuals. The annual meeting of this organization is held in the spring, when representatives of mountaineering and outing clubs from all over New England come together for a full day and evening program of reports, talks, and illustrated lectures on mountain climbing, hiking, and trails and shelters. All sessions are open to the public. The work of the Conference is directed by the chairman, who is elected by the executive committee. For information, contact the secretary, Forrest House, 33 Knollwood Dr., East Longmeadow MA 01028.

ABBREVIATIONS

The following abbreviations are used in trail descriptions.

hr.	hour(s)
min.	minutes(s)
mph	miles per hour
in.	inch(es)
ft.	foot, feet
km.	kilometer(s)
yd.	yard(s)
est.	estimated

AMC	Appalachian Mountain Club
AT	Appalachian Trail
JCC	Jackson Conservation Commission
MMVSP	Mt. Madison Volunteer Ski Patrol
NHDP	New Hampshire Division of Parks
RMC	Randolph Mountain Club
SSOC	Sub Sig Outing Club
USFS	United States Forest Service
USGS	United States Geological Survey
WMNF	White Mountain National Forest

WHITE MOUNTAIN GUIDEBOOK COMMITTEE

Editor
Eugene S. Daniell III

T. Walley Williams III, *ex-officio*
William G. Scheller Jr., *ex-officio*

D. William Baird
Iris Baird
Lawrence R. Blood
Helen Cawood
Gordon Cawood
Debra Y. Clark
Eugene S. Daniell IV
Daniel DeHart
Sharon DeHart
Kathleen Donaghue
Richard M. Dudley
George Dussault
David O. Elliott
Terrence P. Frost
Hal Graham

Angus McEachern
John McHugh
Doris Meyer
Avard Milbury
Kenneth E. Miller
Paul A. Miller
Robert Nesham
William Nichols
Christopher Northrop
Faith Northrop
Herbert G. Ogden Jr.
Anne Peterson
Frank L. Pilar
David H. Raymond
Tom W. Sawyer

Samuel Hagner
Joseph J. Hansen
Mary Hansen
Robert C. Hansen
Alice A. Johnson
Timothy Kennedy
Allen Krause
Albert LaPrade
James R. Lindsley
Forrest Mack
Tom Maguire

Diane D. Sawyer
Roioli Schweiker
Roy R. Schweiker
Kimball Simpson
Vera V. Smith
Dennis Spurling
Audrey Sylvester
Thomas F. Vallette
Guy Waterman
Laura Waterman
David F. Wright

Mount Washington and the Southern Ridges

This section includes the summit of Mt. Washington and the major ridges which run south from it, which constitute the southern portion of the Presidential Range. It is bounded on the north by the Mt. Washington Cog Railway and the Mt. Washington Auto Rd., on the east by NH 16, on the south by US 302, and on the west by US 302 and the Base Rd. The northern portion of the Presidential Range, including Mts. Clay, Jefferson, Adams, and Madison, and the Great Gulf, is covered in Section 2. Many of the trails described in Section 2 also provide routes to Mt. Washington. The AMC Mt. Washington Range map (map 6) covers this entire section.

Three major ridges run southwest or south from Mt. Washington, separated by deep river valleys from each other and from the ranges to the west and east. The most impressive ridge is formed by the Southern Peaks, which run southwest from Mt. Washington, comprising (from northeast to southwest) Mts. Monroe, Franklin, Eisenhower, Pierce (also known as Clinton), Jackson, and Webster, ending abruptly above Crawford Notch at the cliffs of Mt. Webster. On the northwest, the headwaters of the Ammonoosuc River (a Connecticut River tributary) flow across the Fabyan Plain between the Southern Peaks and the much lower Dartmouth Range. The Dry River begins in Oakes Gulf high on Mt. Washington, and runs to the Saco River below Crawford Notch through a deep ravine between the Southern Peaks and the Montalban Ridge. The Montalban Ridge is the longest of all Mt. Washington's subsidiary ridges, extending about 15 mi. from the summit; it first runs south over Boott Spur, Mt. Isolation, Mt. Davis, Stairs Mtn., Mt. Resolution, and Mt. Parker, then swings east to Mts. Langdon, Pickering, and Stanton, the low peaks above the intervales of Bartlett and Glen near the confluence of the Rocky Branch and Saco River. The Bemis Ridge is a significant spur running from Mt. Resolution southwest over Mt. Crawford, then south to Hart Ledge, which overlooks the great bend in the Saco. East of the Montalbans lies the Rocky Branch, and to the east of the Rocky Branch rises the Rocky Branch Ridge, a long, wide-spreading assortment of humps and flat ridges running south from Boott Spur via Slide Peak, with no outstanding summit except Iron Mtn. at the far south end. Still farther east the Ellis River flows down from Pinkham Notch, with NH 16 running through the valley and the ridges of Wildcat Mtn. on the opposite side.

In this section the Appalachian Trail follows the entire Webster Cliff Trail from Crawford Notch to its intersection with the Crawford Path near the summit of Mt. Pierce, then follows the Crawford Path to the summit of Mt. Washington. From there it descends to the Gulfside Trail (see Section 2) via the Trinity Heights Connector. On the way it crosses the summits of Mts. Webster, Jackson, Pierce, and Washington, and passes near Mts. Eisenhower, Franklin, and Monroe. Then, after passing over the Northern Peaks (although it misses most of the summits) and through the Great Gulf (areas covered in Section 2), it returns to Section 1 at the Mt. Washington Auto Rd., following the Old Jackson Road to Pinkham Notch Camp and NH 16.

SUMMIT BUILDINGS

No hotel or overnight lodging for the public is available on the summit of Mt. Washington. From Columbus Day to Memorial Day no buildings are open to hikers for shelter or refuge. The new summit building named in honor of former NH Governor Sherman Adams and operated by the NH Division of Parks and Recreation during the summer season (mid-May to mid-October) has food service, pack room, souvenir shop, public rest rooms, telephone, and a post office. It houses the Mt. Washington Observatory, the Mt. Washington Museum, and facilities for park personnel.

The Yankee Building was built in 1941 to house transmitter facilities for the first FM station in northern New England. It is now leased by WMTW-TV and houses two-way radio equipment for various state, federal, and local organizations. This building is closed to the public.

The transmitter building and powerhouse for WMTW-TV and WHOM-FM, built in 1954, provides living quarters for station personnel and houses television and microwave equipment. The structure, built to withstand winds of 300 mph, is not open to the public.

The Stage Office, built in 1975 to replace a similar building constructed in 1908, is owned by the Mt. Washington Auto Road Company and used only in connection with their operation.

The first Summit House on Mt. Washington was built in 1852. The first Tip Top House hotel, built in 1853, suffered a fire in 1915. It is now owned by the State of New Hampshire and is part of the Mt. Washington State Park. Plans call for restoring this ancient stone building at a future date. Its eventual use has not yet been decided. At present it is closed to all but park use. The second Summit House, 1873–1908, was destroyed by fire.

MOUNT WASHINGTON OBSERVATORY

There has been a year-round weather observatory on Mt. Washington from 1870 to 1886 and from 1932 to the present. The present observatory is operated by a nonprofit corporation, and individuals are invited to become members. For details contact the Mt. Washington Observatory, Membership Secretary, 1 Washington St., Gorham, NH 03581.

THE MOUNT WASHINGTON AUTO ROAD

This road, constructed in 1855–61 and long known as the "Carriage Rd.," extends from the Glen House site on NH 16 to the summit. Automobiles are charged a toll at the foot of the mountain. With long zigzags and an easy grade, it climbs the prominent northeast ridge named for Benjamin Chandler, who died of exposure on the upper part in 1856. Hiking on the road is not forbidden, but despite easier grades and smoother footing than hiking trails, the distance is long and the competition with automobile traffic is annoying and potentially dangerous. In winter ruts from snow vehicle traffic and severe icing and drifting make it a less pleasant and more difficult route than might be anticipated. The emergency shelters that were formerly located along the upper part of the road have been removed.

Because of the continual theft and destruction of trail signs, they are often placed on the trails at some distance from the Auto Rd. The names of some trails are painted on rocks at the point where they leave the road.

The Auto Rd. leaves NH 16 opposite the Glen House site (1600 ft.) and crosses the Peabody River. The Appalachian Trail crosses just above the 2-mi. mark after sharp curves right and then left. To the south, the Appalachian Trail follows the Old Jackson Road (a foot trail), past junctions with the Nelson Crag Trail and the Raymond Path, to Pinkham Notch Camp. To the north it follows the Madison Gulf Trail toward the Great Gulf and Madison Hut. Lowe's Bald Spot, a fine viewpoint about 0.3 mi. from the road, is reached by an easy hike on the Madison Gulf Trail and a side path. The site of the Halfway House (3840 ft.) is on the right at treeline. Just above, where there is a fine view to the north, the road skirts a prominent shoulder, known as the Ledge. A short distance above this point the Chandler Brook Trail to the Great Gulf leaves right. Just above the 5-mi. mark, on the right and exactly at the sharp turn, there are some remarkable folds in the strata of the rocks beside the Auto Rd. At this point, near Cragway Spring, the lower section of the Nelson Crag Trail enters left, and a few yards above, the upper section diverges left. At about 5.5 mi. the road passes through the patch of high scrub in which Dr. B. L. Ball survived two nights in a winter storm in October 1855. A short distance above the 6-mi. mark, the Wamsutta Trail descends right to the Great Gulf, and the Alpine Garden Trail diverges left. The trenchlike structures near the road are the remains of the old Glen House Bridle Path, built in 1853. Just below the 7-mi. mark the Huntington Ravine Trail enters left. Just above, in the middle of a lawn known as the "Cow Pasture," the remains of an old corral are visible. A little beyond on the right are the Cog Railway and the Lizzie Bourne monument at the spot where Bourne perished in September 1855 at the age of 23 (the second recorded fatality on the mountain). The summit is reached at approximately 8 mi. (13 km.).

THE MOUNT WASHINGTON COG RAILWAY

The Mt. Washington Cog Railway, an unusual artifact with a fascinating history, was completed in 1869. Its maximum grade, 13.5 in. to the yd., is equaled by only one other railroad (excluding funicular roads), that on Pilatus in the Alps. The location of the Base Station is called Marshfield, in honor of Sylvester Marsh, an inventor of meat-packing machinery who was the promoter and builder of the railway, and Darby Field. When the cog railway is in operation, walking on the track is not permitted; at other times it is a poor walking route. A new public parking area is located on the Base Rd. about 0.5 mi. west of Marshfield. Hikers who wish to visit the Base Station itself should expect to pay an admission fee.

The cog railway ascends a minor westerly ridge in a nearly straight line to the treeline near Jacob's Ladder (4800 ft.). This trestle, at its highest point about 30 ft. above the mountainside, is the steepest part of the road. After crossing the shoulder toward Mt. Clay, the line curves right and crosses the Westside Trail close to the edge of the Great Gulf. Between the Great Gulf and the cog railway lies the Gulfside Trail, which soon turns right and crosses the tracks. From the Gulf Tank (5600 ft.) there is a fine view across the Gulf toward the Northern Peaks. It is 3 mi. from Marshfield to the summit, and trains ascend in about 1 hr. 10 min.

SKIING IN THE MOUNT WASHINGTON AREA

A number of cross-country ski trails have been constructed in the vicinity of Pinkham Notch Camp, which has become a center for the pursuit of this sport. In addition, a number of the summer trails are suitable for ski-touring. Information on these trails can be obtained at the camp's Trading Post.

The slopes of Tuckerman Ravine and the snowfields on and near the summit cone are justly famous for the opportunities they offer for alpine skiing. The skiing season on the Tuckerman headwall starts about the beginning of March and may last into June in some seasons. The ravine area and the John Sherburne Ski Trail (see below) are patrolled by the USFS and the Mt. Washington Volunteer Ski Patrol. Sections that are unsafe because of ice or possible avalanches are posted in the shelter area. Skiing areas in the ravine, in the Gulf of Slides, or on any other part of the mountain above timberline are subject to wide temperature variations within short periods of time. The difference between corn snow and ice or bathing suits and parkas may be an hour, or even less, when clouds roll in or the afternoon sun drops behind a shoulder of the mountain. Skiers should prepare accordingly. There is a sun deck at Hermit Lake, but no longer a warming room open to the public.

The John Sherburne Ski Trail (WMNF) permits skiers to descend from Tuckerman Ravine to Pinkham Notch Camp. The Tuckerman Ravine Trail affords a good ascent route on foot, as it is normally well packed, but downhill skiing on the Tuckerman Ravine Trail is prohibited since it would endanger persons walking on the trail. The Sherburne Trail is named for John H. Sherburne, Jr., whose efforts contributed greatly to the establishment of this trail. It leaves the south end of the parking lot at Pinkham Notch Camp in company with the Gulf of Slides Ski Trail, and ascends to the Little Headwall of the ravine by a zigzag course, keeping at all times left (south) of the Tuckerman Ravine Trail and the Cutler River. Just below Hermit Lake a short side trail leads right to the Hermit Lake Shelters. From the top of the Little Headwall to the floor of the ravine the trail lies on the north of the stream. It is 10 to 50 ft. wide, and although the slope is suitable for expert and intermediate skiers at some points, even less expert skiers can negotiate this trail because of its width.

The Gulf of Slides, which is situated somewhat similarly to Tuckerman Ravine, receives a large volume of snow that remains in the ravine, so open-slope skiing is possible well into the spring (April and May). Its slopes, though less severe than those in Tuckerman, are more uniform and avalanche frequently. The Gulf of Slides Ski Trail (WMNF) leaves the south end of the parking lot at Pinkham Notch

Camp in company with the John Sherburne Ski Trail, and ascends west 2200 ft. in about 2.5 mi. to the bowl of the Gulf of Slides. Although wet in places, it is used as a hiking trail to the Gulf of Slides in summer.

The Mt. Washington Auto Rd. is not usually suitable for skiing on account of icy spots, windblown bare spots, and ruts from snow vehicle traffic. The areas between the top of the Tuckerman headwall and the summit cone, and Chandler Ridge near the 6-mi. mark on the Auto Rd., afford good spring skiing at all levels of experience, but are hard to reach because of their elevation. The Old Jackson Road is a good run for all levels. It drops 650 ft. and can be run in 30 min. The ascent takes 1 hr. Skiers should use the old trail instead of the relocation; enter the Old Jackson Road below the 2-mi. mark, about 0.2 mi. below where the relocation and the Madison Gulf Trail meet at the Auto Rd. The Raymond Path is not a ski run, but it affords a route between Tuckerman Ravine Trail and the Auto Rd. It is wide on the level sections, but narrow and difficult on the steep pitches. In deep snow, the trail is often obscured. It drops, not uniformly, about 1100 ft. toward the north and east.

MOUNTAIN SAFETY

Caution. Mt. Washington has a well-earned reputation as the most dangerous small mountain in the world. Storms increase in violence with great rapidity toward the summit. The highest wind velocity ever recorded at a surface weather station (231 mph on 12 April 1934) was attained on Mt. Washington. Judged by the wind-chill temperatures, the worst conditions on Mt. Washington are approximately equal to the worst reported from Antarctica, although actual temperatures on Mt. Washington are not as low. If you begin to experience difficulty from the weather, remember that the worst is yet to come, and turn back, without shame, before it is too late. (This warning applies to all peaks above timberline, particularly the Northern Peaks.) Each hiker should carry, as a bare minimum, a good rain suit with a hood (or equivalent outfit) which will also protect from wind, an extra sweater, wool hat, and mittens.

Ascents of the mountain in winter are sometimes easy enough to deceive inexperienced hikers into false confidence, but the worst conditions in winter are inconceivably brutal and can materialize with little warning. Safe ascent of the mountain in winter requires much warm clothing, some special equipment, and experienced leadership. From Columbus Day to Memorial Day no building is open to provide shelter or refuge to hikers.

Inexperienced hikers sometimes misjudge the difficulty of climbing Mt. Washington by placing too much emphasis on the relatively short distance from the trailhead to the summit. To a person used to walking around the neighborhood, the trail distance of 4 mi. or so sounds rather tame. But the most important factor in the difficulty of the trip is the altitude gain of 4000 ft., give or take a few hundred, from base to summit. To a person unused to mountain trails, and in less than excellent physical condition, this unrelenting uphill grind can be grueling and intensely discouraging. If you are not an experienced climber or a trained athlete, you will almost certainly enjoy the ascent of Mt. Washington a great deal more if you build up to it with lesser climbs.

The visitor who ascends the mountain on foot should carry a compass and should take care to stay on trails. The hiker who becomes lost from the trail above treeline in a cloud or "white-out," particularly if the weather is rapidly deteriorating, is in a grave predicament. There is no completely satisfactory course of action in this situation, since the object is to get below treeline, with or without a trail, and the weather exposure is generally worse to the west, while cliffs are more prevalent in the ravines to the east. If you know where the nearest major trail should be, then it is probably best to try to find it. If you have adequate clothing, it may be best to find a scrub patch and shelter yourself in it. In the absence of alternatives, take note that the cog railway on one slope and the Mt. Washington Auto Rd. on another make a line, although a very crooked one, from west to east. Remember which side of the mountain you are on, and go north or south, as the case may be, skirting the heads of ravines; sooner or later you will approach the road or the railroad, landmarks that cannot be missed in the darkest night or the thickest fog, except in winter when they may be obliterated by snow. Given a choice, avoid the railroad, as it is on the side of the mountain facing the prevailing winds.

Whether Mt. Washington has the worst weather in the world, or in North America, is subject to debate. But the dozens of people who have died on its slopes in the last century furnish adequate proof that the weather is vicious enough to kill those who are foolish enough to challenge the mountain at its worst. This appalling and needless loss of life has been due almost without exception to the failure of robust but incautious hikers to realize that wintry storms of incredible violence occur frequently, even during the summer months. Winds of hurricane force exhaust even the strongest hiker, and rain driven horizontally by the wind penetrates clothing and drains heat from the body. The temperature may or may not drop below freezing, but temperatures just above freezing are every bit as dangerous as those below, although sleet and freezing rain on rocks may obstruct a belated attempt to return to safety. As the victim's body temperature falls, brain function quickly deteriorates; this is one of the first, and most insidious, effects of excessive heat loss (hypothermia). Eventually the victim loses coordination, staggers, and then falls, numb and dazed, never to rise again. At this point, even immediate access to the best medical treatment obtainable will not assure the victim's survival. Prevention is the only sure cure. Most of those who misjudge conditions and their own endurance get away with their mistakes, and thus many are lulled into carelessness. The mountain spares most fools, but now and then claims one or two without mercy.

All water sources in this heavily used area should be suspected of being unfit to drink; the safest course is to avoid drinking from trailside sources. Water is available at the Sherman Adams summit building during the months that it is open.

GEOGRAPHY

Mt. Washington (6288 ft.), the highest peak east of the Mississippi and north of the Carolinas, was seen from the ocean as early as 1605. Its first recorded ascent was in June 1642 by Darby Field, of Exeter NH, and two Native Americans, who probably made the ascent by way of the Ellis River valley and Boott Spur. The mountain has had several hotels, a road and a railway, a weather observatory, a daily newspaper, a radio station and a television station, and has been the site of auto, foot, and ski races. *The Story of Mt. Washington* by F. Allen Burt treats the fascinating (and frequently unusual) human history of the mountain in great detail, while Peter Randall's *Mount Washington* is a much shorter and less detailed handbook of human and natural history.

Mt. Washington is a broad, massive mountain with great ravines cut deeply into its steep sides, leaving buttress ridges which reach up through the timberline and support the great upper plateau. The timberline occurs at an elevation of 4500 to 5000 ft., depending on the degree of exposure to the mountain's fierce weather. The upper plateau, which varies in elevation from 5000 to 5500 ft., bears comparatively gentle slopes interspersed with "lawns"—wide grassy areas strewn with rocks; the summit cone, covered with fragments of rock and almost devoid of vegetation, rises steeply above the plateau. The upper part of the mountain has a climate similar to that of northern Labrador, and its areas of alpine tundra support a fascinating variety of plant and animal life, species adapted to the extreme conditions of the alpine environment. Many of these species are found only on other high mountaintops or in the tundra many hundreds of miles farther north, and a few are found only or primarily on the Presidential Range. The plant species in particular have attracted many professional and amateur botanists (including Henry David Thoreau), and many of the features of the mountain are named for early botanists, such as Manasseh Cutler, Jacob Bigelow, Francis Boott, William Oakes, and Edward Tuckerman. Great care should be exercised not to damage the plant life in these areas, as their struggle for survival is already sufficiently severe. Hikers should avoid unnecessary excursions away from the trails, and should step on rocks rather than vegetation wherever possible. The AMC publishes the *AMC Field Guide to Mountain Flowers of New England,* an illustrated guide to all plants which normally grow above or near treeline, and *At Timberline,* a handbook that covers geology and animal life as well as plants. The NH Department of Resources and Economic Development (PO Box 856, Concord, NH 03301) publishes geological booklets intended for the general public; the Presidential Range area is covered by *The Geology of the Mt. Washington Quadrangle* and *The Geology of the Crawford Notch Quadrangle* ($2.50 and $2.00, respectively, in 1986).

The slopes of Mt. Washington are drained by tributaries of three major rivers: the Androscoggin, the Connecticut, and the Saco. The high, massive Northern Peaks continue the rocky alpine terrain of Mt. Washington to the north and northeast in an arc which encloses the Great Gulf, the largest glacial cirque in the White Mtns. Moving clockwise from the Great Gulf toward the east side of the mountain, Chandler Ridge (which is ascended by the Mt. Washington Auto Rd.) and the low peak of Nelson Crag form the northern boundary of a lawn called the "Alpine Garden," and divide the Great Gulf from the great ravines of the east face: Huntington Ravine, the Ravine of Raymond Cataract, and Tuckerman Ravine. The latter is one of the finest examples of the glacial cirque.

Raymond Cataract falls through a series of wild and beautiful cascades in the Ravine of Raymond Cataract. Brush has covered a former footway, so the Cataract can only be reached by those intrepid explorers who are skilled in off-trail travel. Easier to visit is Glen Ellis Falls, reached from NH 16 by a gravel path with rock steps and handrails, which leaves the parking area 0.8 mi. south of Pinkham Notch Camp, passes under the highway through a tunnel, and reaches the falls in 0.3 mi. (This path is not described as a hiking trail in this guide.) The main fall is 70 ft. high, and below it are several pools and smaller falls.

Boott Spur, the great southeast shoulder of Mt. Washington, forms the south wall of Tuckerman Ravine and the north wall of the Gulf of Slides, and the flat ridge connecting it with the cone of Mt. Washington bears Bigelow Lawn, the largest of the Presidential Range lawns. Both the Montalban Ridge and the Rocky Branch Ridge descend from Boott Spur and quickly drop below treeline, continuing south in thick woods with occasional open summits. Oakes Gulf, at the headwaters of the Dry River, lies west of Boott Spur and east of Mt. Monroe. The Southern Peaks, running southwest from Mt. Washington, form the second most prominent ridge in the range (after the Northern Peaks), dropping to the treeline slowly and rising above it again several times before the final descent into the woods below Mt. Pierce. The Mt. Washington Cog Railway ascends the unnamed ridge between the less spectacular ravines of the western face, Ammonoosuc Ravine and Burt Ravine, which lie between the Southern Peaks and the Northern Peaks.

Day trips to the summit of Mt. Washington can be made by several different routes, but the vast majority of climbers use only a very few trails. From the west, the mountain is ascended from a parking area (2500 ft.) on the Base Rd. near the Cog Railway by the Ammonoosuc Ravine Trail and the Crawford Path, or by the Jewell and Gulfside trails (see Section 2), or by a loop using both routes. The Ammonoosuc Ravine Trail has a long, very steep section but offers the shelter of Lakes of the Clouds Hut, just above treeline, if a storm arises. The Jewell Trail provides an easier ascent or descent, but reaches the Gulfside Trail on the slope of Mt. Clay, a more dangerous place in bad weather. Both of these trails are used heavily. Because of the very high elevation of its trailhead (3000 ft.) on the Jefferson Notch Rd., the Caps Ridge Trail is frequently used for a one-day hike to Mt. Washington, in combination with the Gulfside Trail and the Cornice (see Section 2). It offers fine scenery and the opportunity to also climb Mt. Jefferson with little extra effort, but this longer, rougher route to Mt. Washington is more exposed to bad weather and saves no exertion. The Boundary Line Trail (see Section 2) connects the Base Rd. parking area with the Jefferson Notch Rd., and thus makes possible loop trips involving the Caps Ridge Trail and the Ammonoosuc Ravine or Jewell trails.

Most hikers ascend from the east. The Tuckerman Ravine Trail from Pinkham Notch Camp (2000 ft.) is by far the most popular route, affording what is probably the easiest ascent of Mt. Washington, with moderate grades for most of its length and spectacular views of the ravine. It also provides easy access to Crystal Cascade, a beautiful waterfall not far from Pinkham Notch Camp. In the spring and fall this trail is often closed by the WMNF on account of dangerous snow or ice conditions; notice of its closure is posted at the top and bottom. In this case the Lion Head Trail is usually the best alternative. The Lion Head Trail runs along the prominent and aptly named ridge north of Tuckerman Ravine; an older route of this trail, closed for summer hiking, is the most popular and least dangerous route of ascent in winter. Routes other than the Tuckerman Ravine Trail are all somewhat longer, or steeper, or both, but have good views and are less crowded.

The Southern Presidentials form a great ridge that extends about 8 mi. southwest from the summit of Mt. Washington to the Webster Cliffs above Crawford Notch. The Ammonoosuc River lies to the northwest, and the Dry River to the southeast. The summits on this ridge decrease steadily in elevation from northeast to southwest.

Mt. Monroe (5384 ft.), the highest, is a sharply pointed pyramid rising abruptly from the flat area around the Lakes of the Clouds, with a secondary summit, a small crag sometimes called Little Monroe (5207 ft.), on its west ridge. It is completely above treeline, and affords fine views of the deep chasm of Oakes Gulf on the east, the beautiful Lakes of the Clouds, and the nearby summit of Mt. Washington. The flats between Mt. Monroe and the Lakes of the Clouds support a bountiful number of alpine plants, making it the most significant, and most vulnerable, habitat in the White Mtns. Part of this area is closed to all public entry due to damage caused in the past by hikers coming to admire these plants, which can withstand the full violence of above-treeline weather but not the tread of hikers' boots. Sadly, we can now pay homage to some of these rare survivors only from a distance. The summit of Mt. Monroe is crossed by the Mount Monroe Loop.

Mt. Franklin (5004 ft.) is a rather flat shoulder of
Monroe, which appears impressive only when seen from
below, in the Franklin—Pleasant col. The exact location of
the summit is not obvious, but the summit does exists and
lies a short distance off the Crawford Path.

Mt. Eisenhower (4761 ft.), formerly called Mt. Pleasant,
was renamed after the former President's death. While
there is a good deal of scrub on the lower slopes of this
dome-shaped mountain, the top is completely bald. Its
summit is crossed by the Mount Eisenhower Loop.

Mt. Pierce (4310 ft.) was named for Franklin Pierce, the
only President born in NH, by act of the NH Legislature in
1913. Although this name appears on all USGS maps it was
not universally accepted, and the mountain's former name,
Mt. Clinton, persists in the Mt. Clinton Rd. and the Mount
Clinton Trail, which ascends the southeast slopes of the
mountain. Mt. Pierce is wooded almost to the top of its flat
summit on the west, but a broad open area on the east side
affords fine views. Its summit lies on the Webster–Cliff
Trail, just off the Crawford Path.

Mt. Jackson (4052 ft.), named for NH State Geologist
Charles Jackson and not for President Andrew Jackson,
has a square, ledgy summit with steep sides and a flat top,
and possibly the finest views overall of all the Southern
Peaks. Its summit is crossed by the Webster Cliff Trail and
is also reached by the Jackson branch of the Webster–
Jackson Trail.

Mt. Webster (3910 ft.), once called Notch Mtn., was
renamed for Daniel Webster, the great US Senator and
Secretary of State, an illustrious orator who was probably
the best-known native of NH. The summit is crossed by the
Webster Cliff Trail, which is intersected by the Webster
branch of the Webster–Jackson Trail not far from the top.

To the southeast of the Southern Peaks lies the Dry
River, running down the central valley of the Presiden-

tial–Dry River Wilderness Area. This river has also been called the Mt. Washington River, but Dry River has won the battle, possibly because of the ironic quality of the name. The Dry River runs from Oakes Gulf to the Saco through a deep, narrow, steep-walled ravine. Though in a dry season the flow is a bit meager, with lots of rocks lying uncovered in the stream bed, its watershed has extremely rapid runoff, and its sudden floods are legendary. It has killed hikers. No other logging railroad ever constructed in the White Mtns. has ever had as many river crossings in so short a distance as the railroad which was built up this valley, and no other logging railroad has ever had all its trestles swept away so quickly after ceasing operations.

Access to the Dry River area has always been somewhat difficult, and ascents of the Southern Peaks from this side have always been relatively arduous, but since the Wilderness Area was established and the number of wilderness-seeking visitors increased sharply, the WMNF has made access somewhat easier by eliminating many river crossings through trail relocations and the construction of a bridge. It is still an area where visitors need to keep a careful watch on the weather, including that of the last few days.

The Montalban Ridge extends southward from Boott Spur, forming the longest subsidiary ridge in the Presidential Range, running for about 15 mi. between the Rocky Branch on the east and the Dry River and Saco River on the west. At Mt. Resolution the main ridge curves to the east along the Saco valley, while the short Bemis Ridge carries the line of the upper ridge south to the great bend in the Saco. The peaks of the Montalban Ridge, in order from the north, include Mt. Isolation (4005 ft.), Mt. Davis (3840 ft.), Stairs Mtn. (3460 ft.), Mt. Resolution (3428 ft.), Mt. Parker (3015 ft.), Mt. Langdon (2423 ft.), Mt. Pickering (1942 ft.), and Mt. Stanton (1748 ft.). The peaks of the Bemis Ridge include

Mt. Crawford (3129 ft.), Mt. Hope (2520 ft.), and Hart Ledge (2040 ft.). Cave Mtn. (1460 ft.), a low spur of the range near Bartlett village, is much better known for the cave on its south face than for its summit.

East of the Montalban Ridge, across the Rocky Branch and west of the Ellis River, lies the Rocky Branch Ridge. This heavily wooded ridge runs south from Gulf Peak, and is sharply defined for only about 3 mi., then spreads out and flattens. It has no important peaks. Iron Mtn. (2716 ft.), near Jackson, is the most significant summit on the ridge between the Rocky Branch and the Ellis River, but the Rocky Branch Ridge ceases to be a prominent ridge long before it reaches Iron Mtn.

The views from the summits of Mts. Isolation, Davis, and Crawford are among the finest in the White Mtns., and Mt. Resolution and Mt. Parker also offer excellent outlooks. The Giant Stairs are a wild and picturesque feature of the region, offering a spectacular view from the top of the cliff that forms the upper stair. These two great steplike ledges at the south end of the ridge of Stairs Mtn. are quite regular in form, and are visible from many points. A third and somewhat similar cliff, sometimes called the "Back Stair," lies east of the main summit, but there is no trail. Mt. Stanton and Mt. Pickering are wooded but have frequent open ledges which afford interesting views in various directions. Iron Mtn. has a fine north outlook, and a magnificent open ledge at the top of the south cliffs.

All of the peaks named above are reached by well-maintained trails, except Mt. Hope and Hart Ledge. Mt. Hope is heavily wooded, pathless, and very seldom climbed. The fine cliff of Hart Ledge rises more than 1000 ft. above the meadows at the great bend in the Saco River just above Bartlett and affords commanding views to the east, west, and south. There is no regular trail, but intrepid bushwhackers may follow the roads west along the north side of the river, passing under the cliffs, then climb up the slope well to the west of the cliffs.

HUTS, SHELTERS, AND CAMPING

Note: No hotel or overnight lodging for the public is available on the summit of Mt. Washington. No camping is permitted above treeline between 1 May and 1 November.

HUTS

Pinkham Notch Camp (AMC)

Pinkham Notch Camp is a unique mountain facility in the heart of the WMNF. This camp, originally built in 1920 and greatly enlarged since then, is located on NH 16 practically at the height-of-land in Pinkham Notch, about 20 mi. north of Conway and 11 mi. south of Gorham. It is also 0.8 mi. north of Glen Ellis Falls and 1 mi. south of the base of the Wildcat Mtn. Ski Area. Pinkham Notch Camp offers food and lodging to the public throughout the year and is managed similarly to the AMC huts. The telephone number is 603-466-2727. Concord Trailways offers daily bus service to and from South Station in Boston, and the AMC operates a hiker shuttle bus during the summer.

The Joe Dodge Center, which accommodates over a hundred guests in rooms with two, three, or four bunks, also offers a library that commands a spectacular view of the nearby Wildcat Ridge, and a living room where accounts of the day's activities can be shared by an open fireplace. The Center features a 65-seat conference room equipped with audiovisual facilities.

The Trading Post, a popular meeting place for hikers, has been a center of AMC educational and recreational activities since 1920. Weekend workshops, seminars, and lectures are conducted throughout the year. The building houses a dining room, and an information desk where basic equipment and guidebooks are available. The packroom downstairs is open 24 hours a day for hikers to stop in, relax, shower, and repack their gear.

Pinkham Notch Camp is the most important trailhead on the east side of Mt. Washington, and free public parking is available, although sleeping in cars is not permitted. The Tuckerman Ravine Trail, the Lost Pond Trail, and the Old Jackson Road all start at the camp, giving access to many more trails, and a number of walking trails have been constructed for shorter, easier trips in the Pinkham vicinity. Among these are the Crew-Cut Trail, Liebeskind's Loop, and the Square Ledge Trail. There are also several ski-touring trails; for information consult personnel at the Camp Trading Post.

Crawford Notch Hostel (AMC)

Low-cost, self-service lodging is available in historic Crawford Notch. The main hostel holds thirty people in one large bunkroom. There is also a kitchen, bathrooms, and a common area. Three adjacent cabins accommodate eight persons each.

The hostel is open to the public. AMC members receive a discount on lodging. Overnight lodging is available year-round. Reservations are encouraged. Guests must supply food and sleeping bags; stoves and cooking equipment are provided. The hostel is an excellent choice for families and small groups and offers a wide range of hiking and outdoor experiences.

Lakes of the Clouds Hut (AMC)

The original stone hut, greatly enlarged since, was built in 1915. It is located on a shelf near the foot of Mt. Monroe about 50 yd. west of the larger lake at an elevation of about 5050 ft. It is reached by the Crawford Path or the Ammonoosuc Ravine Trail, and has accommodations for ninety guests. The hut is open to the public from mid-June to mid-September, and closed at all other times. Space for backpackers is available at a lesser cost. A refuge room in the cellar is left open in the winter for emergency use only.

Mizpah Spring Hut (AMC)

The newest of the AMC huts was completed in 1965 and is located at about 3800 ft. elevation, on the site formerly occupied by the Mizpah Spring Shelter, at the junction of the Webster Cliff Trail and the Mount Clinton Trail, near the Mizpah Cutoff. The hut accommodates sixty guests, with sleeping quarters in eight rooms containing from four to ten bunks. This hut is open to the public from mid-June to mid-October. There are tentsites nearby (caretaker, fee charged).

For current information on AMC huts, Pinkham Notch Camp, or Crawford Notch Hostel, contact Reservation Secretary, Pinkham Notch Camp, Box 298, Gorham, NH 03581 (603-466-2727).

CAMPING

Presidential Range–Dry River Wilderness

In this area, camping and fires are prohibited above tree-line, and within 200 ft. of any trail except at designated sites. No campsite can be used by more than ten persons at any one time. Many shelters have been removed, and the remaining ones will be removed when major maintenance is required; do not count on using these shelters.

Restricted Use Areas

The WMNF has established a number of Restricted Use Areas (RUA's) where camping and wood or charcoal fires are prohibited from 1 May to 1 November. The specific areas are under continual review, and areas are added to or subtracted from the list in order to provide the greatest amount of protection to areas subject to damage by excessive camping, while imposing the lowest level of restrictions possible. A general list of RUA's follows, but one should obtain a map of current RUA's from the WMNF.

(1) No camping is permitted above treeline (where trees are less than 8 ft. tall). The point where the restricted area begins is marked on most trails with small signs, but the absence of such signs should not be construed as proof of the legality of a site.

(2) No camping is permitted within one-quarter mile of most facilities, such as huts, cabins, shelters, or tentsites, except at the facility itself.

(3) No camping is permitted within 200 ft. of certain trails. In 1986, designated trails included the Ammonoosuc Ravine Trail, Edmands Path, the Crawford Path from US 302 to Mt. Pierce, and those parts of the Webster Cliff Trail and Webster–Jackson Trail which are not in the State Park (where camping is absolutely prohibited).

(4) In Tuckerman and Huntington ravines (Cutler River drainage), camping is prohibited throughout the year except at the Hermit Lake Shelters; the Hermit Lake tentsites are available in winter only. The Hermit Lake Shelters are lean-tos open to the public. Tickets for shelter space (nontransferable and nonrefundable) must be purchased at Pinkham Notch Camp in person (first come, first served) for a nominal fee, for a maximum of seven consecutive nights. Overnight use is limited to the 86 spaces in the shelters. Ten tentsites for forty people are available between 1 December and 1 April. Fee is $1.75 per person per night. Users may no longer kindle charcoal or wood fires; people intending to cook must bring their own small stoves. Day visitors and shelter users alike are required to carry out all their own trash and garbage. No receptacles are provided. This operating policy is under continual review, so it can

change from time to time. Information is available at the caretaker's residence. There is no warming room open to the public, and refreshments are not sold.

Crawford Notch State Park

No camping is permitted in Crawford Notch State Park, except at the public Dry River Campground (fee charged).

Established Trailside Campsites

Mizpah Tentsite (AMC) has seven tent platforms at Mizpah Spring Hut. There is a caretaker, and a fee is charged in summer.

Lakes of the Clouds Hut (AMC) has limited space available for backpackers at a substantially lower cost than the normal hut services.

Rocky Branch Shelter #1 and Tentsite (WMNF) is located near the junction of the Rocky Branch and Stairs Col trails, just outside the Presidential Range–Dry River Wilderness.

Mt. Langdon Shelter (WMNF) is located at the junction of the Mount Langdon and Mount Stanton trails, at the edge of the Presidential Range–Dry River Wilderness.

Rocky Branch Shelter #2 (WMNF) is located at the junction of the Rocky Branch and Isolation trails, within the Presidential Range–Dry River Wilderness. Following the established policy for management of wilderness, this shelter will be removed when major maintenance is required.

Dry River Shelter #3 (WMNF) is located on the Dry River Trail, 6.3 mi. from US 302, within the Presidential Range–Dry River Wilderness. This shelter will be removed when major maintenance is required.

Resolution Shelter (AMC) is located on a spur path which leaves the Davis Path at its junction with the Mount Parker Trail, within the Presidential–Dry River Wilderness.

The water source is scanty in dry seasons. This shelter will be removed when major maintenance is required.

THE TRAILS

Tuckerman Ravine Trail (WMNF)

This trail is the most popular route of ascent on Mt. Washington. From Pinkham Notch Camp to the floor of Tuckerman Ravine it uses a rocky tractor road. It is a well-graded path from there to the top of the headwall, steady but not excessively steep. Its final section ascends the cone of Mt. Washington steeply over fragments of rock. In the spring and fall the WMNF often closes the section of trail on the headwall because of snow and ice, and notice is posted at the top and bottom. In these circumstances, the Lion Head Trail is usually the most convenient alternative route. In the winter this section is often impassable except by experienced and well-equipped snow and ice climbers, and it is frequently closed even to such climbers by the WMNF.

The trail leaves the west side of NH 16 behind the Trading Post at Pinkham Notch Camp. Be careful to avoid numerous side paths in this area. In 0.3 mi. it crosses a bridge to the south bank of Cutler River, and soon climbs to a side path 20 yds. right to the best viewpoint of the Crystal Cascade. At a curve to the right 0.4 mi. from Pinkham Notch Camp, the Boott Spur Trail leaves left. After two long switchbacks, the path continues west, ascending by steady grades. At 1.3 mi. the Huntington Ravine Trail diverges right. At 1.5 mi. the trail crosses a tributary, then at 1.6 mi. the main branch, of the Cutler River. Soon the Huntington Ravine Fire Rd., which is the best route to Huntington Ravine in winter, leaves right. At 2.1 mi. the Raymond Path enters right, at a point where the Tuckerman trail turns sharply left. At a crossroads at 2.3 mi. the Boott Spur Link turns left, and directly opposite the Lion Head Trail turns right.

In another 0.1 mi. the trail reaches the buildings in the floor of Tuckerman Ravine near Hermit Lake. The cliff on the right is Lion Head, so called because of its appearance from the Glen House site. The more distant crags on the left are the Hanging Cliffs of Boott Spur.

The main trail keeps to the right (north) of the stream and ascends a well-constructed footway into the floor of the ravine, and finally, at the foot of the headwall, bears right and ascends a steep slope where the Snow Arch can be found on the left in the spring and early summer. In the spring the snowfield above the Snow Arch usually extends across the trail, and the trail is often closed. Some snow may persist in the ravine until late summer. The arch (which does not always form) is carved by a stream of snow meltwater which flows under the snowfield. **Caution.** Do not approach too near the arch and under no circumstances cross or venture beneath it: one death and some narrow escapes have already resulted. Sections weighing tons may break off at any moment. When ascending the headwall, be careful not to start rocks rolling, since such carelessness may put others in serious danger.

Turning sharp left at the top of the debris slope and traversing under a cliff, the trail emerges from the ravine and climbs almost straight west up a grassy, ledgy slope. A short distance above the top of the headwall, the Alpine Garden Trail diverges right. At Tuckerman Junction, at the top of the plateau, the Tuckerman Crossover leads almost straight ahead (southwest) to the Crawford Path near the Lakes of the Clouds Hut; the Southside Trail leads west and northwest, skirting the cone to the Davis Path; and the Lawn Cutoff leads left (south) toward Boott Spur. The Tuckerman Ravine Trail turns sharp right and ascends the steep rocks, marked by cairns and paint on ledges. About a third of the way up the cone, at Cloudwater Spring, the Lion Head Trail enters right. The Tuckerman trail continues to ascend to the Auto Rd. a few yards below the lower parking area, just below the summit.

Tuckerman Ravine Trail (map 6:F9)
Distances from Pinkham Notch Camp
  to Boott Spur Trail: 0.4 mi., 20 min.
  to Huntington Ravine Trail: 1.3 mi., 1 hr. 10 min.
  to Raymond Path: 2.1 mi., 1 hr. 50 min.
  to Lion Head Trail and Boott Spur Link: 2.3 mi., 2 hr. 5 min.
  to Hermit Lake shelters: 2.4 mi., 2 hr. 10 min.
  to Snow Arch: 3.1 mi., 2 hr. 50 min.
  to Tuckerman Junction: 3.6 mi., 3 hr. 30 min.
  to Mt. Washington summit: 4.1 mi. (6.6 km.), 4 hr. 15 min.

Lion Head Trail (AMC)

The Lion Head Trail follows the steep-ended ridge that forms the north wall of Tuckerman Ravine. It begins and ends on the Tuckerman Ravine Trail and thus provides an alternative route, although it is much steeper in parts. It is especially important as an alternative when the Tuckerman Ravine Trail over the headwall is closed on account of snow or ice hazard. An older route of the trail, closed to summer hiking, is considered the least dangerous route to Mt. Washington in winter conditions, and is the most frequently used winter ascent route. The signs and markings are changed at the beginning and end of the winter season to ensure that climbers take the proper route for prevailing conditions.

This trail diverges right from the Tuckerman Ravine Trail 2.3 mi. from Pinkham Notch Camp and 0.1 mi. below Hermit Lake, opposite the foot of the Boott Spur Link. Running north, it passes a side path left to one of the Hermit Lake shelters and crosses the outlet of Hermit Lake. In 0.1 mi. the winter route diverges left, and the summer trail soon begins to climb the steep slope by switchbacks, scrambling up several small ledges with very rough footing, and reaches treeline at 0.4 mi. It then bears left, ascends the open slope to the left, and the winter route rejoins at 0.7 mi., just below the lower Lion Head. (The winter route is 0.2 mi. shorter.) The trail continues to the upper Lion Head at 0.9 mi., then runs mostly level, with impressive views from the open spur, until it crosses the Alpine Garden Trail at 1.1 mi. After passing through a belt of scrub, it ascends to the Tuckerman Ravine Trail, which it enters at Cloudwater Spring about a third of the way up the cone of Mt. Washington.

Lion Head Trail (map 6:F9)
Distances from lower junction with Tuckerman Ravine Trail
to Alpine Garden Trail: 1.1 mi. (1.8 km.), 1 hr. 15 min.

to upper junction with Tuckerman Ravine Trail: 1.6 mi. (2.5 km.), 1 hr. 45 min.

Distance from Pinkham Notch Camp
to summit (via summer route): 4.3 mi. (7.0 km.), 4 hr. 20 min.

Huntington Ravine Trail (AMC)

Caution. This is the most difficult trail in the White Mtns. Many of the ledges demand proper use of handholds for safe passage. Although experienced hikers who are comfortable on steep rock probably will encounter little difficulty when conditions are good, the exposure on several of the steepest ledges is likely to prove extremely unnerving to novices and to those who are uncomfortable in steep places. Do not attempt this trail if you tend to feel queasy or have difficulty on ledges on ordinary trails. Persons encumbered with large or heavy packs may experience great difficulty in some places. This trail is very dangerous when wet or icy. Extreme caution must be exercised at all times. Descent by this trail is strongly discouraged. Since retreat under unfavorable conditions can be extremely difficult and hazardous, one should never venture beyond the "Fan" in deteriorating conditions or when weather on the Alpine Garden is likely to be severe. During late fall, winter, and early spring, this trail (and any part of the ravine headwall) should be attempted only by those with full technical ice-climbing gear and training. In particular, the ravine must not be regarded as a viable "escape route" from the Alpine Garden in severe winter conditions.

The trail diverges right from the Tuckerman Ravine Trail 1.3 mi. from Pinkham Notch Camp. In 0.2 mi. it crosses the Cutler River and, at 0.3 mi., the brook that drains Huntington Ravine. At 0.5 mi. it goes straight across the Raymond Path, a junction that might not be well signed. Above this junction it crosses the brook and the Huntington Ravine Fire

Rd. several times, and care should be used to distinguish the trail from the road. At 1.3 mi. it reaches the first-aid cache in the floor of the ravine. Just beyond here there are some interesting boulders near the path whose tops afford good views of the ravine. Beyond the scrubby trees is a steep slope covered with broken rock, known as the "Fan," whose tip lies at the foot of the deepest gully. To the left of this gully are precipices, the lower known as the "Pinnacle." After passing through the boulders the path ascends the left side of the Fan for about 60 ft. It then turns right, and, marked by yellow blazes on the rocks, crosses a stream and ascends the north (right) side of the Fan to its tip at 1.8 mi. The trail then climbs the rocks to the right of the main gully. The first pitch above the Fan—a large, steeply sloping slab—is probably the most difficult scramble on the trail. The trail now climbs about 650 ft. in 0.3 mi. The route follows the line of least difficulty and should be followed carefully over the ledges, which are dangerous, especially when wet. Above the first ledges the trail climbs steeply through scrub and over short sections of rock, with some fairly difficult scrambles. About two-thirds of the way up it turns sharp left at a promontory with a good view, then continues to the top of the headwall where it crosses the Alpine Garden Trail at 2.1 mi. From this point it ascends moderately, crossing the Nelson Crag Trail at 2.3 mi., and reaches the Mt. Washington Auto Rd. just below the 7-mi. mark, 1.1 mi. below the summit.

Huntington Ravine Trail (map 6:F9)
Distances from Tuckerman Ravine Trail
   to Raymond Path: 0.5 mi., 30 min.
   to first-aid cache in ravine floor: 1.3 mi., 1 hr. 15 min.
   to Alpine Garden Trail crossing: 2.1 mi., 2 hr. 20 min.
   to Auto Rd.: 2.4 mi. (3.8 km.), 2 hr. 35 min.

Distance from Pinkham Notch Camp
   to Mt. Washington Summit (via Nelson Crag Trail): 4.3
   mi. (6.9 km.), 4 hr. 20 min.

Nelson Crag Trail (AMC)

   This trail leaves the Auto Rd. on the left in common with
the Old Jackson Road and Raymond Path, just above the
2-mi. mark and opposite the Madison Gulf Trail. It soon
diverges right and bears southwest, then almost due west,
climbing steadily with some sharp ascents. After about 1
mi. it rises steeply out of the scrub, emerging on a watershed ridge from which there is an unusual view of Pinkham
Notch in both directions. From here on it is above treeline
and very exposed to the weather. It then bears slightly
north, climbs moderately over open ledges, and joins the
Auto Rd. near Cragway Spring, at the sharp turn about 0.3
mi. above the 5-mi. mark. A few yards above, the trail
again diverges left from the Auto Rd. and climbs steeply to
the crest of the ridge. It travels over Nelson Crag, crosses
the Alpine Garden Trail, then swings left and follows a
newly relocated route across the Huntington Ravine Trail
and up the rocks to Ball Crag (6106 ft.), then runs to the
summit, crossing the Auto Rd. and the Cog Railway.

   Nelson Crag Trail (map 6:F9)
Distances (est.) from two-mile mark on Auto Rd.
   to its middle junction with the Auto Rd.: 1.6 mi., 1 hr.
   40 min.
   to the summit of Mt. Washington: 3.7 mi. (6.0 km.), 3
   hr. 40 min.

Boot Spur Trail (AMC)

   This trail runs from the Tuckerman Ravine Trail near
Pinkham Notch Camp to the Davis Path near the summit
of Boot Spur. It follows the long ridge that forms the
south wall of Tuckerman Ravine and affords fine views.

The trail diverges left from the Tuckerman Ravine Trail at a sharp right turn 0.4 mi. from Pinkham Notch Camp, about 150 yd. above the side path to Crystal Cascade. It crosses the John Sherburne Ski Trail, bears right, soon crosses a small brook, bears sharp left at the base of a rocky ledge, and, a short distance beyond, makes a sharp right turn and ascends an old logging road for about 0.3 mi. Descending slightly, the trail shortly makes a sharp right turn, where a side trail (left) leads in 50 yd. down to a restricted view east. The trail then passes through some interesting woods, ascends to the south side of a small wooded ridge, crosses a south outlook and turns right. It soon reaches a short moist area and ascends northwest up a steep slope. Halfway up the slope a side trail leads left 100 yd. to a brook (last water). At the top of this slope, at 1.0 mi. from the Tuckerman Ravine Trail, a side trail leads right (east) 25 yd. to an interesting outlook. At this junction the trail turns left, continues upward at moderate grades, heads more north, and shortly makes a sharp left turn. Turning more to the west, the trail ascends steadily, and at 1.7 mi. a short side trail right leads in 30 yd. to Ravine Outlook, with a view of Tuckerman Ravine, and of Lion Head directly in front of the summit of Mt. Washington.

The main trail emerges from the trees at 1.9 mi., soon bears left and slabs the ridge to Split Rock, which you can pass through or go around, at 2.2 mi. The trail then turns right, rises steeply over two minor humps to a broad, flat ridge, where, at 2.2 mi., Boott Spur Link descends on the right to the Tuckerman Ravine Trail near Hermit Lake. Above this point the trail follows the ridge, which consists of a series of steplike levels and steep slopes. The views of the ravine are excellent, particularly where the path skirts the dangerous Hanging Cliff, 1500 ft. above Hermit Lake. After passing just right (north) of the summit of the Spur, the trail ends at the Davis Path.

Boott Spur Trail (map 6:F9)
Distances from Tuckerman Ravine Trail
- *to* Ravine Outlook: 1.7 mi., 1 hr. 45 min.
- *to* Split Rock: 2.0 mi., 2 hr.
- *to* Boott Spur Link: 2.2 mi., 2 hr. 20 min.
- *to* Davis Path junction: 2.9 mi. (4.7 km.), 3 hr.

Distances from Pinkham Notch Camp
- *to* Davis Path junction: 3.4 mi., 3 hr. 25 min.
- *to* Mt. Washington summit (via Davis and Crawford paths): 5.5 mi. (8.9 km.), 5 hr.

Boott Spur Link (AMC)

This trail diverges south from the Tuckerman Ravine Trail 2.3 mi. from Pinkham Notch Camp and 0.1 mi. below Hermit Lake, opposite the foot of the Lion Head Trail. It immediately crosses two branches of Cutler River and the John Sherburne Ski Trail, then runs straight up the side of the ridge very steeply through scrub until it tops the ridge, and ends in a few yards at Boott Spur Trail.

Boott Spur Link (map 6:F9)
Distance from Tuckerman Ravine Trail
- *to* Boott Spur Trail: 0.6 mi. (1.0 km.), 45 min.

Glen Boulder Trail (AMC)

This trail runs from NH 16 to the Davis Path 0.4 mi. below Boott Spur. It is rough in parts, but reaches treeline and views relatively quickly.

The trail leaves the west side of NH 16 at the parking area near Glen Ellis Falls. It ascends gradually for about 0.4 mi. to the base of a small cliff. You can go up the cliff via the rather muddy and unappealing Chimney Route or, preferably, take the Chimney Bypass, which goes around to the right of the cliff. The Bypass makes a short, steep climb and then meets the Direttissima, which enters from the right (north) from Pinkham Notch Camp. The Chimney Bypass swings south, the Chimney Route enters left, and then a short branch trail leads left to an outlook on the brink of a cliff, which commands a fine view of Wildcat Mtn. and Pinkham Notch. The main trail turns west, rises gradually, then steepens. At 0.8 mi. it crosses the Avalanche Brook Ski Trail, which is marked with blue plastic markers and is not suitable for hiking. The Glen Boulder Trail soon reaches the north bank of a brook draining the minor ravine south of the Gulf of Slides. After following the brook, which soon divides, the trail then turns southwest and crosses both branches. It is level for 200 yd., then rapidly climbs the northeast side of the spur through evergreens, giving views of the minor ravine and spur south of the Gulf of Slides. Leaving the trees, it climbs over open rocks and, at 1.6 mi., reaches the Glen Boulder, an immense rock perched on the end of the spur, which is a familiar landmark for travelers through Pinkham Notch. The view is wide, from Chocorua around to Mt. Washington, and is particularly fine of Wildcat Mtn.

From the boulder the trail climbs steeply up the open spur to its top at 2.0 mi., re-enters high scrub and ascends moderately. At 2.3 mi. a side trail descends right about 60 yd. to a fine spring. The main trail continues to Gulf Peak (sometimes called Slide Peak), the rather insignificant peak heading the Gulf of Slides, at 2.6 mi. It then turns north, descends slightly, soon leaves the scrub, and runs entirely above treeline—greatly exposed to the weather—to the Davis Path just below a minor crag.

Glen Boulder Trail (map 6:F9)
Distances from Glen Ellis Falls parking area on NH 16
  to Chimney: 0.4 mi., 20 min.

to Avalanche Brook Ski Trail: 0.8 mi., 45 min.

to Glen Boulder: 1.6 mi., 1 hr. 40 min.

to Slide Peak: 2.6 mi., 2 hr. 45 min.

to Davis Path junction: 3.2 mi. (5.2 km.), 3 hr. 15 min.

to Boott Spur Trail (via Davis Path): 3.7 mi., 3 hr. 35 min.

to Mt. Washington summit (via Davis and Crawford paths): 5.8 mi. (9.3 km.), 5 hr. 5 min.

The Direttissima (MMVSP)

For hikers desiring access to the Glen Boulder Trail from Pinkham Notch Camp, this nearly level trail eliminates a road walk on NH 16. It begins just south of the highway bridge over the Cutler River near Pinkham Notch Camp, indicated by a sign at the edge of the woods. Marked by paint blazes, the trail turns sharp left about 10 yd. into the woods and follows a cleared area south. It turns slightly west at the end of this clearing and winds generally south, crossing a small brook, skirts through the upper (west) end of a gorge, and then crosses the New River. The trail continues past an excellent viewpoint looking down the Notch, climbs alongside a cliff, crosses another small brook, and ends on the Chimney Bypass near its upper junction with the regular (Chimney) route of the Glen Boulder Trail.

The Direttissima (map 6:F9-G9)
Distance (est.) from Pinkham Notch Camp

to Glen Boulder Trail: 0.6 mi. (1.0 km.), 35 min.

Alpine Garden Trail (AMC)

This trail leads from the Tuckerman Ravine Trail through a grassy lawn called the Alpine Garden to the Mt. Washington Auto Rd. It forms a convenient connecting link between the trails on the east side of the mountain. Although its chief value is its beauty, it also affords various combinations of routes to those who do not wish to visit the summit. It is completely above treeline and exposed to bad weather, although it is on the mountain's east side, which is usually more sheltered.

The tiny alpine flowers here are best seen in late June. Especially prominent in this area are the five-petaled white Diapensia, the bell-shaped pink-magenta Lapland Rosebay, and the very small pink flowers of the Alpine Azalea. (See the AMC's *Field Guide to Mountain Flowers of New England* and *At Timberline: A Nature Guide to the Mountains of the Northeast*.) No plants should ever be picked or otherwise damaged. Hikers are urged to stay on trails or walk very carefully on rocks so as not to kill the fragile alpine vegetation.

The trail diverges right from the Tuckerman Ravine Trail a short distance above the ravine headwall, about 0.1 mi. below Tuckerman Junction. It leads northeast, bearing toward Lion Head, and crosses the Lion Head Trail. Beyond the crossing the trail leads north, its general direction until it ends at the road. It traverses the Alpine Garden and crosses a tiny stream, which is the headwater of Raymond Cataract. (This water is unfit to drink: it consists largely of drainage from the summit buildings.) The trail soon approaches the top of Huntington Ravine and crosses the Huntington Ravine Trail. Here, a little off the trail, there is a fine view of this impressive ravine. Rising to the top of the ridge, the trail crosses the Nelson Crag Trail, then descends and soon enters the old Glen House Bridle Path, constructed in 1853, whose course is still plain although it was abandoned about a century ago. In a short distance the Alpine Garden Trail leads left and in a few yards enters the Auto Rd. a short distance above the 6-mi. mark and opposite the upper terminus of the Wamsutta Trail.

Alpine Garden Trail (map 6:F9)
Distances (est.) from Tuckerman Ravine Trail
   to Lion Head Trail: 0.3 mi., 10 min.

> *to* Huntington Ravine Trail: 1.3 mi., 45 min.
> *to* Nelson Crag Trail: 1.5 mi., 50 min.
> *to* Auto Rd. junction: 1.8 mi. (2.9 km.), 1 hr.

Southside Trail (AMC)

This trail forms a link between Tuckerman Ravine and the Crawford Path and Westside Trail. It diverges right (west) from Tuckerman Crossover about 10 yd. southwest of Tuckerman Junction and, skirting the southwest side of the cone of Mt. Washington, enters the Davis Path near its junction with the Crawford Path.

Southside Trail (map 6:F9)
Distance (est.) from Tuckerman Junction
> *to* Davis Path: 0.2 mi. (0.3 km.), 10 min.

Tuckerman Crossover (AMC)

This trail connects Tuckerman Ravine with Lakes of the Clouds Hut. It is totally above treeline, and crosses a high ridge where there is much exposure to westerly winds. It leaves the Tuckerman Ravine Trail left (southwest) at Tuckerman Junction, where the latter trail turns sharply right to ascend the cone. It rises gradually across Bigelow Lawn, crosses the Davis Path, then descends moderately to the Crawford Path, which it meets along with the Camel Trail a short distance above the upper Lake of the Clouds. Turning left on the Crawford Path, the Lakes of the Clouds Hut is reached in 0.2 mi.

Tuckerman Crossover (map 6:F9)
Distances from Tuckerman Junction
> *to* Crawford Path: 0.8 mi. (1.3 km.), 25 min.
> *to* Lakes of the Clouds Hut (via Crawford Path): 1.0 mi. (1.6 km.), 30 min.

Lawn Cutoff (AMC)

This trail provides a direct route between Tuckerman Junction and Boott Spur. It is entirely above treeline. It leaves the Tuckerman Ravine Trail at Tuckerman junction and leads south across Bigelow Lawn to the Davis Path about 0.5 mi. north of Boott Spur.

Lawn Cutoff (map 6:F9)
Distance from Tuckerman Junction
 to Davis Path: 0.4 mi. (0.6 km.), 15 min.

Camel Trail (AMC)

This trail, connecting Boott Spur with the Lakes of the Clouds Hut, is named for ledges on Boott Spur which resemble a kneeling camel when seen against the skyline.

The trail is the right of the two that diverge right (east) from the Crawford Path 0.2 mi. northeast of Lakes of the Clouds Hut (the Tuckerman Crossover is the left of the diverging trails). It ascends easy grassy slopes, crosses the old location of the Crawford Path, and continues in a practically straight line across the level stretch of Bigelow Lawn. It aims directly toward the ledges forming the camel, passes under the camel's nose, and joins the Davis Path about 100 yd. northwest of the Lawn Cutoff.

Camel Trail (map 6:F9)
Distance from Crawford Path
 to Davis Path: 0.6 mi. (1.0 km.), 30 min.

Westside Trail (WMNF)

This trail was partially constructed by pioneer trailmaker J. Rayner Edmands; many segments are paved with carefully placed stones. It is wholly above timberline, and is very much exposed to the prevailing west and northwest winds. By avoiding the summit of Mt. Washington, it saves nearly 1 mi. in distance and 600 ft. in elevation between points on the Northern Peaks and on the Crawford Path.

The trail diverges left from the Crawford Path, where the latter path begins to climb the steep part of the cone of Mt. Washington. It skirts the cone, climbing for 0.6 mi. at an easy grade, then descends moderately, crosses under the Mt. Washington Cog Railway, and soon ends at the Gulfside Trail.

Westside Trail (map 6:F9)
Distance from Crawford Path
  to Gulfside Trail: 0.9 mi. (1.4 km.), 30 min.

Trinity Heights Connector (NHDP)

This newly constructed trail allows the Appalachian Trail to make a loop over the summit of Mt. Washington. From the true summit (marked by a large sign) it runs approximately northwest to the Gulfside Trail, not far from its junction with the Crawford Path.

Trinity Heights Connector (map 6:F9)
Distance (est.) from true summit of Mt. Washington
  to Gulfside Trail: 0.2 mi. (0.3 km.), 5 min.

Raymond Path (AMC)

This old trail leaves the Auto Rd. along with the Old Jackson Road and the Nelson Crag Trail just above the 2-mi. mark, opposite the Madison Gulf Trail, and extends to the Tuckerman Ravine Trail about 0.3 mi. below Hermit Lake. Its grades are mostly easy to moderate.

It is the second trail to diverge right from the Old Jackson Road just south of the Auto Rd. (the first one is the Nelson Crag Trail). It crosses several streams—first a branch of the Peabody and then branches of the Cutler River. It crosses the Huntington Ravine Trail near the largest stream (this junction may not be well signed), then soon crosses the brook that drains the Ravine of Raymond Cataract, and ends about 0.4 mi. beyond at the Tuckerman Ravine Trail.

Raymond Path (map 6:F9)
Distances from Old Jackson Road

to Huntington Ravine Trail: 1.8 mi., 1 hr. 20 min.

to Tuckerman Ravine Trail: 2.4 mi. (3.9 km.), 1 hr. 50 min.

to Hermit Lake (via Tuckerman Ravine Trail): 2.7 mi., 2 hr.

Old Jackson Road (AMC)

This trail runs north from Pinkham Notch Camp to the Mt. Washington Auto Rd. It is part of the Appalachian Trail and is blazed in white. It diverges right from the Tuckerman Ravine Trail about 50 yd. from the camp. After about 0.3 mi. it begins to ascend steeply and steadily and the Crew-Cut Trail leaves right (east). At about 0.6 mi. the Blanchard Loop Ski Trail crosses. Upon reaching the height-of-land, where the George's Gorge Trail leaves right (east), the Old Jackson Road descends slightly, crosses several brooks, and at a large one takes a sharp left uphill. After a short, steep climb it slabs the slope, and the Raymond Path enters left, several small brooks are crossed, and then the Nelson Crag Trail enters left. Continuing north the trail climbs slightly, continues through an old gravel pit and meets the Auto Rd. just above the 2-mi. mark, opposite the Madison Gulf Trail.

Old Jackson Road (map 6:F9)
Distance from Pinkham Notch Camp

to Mt Washington Auto Rd.: 1.8 mi. (2.9 km.), 1 hr. 15 min.

Crew-Cut Trail (MMVSP)

The Crew-Cut Trail starts at the Old Jackson Road, leaving right about 0.3 mi. from Pinkham Notch Camp, after a stream crossing near where the abandoned section of the old road enters on the right from NH 16, as the Old Jackson Road starts to climb steeply. It is called "Brad's Trail" on some signs. After crossing a stony, dry brook bed it runs generally east-northeast, crossing two small brooks. On the east bank of the second brook, at 0.2 mi., the George's Gorge Trail leaves left.

The Crew-Cut Trail continues its same general line, rising gradually through open woods in a long slabbing of the slope and crossing several gullies. It skirts southeast of the steeper rocky outcroppings until it reaches the base of a cliff. At this point the main trail turns sharply right (south) while a very short side trail leads straight ahead and directly up to a lookout, "Lila's Ledge." From this ledge you can look straight in at the Wildcat ski-trail complex, down Pinkham Notch over the AMC buildings, and up at Mt. Washington over Huntington Ravine.

The main trail makes a sharp turn around the nose of the cliff and then resumes its generally east-northeast direction. In about 50 ft., and 0.5 mi. from the Old Jackson Road, Liebeskind's Loop enters left, coming down from the knob at the high point on the George's Gorge Trail. The Crew-Cut Trail continues its descent over a few small ledges and through open woods until it passes east of a small high-level bog formed by an old beaver dam. Shortly thereafter, it goes through open woods again, emerging at the top of the grassy slope on NH 16 almost exactly opposite the south end of the Wildcat Ski Area parking lot.

Crew-Cut Trail (map 6:F9-F10)
Distances (est.) from Old Jackson Road
to George's Gorge Trail: 0.2 mi., 5 min.

to Liebeskind's Loop: 0.5 mi., 25 min.
to NH 16: 0.7 mi. (1.1 km.), 35 min.

Liebeskind's Loop (MMVSP)

Liebeskind's Loop makes possible a loop hike (using the Crew-Cut, George's Gorge, Loop, and Crew-Cut trails) without resorting to returning either by NH 16 or by the steep section of the Old Jackson Road. This loop hike is best made in the direction described, since the Gorge is more interesting on the ascent and the Loop is more interesting on the descent.

Liebeskind's Loop leaves right (east) near the top of the George's Gorge Trail 0.2 mi. from Old Jackson Road, just before George's Gorge Trail makes the final short ascent to the knob. From this knob a short spur to the left (south) leads to an excellent view of Wildcat Mtn. and Huntington and Tuckerman ravines. Liebeskind's Loop descends to a swampy flat, then rises through a spruce thicket to the top of a cliff, where there is a fine lookout with a good view down Pinkham Notch. Here the trail turns left and runs along the edge of the cliff, finally descending by an easy zigzag in a gully to a beautiful open grove of birches. The trail continues east, descending through two gorges and skirting the east end of rises until it finally climbs a ridge and descends 50 yd. on the other side to join the Crew-Cut Trail just east of Lila's Ledge. The Crew-Cut Trail can then be followed back to the starting point.

Liebeskind's Loop (map 6:F9-F10)
Distance (est.) from George's Gorge Trail
to Crew-Cut Trail: 0.5 mi. (0.8 km.), 15 min.

George's Gorge Trail (MMVSP)

This trail leaves the Crew-Cut Trail to the left on the east bank of a small brook 0.2 mi. from the Old Jackson Road, and leads up the brook, steeply in places, passing Chuda-coff Falls. Liebeskind's Loop enters right at 0.6 mi., and in a very short distance George's Gorge Trail passes a spur path right (south) to an excellent view of Wildcat Mtn. and Huntington and Tuckerman ravines. From here it descends west to the Old Jackson Road in its upper, flat section, about 1 mi. from Pinkham Notch Camp.

George's Gorge Trail (map 6:F9-F10)
Distances (est.) from Crew-Cut Trail
to Liebeskind's Loop: 0.6 mi., 40 min.
to Old Jackson Road: 0.8 mi. (1.3 km.), 45 min.

Crawford Path (WMNF)

Caution. Parts of this trail are dangerous in bad weather. Below Mt. Eisenhower there are a number of ledges exposed to the weather, but they are scattered and shelter is usually available in nearby scrub. From the Eisenhower-Franklin col it lies completely above treeline, exposed to the full force of all storms. The most dangerous part of the path is the section on the cone of Mt. Washington, beyond Lakes of the Clouds Hut. Several lives have been lost on the Crawford Path through failure to observe proper precautions. Always carry a compass and study the map before starting. If trouble arises on or above Mt. Monroe, use the Lakes of the Clouds Hut or go down the Ammonoosuc Ravine Trail. If the path should be lost in cloudy weather, go northwest if you are below Mt. Monroe, west if you are above, descending into the woods and following water. On the southeast, toward the Dry River valley, nearly all the slopes are more precipitous, the river crossings potentially dangerous, and the distance to a highway is much greater.

This trail is considered to be the oldest continuously maintained footpath in America. The first section, a footpath leading up Mt. Pierce (Mt. Clinton), was cut in 1819 by Abel Crawford and his son Ethan Allen Crawford. In 1840 Thomas J. Crawford, a younger son of Abel, converted the footpath into a bridle path, although it has not been used for horses for many decades. The trail still follows the original path, except for the section between Mt. Monroe and the Westside Trail. From Mt. Pierce to the summit of Mt. Washington, the Crawford Path is part of the Appalachian Trail, and so it is blazed in white.

The path leaves US 302 opposite the Crawford House site, just south of the parking area near the junction with the Mt. Clinton Rd. It passes a short side trail to a view of a small flume in Gibbs Brook, and at 0.2 mi. from US 302 a side trail leads left to Crawford Cliff. This side path immediately crosses Gibbs Brook and follows it to a small flume and pool. It climbs steeply above the brook, then turns left at an old sign, becomes very rough, and reaches a ledge with an outlook over Crawford Notch and the Willey Range, 0.4 mi. (20 min.) from the Crawford Path.

There are plans to build a short link path to the Webster–Jackson Trail from this vicinity. The main trail continues along the south bank of Gibbs Brook, and at 0.4 mi. a side path leads 40 yd. left to Gibbs Falls. Soon the trail passes an information sign for the Gibbs Brook Scenic Area, and climbs moderately but steadily. At about 1 mi. from US 302 the trail climbs away from the brook and slabs the side of the valley. At 1.7 mi. the Mizpah Cutoff diverges east for Mizpah Spring Hut. The Crawford Path continues to ascend at easy to moderate grades, crossing several small brooks, then reaches its high point on the shoulder of Mt. Pierce and runs almost level, breaking into the open with fine views, and at 2.9 mi. reaches its junction with the Webster Cliff Trail, which leads right (south) to the summit of Mt. Pierce in about 0.1 mi.

From Mt. Pierce to Mt. Eisenhower the path runs through patches of scrub and woods with many open ledges that give magnificent views in all directions. Cairns and the marks of many feet on the rocks indicate the way. The path winds about fairly near the crest of the broad ridge, which is composed of several rounded humps. The general direction in ascending is northeast. At 3.6 mi. the trail crosses a small brook in the col, then ascends mostly on ledges to the junction with the Mount Eisenhower Loop, which diverges left at 4.1 mi. The trip over this summit adds only 0.2 mi. and 300 ft. of climbing to the trip, and the view is excellent in good weather. The Crawford Path continues right and slabs through scrub on the southeast side of the mountain; this is the better route in bad weather. In the col between Mts. Eisenhower and Franklin the path passes close to the right of stagnant Red Pond, and just beyond the Mount Eisenhower Loop rejoins the Crawford Path on the left. In another 100 yds., at 4.7 mi., the Edmands Path also enters left, and at 4.8 mi. the Mount Eisenhower Trail from the Dry River enters right.

The trail then begins the ascent of the shoulder called Mt. Franklin, first moderately, then steeply for a short distance near the top. At 5.3 mi. the trail reaches the relatively level shoulder and continues past an unmarked path at 5.8 mi. which leads in 130 yds. to the barely noticeable summit of Mt. Franklin, from which there are good views. At 6.1 mi. the Mount Monroe Loop diverges left to cross both summits of Monroe, affording excellent views. It is about the same length as the parallel section of the Crawford Path but requires about 350 ft. more climbing. The Crawford Path is safer in bad weather, as it is much less exposed to the weather. The Crawford Path continues along the edge of the precipice that forms the northwest wall of Oakes Gulf, then follows a relocated section, passing an area that has been closed to public entry to preserve an endangered species of plant. The area between the two ends of the Mount Monroe Loop is one of great botanical importance and fragility. To protect this area, the most scrupulous care is required on the part of visitors. At 6.7 mi. the Mount Monroe Loop rejoins on the left, and the path descends easily to Lakes of the Clouds Hut.

The Ammonoosuc Ravine Trail diverges left at the corner of the hut and in another 30 yd. the Dry River Trail diverges right. The Crawford Path crosses the outlet of the larger lake and passes between it and the second lake, where the Camel Trail to Boott Spur and the Tuckerman Crossover to Tuckerman Ravine diverge right. The path then ascends gradually, always some distance below (northwest) the crest of the ridge. The Davis Path, which here follows the original location of the Crawford Path, enters at 7.7 mi., at the foot of the cone of Mt. Washington. In another 50 yd. the Westside Trail to the Northern Peaks diverges left. The Crawford Path turns straight north, switching back and forth as it climbs the steep cone through a trench in the rocks. At the ridge top it meets the Gulfside Trail at 8.0 mi., then turns right, passes through the pen in which saddle horses from the Glen House used to be kept, and from there ascends to the summit, marked by frequent cairns. (Descending, the path is on the right (north) side of the railroad track. Beyond the buildings it leads generally northwest, then swings west. Avoid random side paths toward the south.)

Crawford Path (map 6:G8-F9)
Distances from US 302 near Crawford House site
> *to* Mizpah Cutoff: 1.7 mi., 1 hr. 20 min.
> *to* Webster Cliff Trail: 2.9 mi., 2 hr.
> *to* south end of Mount Eisenhower Loop: 4.1 mi., 2 hr. 45 min.
> *to* Edmands Path: 4.8 mi., 2 hr. 55 min.
> *to* Mt. Franklin summit: 5.8 mi., 3 hr. 45 min.

to south end of Mount Monroe Loop: 6.1 mi., 4 hr. 5 min.

to Lakes of the Clouds Hut: 6.8 mi., 4 hr. 30 min.

to Westside Trail: 7.7 mi., 5 hr. 20 min.

to Gulfside Trail: 8.0 mi., 5 hr. 50 min.

to Mt. Washington summit: 8.2 mi. (13.2 km.), 6 hr.

Mount Eisenhower Loop (AMC)

This short trail parallels the Crawford Path and crosses over the bare, flat summit of Mt. Eisenhower, which provides magnificent views. It diverges from the Crawford Path 4.1 mi. from US 302 at the south edge of the summit dome, climbs easily for 0.1 mi., then turns sharp left in a flat area and ascends steadily to the summit at 0.4 mi. It then descends moderately to a ledge overlooking Red Pond, drops steeply and passes through a grassy sag just to the left of Red Pond, and finally climbs briefly to rejoin the Crawford Path on a small, rocky knob.

Mount Eisenhower Loop (map 6:G8)
Distances from south junction with Crawford Path

to summit of Mt. Eisenhower: 0.4 mi., 20 min.

to north junction with Crawford Path: 0.8 mi. (1.2 km.), 35 min.

Mount Monroe Loop (AMC)

This short trail runs parallel to the Crawford Path and passes over the summits of Mt. Monroe and Little Monroe. The views are fine but the summits are very exposed to the weather. The trail diverges from the Crawford Path 6.1 mi. from US 302 and quickly ascends the minor crag called Little Monroe and descends into the shallow, grassy sag beyond. It then ascends steeply to the summit of Mt. Monroe at 0.3 mi., follows the northeast ridge to the end

of the shoulder, and drops sharply to the Crawford Path
0.1 mi. south of Lakes of the Clouds Hut.

Mount Monroe Loop (map 6:F9)
Distances (est.) from south junction with Crawford Path
   to summit of Mt. Monroe: 0.3 mi., 20 min.
   to north junction with Crawford Path: 0.6 mi. (1.0
   km.), 30 min.

Ammonoosuc Ravine Trail (WMNF)
   The Ammonoosuc Ravine Trail runs from the Base Rd.
to Lakes of the Clouds Hut, following the headwaters of
the Ammonoosuc River with many fine falls, cascades, and
pools, and affords fine views from its upper section. It is
the most direct route to Lakes of the Clouds Hut, and the
best route in bad weather, since it lies in woods or scrub
except for the last 200 yd. to the hut. The section above
Gem Pool is extremely steep and rough, and is likely to
prove quite arduous to many hikers; it is also somewhat
unpleasant to descend this section, on account of the steep,
often slippery rocks. Together with the upper section of the
Crawford Path it provides the shortest route to Mt. Washington from the west. It can also be reached on foot from
the Jefferson Notch Rd. via the Boundary Line Trail (see
Section 2).
   The trail begins at a newly constructed parking lot on the
Base Rd. about 1 mi. east of its junction with the Mt.
Clinton Rd. and the Jefferson Notch Rd. It follows a newly
cut path through the woods, crossing Franklin Brook at 0.3
mi., then passing over a double pipeline as it skirts around
the Base Station Area. It joins the old route of the trail at
the edge of the Ammonoosuc River at 1.0 mi., after a slight
descent, and bears right along the river, following the old
trail for the rest of the way. It ascends mostly by easy
grades, with some rough footing, crosses Monroe Brook at

1.7 mi., and at 2.1 mi. crosses the outlet of Gem Pool, a beautiful pool at the foot of a cascade.

Now the very steep, rough ascent begins. At 2.3 mi. a side path (sign) leads right about 80 yd. to a spectacular viewpoint at the foot of the gorge. Above this point the main brook falls about 600 ft. down a steep trough in the mountainside at an average angle of 45 degrees. Another brook a short distance to the north does the same, and these two spectacular waterslides meet at the foot of the gorge, forming a pool at the base. The main trail continues its steep ascent, passes an outlook over the falls to the right of the trail, and continues to the main brook, which it crosses at 2.5 mi. on flat ledges at a striking viewpoint at the head of the highest fall. The grade now begins to ease, and the trail crosses several brooks as ledges become more frequent and the scrub becomes smaller and sparse. At 3.0 mi. the trail emerges from the scrub and follows a line of cairns directly up some rock slabs (which are slippery when wet), passes through one last patch of scrub, and reaches the Crawford Path at the south side of Lakes of the Clouds Hut.

Ammonoosuc Ravine Trail (map 6:F8-F9)
Distances from the Base Rd. parking lot
to Gem Pool: 2.1 mi., 1 hr. 30 min.
to brook crossing on flat ledges: 2.5 mi., 2 hr. 10 min.
to Lakes of the Clouds Hut: 3.1 mi. (5.0 km.), 2 hr. 55 min.

Edmands Path (WMNF)

The Edmands Path leads from the Mt. Clinton Rd. to the Crawford Path in the Eisenhower–Franklin col. It provides the shortest route to the summit of Mt. Eisenhower, and an easy access to the middle portion of the Crawford Path. The last 0.2 mi. segment before the Crawford Path junction is very exposed to northwest winds and, although short, could pose problems in bad weather. J. Rayner Edmands, the pioneer trailmaker, relocated and reconstructed this trail in 1909. The rock cribbing and paving in the middle and upper sections of the trail testify to the infinite pains that Edmands expended to construct a trail with constant comfortable grades in rather difficult terrain. Most of his work has survived the weather and foot traffic of many decades well, and the trail retains what is probably the best grade and footing of any comparable trail in the White Mtns. The trail is nearly always comfortable, and almost never challenging.

The path leaves the east side of the Mt. Clinton Rd. 2.3 mi. north of the Crawford House site. It runs nearly level across two small brooks, then at 0.4 mi. it crosses Abenaki Brook and turns sharp right onto an old logging road on the far bank. At 0.7 mi. the trail diverges left off the old road and crosses a wet area. Soon it begins to climb steadily, undulating up the west ridge of Mt. Eisenhower, carefully searching out the most comfortable grades. At 2.2 mi. the trail swings left and slabs up the hillside on a footway supported by extensive rock cribbing, then passes through a little stone gateway. At 2.5 mi. it crosses a small brook running over a ledge, and soon the grade becomes almost level as the trail contours around the north slope of Mt. Eisenhower, affording excellent views out through the trees. At 2.8 mi. it breaks into the open, crosses the nose of a ridge on a footway paved with carefully placed stones, and reaches the Crawford Path after a slight descent.

Edmands Path (map 6:G8)
Distances from Mt. Clinton Rd.

to stone gateway: 2.3 mi., 2 hr. 10 min.

to Crawford Path junction: 3.1 mi. (4.9 km.), 2 hr. 45 min.

Webster–Jackson Trail (AMC)

This trail connects US 302 at the Crawford Depot information center with the summits of both Mt. Webster and Mt. Jackson, and provides the opportunity for many interesting loop trips from this vicinity. The two summits are linked by the Webster Cliff Trail.

The trail, blazed in blue, leaves the east side of US 302 0.1 mi. south of the Crawford Depot and 0.1 mi. north of the Gate of the Notch. The trail runs through a clearing, enters the woods, and passes the side path leading right to Elephant Head at 0.1 mi. from US 302.

Elephant Head is an interesting ledge forming the east side of the Gate of the Notch, with veins of white quartz in the gray rock providing a remarkable likeness to an elephant's head. The path runs through the woods parallel to the highway at an easy grade, then ascends across the summit of the knob and descends 40 yd. to the top of the ledge—which overlooks Crawford Notch with fine views— 0.2 mi. (10 min.) from the Webster–Jackson Trail.

The main trail runs above Elephant Head Brook, then turns right, away from the brook, at 0.2 mi. There are plans to construct a short trail from this point to the lower part of the Crawford Path. The trail continues up the slope, crosses Little Mossy Brook at 0.3 mi., and continues in the same general direction, nearly level stretches alternating with sharp pitches. At 0.6 mi. from US 302 a side path leads right 60 yd. to Bugle Cliff, a massive ledge overlooking Crawford Notch, where the view is well worth the slight extra effort required; if there is ice present, exercise extreme caution. The main trail rises fairly steeply and crosses Flume Cascade Brook at 0.9 mi. At 1.4 mi., within sound of Silver Cascade Brook, the trail divides, the left branch for Mt. Jackson and the right (straight ahead) for Mt. Webster.

Mount Webster

The Webster (right) branch immediately descends steeply to Silver Cascade Brook, crosses it just below a beautiful cascade and pool, bears left and climbs the bank steeply. The trail then climbs steadily south 1.0 mi., meeting the Webster Cliff Trail on the high plateau northwest of the summit of Mt. Webster, 2.4 mi. from US 302. The ledgy summit of Mt. Webster, with an excellent view of Crawford Notch and the mountains to the west and south, is 0.1 mi. right (south); turn left for Mt. Jackson.

Mount Jackson

The Jackson (left) branch ascends easily until it comes within sight of the brook and begins to climb steadily. About 0.5 mi. above the junction, it crosses three branches of the brook in quick succession. At 1.0 mi. from the junction it passes Tisdale Spring (unreliable, often scanty and muddy), a short distance below the base of the rocky cone. The trail climbs, soon ascending steep ledges to the open summit, 2.6 mi. from US 302.

Webster–Jackson Trail (map 6:G8)
Distances from US 302

  to Elephant Head side path: 0.1 mi., 5 min.
  to Bugle Cliff: 0.6 mi., 35 min.
  to Flume Cascade Brook: 0.9 mi., 45 min.
  to Mt. Webster–Mt. Jackson fork: 1.4 mi., 1 hr. 10 min.
  to Webster Cliff Trail (via Webster branch): 2.4 mi., 2 hr. 15 min.
  to summit of Mt. Webster (via Webster Cliff Trail): 2.5 mi. (4.1 km.), 2 hr. 20 min.
  to summit of Mt. Jackson (via Jackson branch): 2.6 mi. (4.2 km.), 2 hr.
  for loop trip over summits of Webster and Jackson (via Webster Cliff Trail): 6.5 mi. (10.5 km.), 4 hr. 30 min.

Webster Cliff Trail (AMC)

This trail, a part of the Appalachian Trail, leaves the east side of US 302 opposite the road to Willey House Station, about 1 mi. south of the Willey House Recreation Area at the Willey House site. It ascends along the edge of the spectacular cliffs which form the east wall of Crawford Notch, then leads over Mts. Webster, Jackson, and Pierce to the Crawford Path 0.1 mi. north of Mt. Pierce.

From US 302, it runs nearly east 0.1 mi. to a bridge across the Saco River. Then the trail climbs steadily up the south end of the ridge, winding up the steep slope, growing steeper and rougher as it approaches the cliffs and swinging more to the north. At 1.8 mi. from US 302 it reaches the first open ledge, and from here on, as the trail ascends the ridge with easier grades, there are frequent outlook ledges giving ever-changing perspectives of the notch and the mountains to the south and west. At 2.4 mi. a ledge affords a view straight down to the State Park buildings, and at 3.3 mi. the jumbled, ledgy summit is reached.

The trail then descends north, and in 0.1 mi. the Webster branch of the Webster–Jackson Trail from Crawford Depot on US 302 enters left. The Webster Cliff Trail swings east and crosses numerous wet gullies, finally ascending the steep, ledgy cone of Mt. Jackson, reaching the summit at 4.7 mi., where the Jackson branch of the Webster–Jackson Trail enters left.

The trail leaves the summit of Mt. Jackson toward Mt. Pierce, following a line of cairns running north, and descends the ledges at the north end of the cone quite rapidly into the scrub, then enters and winds through open alpine meadows. At 5.2 mi., where a side path leads right 40 yd. to an outlook, the trail turns sharp left and drops into the woods. It continues up and down along the ridge toward Mt. Pierce, then descends gradually to the junction at 6.3 mi. with the Mizpah Cutoff, which leads left (west) to the

Crawford Path. At 6.4 mi. Mizpah Spring Hut (which also has tentsites) is reached, and the Mount Clinton Trail to the Dry River diverges right (southeast) diagonally down the hut clearing. Continuing west of the hut, the trail ascends very rapidly, passes an outlook toward Mt. Jackson, and reaches an open ledge with good views at 6.6 mi. The grade lessens, and after a sharp right turn in a ledgy area the trail reaches the summit of the southwest knob of Mt. Pierce, which affords a view of the summit of Mt. Washington rising over Mt. Pierce. The trail descends into a sag, ascends easily through scrub to the summit of Mt. Pierce at 7.2 mi., where it comes into the open. It then descends moderately in the open in the same direction (northeast), to its junction with the Crawford Path.

Webster Cliff Trail (map 6:G8)
Distances from US 302
to first open ledge: 1.8 mi., 1 hr. 50 min.
to summit of Mt. Webster: 3.3 mi., 3 hr.
to summit of Mt. Jackson: 4.7 mi., 4 hr.
to Mizpah Spring Hut: 6.4 mi., 5 hr. 10 min.
to Crawford Path: 7.3 mi. (11.7 km.), 5 hr. 35 min.

Mizpah Cutoff (AMC)
This short trail provides a direct route from US 302 near the AMC Crawford Notch Hostel to Mizpah Spring Hut. It diverges right (east) from the Crawford Path 1.7 mi. from US 302, climbs the ridge at a moderate grade, passes through a fairly level area, and descends slightly to join the Webster Cliff Trail 0.1 mi. south of Mizpah Spring Hut.

Mizpah Cutoff (map 6:G8)
Distance from Crawford Path
to Mizpah Spring Hut: 0.7 mi. (1.1 km.), 30 min.

Distance from US 302
  to Mizpah Spring Hut (via Crawford Path and Mizpah
    Cutoff): 2.4 mi. (3.9 km.), 1 hr. 50 min.

Saco Lake Trail (AMC)

This very short trail makes a loop around the east shore
of Saco Lake, beginning and ending on US 302. It starts
opposite the AMC Crawford Notch Hostel and ends after
crossing the dam at the south end of Saco Lake. In addition to being an attractive short walk, it provides an alternative to part of the road walk between the Crawford Path
and Webster–Jackson Trail.

Saco Lake Trail (map 6:G8)
Distance (est.) from north junction with US 302
  to south junction with US 302: 0.4 mi. (0.6 km.), 15
    min.

Dry River Trail (WMNF)

The Dry River Trail is the main trail from US 302 up the
valley and through Oakes Gulf to Lakes of the Clouds Hut,
with access to Mt. Washington, the Southern Peaks, and the
upper portion of the Montalban Ridge. The first 5 mi.
roughly follows the route of an old logging railroad, although the river and its tributaries have eradicated much of
the old roadbed, and the relocations cut to eliminate the
numerous, potentially hazardous river crossings have by-
passed much of the remaining grade. The few river crossings
that remain can be very difficult when water is high. The trail
is somewhat rougher than most similar valley trails elsewhere
in the White Mtns. This trail is almost entirely within the
Presidential Range-Dry River Wilderness. Dry River Shelters
#1 and #2 have been removed; Dry River Shelter #3 will be
removed whenever major maintenance is required.

The trail leaves the east side of US 302, 0.3 mi. north of
the entrance to Dry River Campground. From the highway

the trail follows a wide wood road, generally northeast, for 0.5 mi. to its junction with the bed of the old logging railroad. From here the trail follows the railroad bed, passes the Wilderness Area boundary at 0.7 mi., and leaves the railroad grade sharp left at 0.9 mi, staying on the west side of the river (the railroad crossed it). Just downstream from this point there is a pleasant pool. The trail turns left and climbs over a low bluff, rejoins the roadbed, then leaves it again and climbs over a higher bluff, where there is a restricted but beautiful outlook up the Dry River to Mt. Washington, Mt. Monroe, and the headwall of Oakes Gulf. At 1.7 mi. the trail crosses the Dry River on a suspension bridge, and continues up the east bank, occasionally using portions of the old railroad grade. At 2.9 mi. the Mount Clinton Trail diverges left to ascend to Mizpah Spring Hut. At 4.2 mi. the trail makes a sharp turn away from the river, then turns left and continues along the bank at a higher level. At 4.9 mi. the trail crosses Isolation Brook, turns right along the bank, and in 60 yd. the Isolation Trail diverges right.

The Dry River Trail continues straight along the high river bank on a recently cut path, passes a cleared outlook over the river, and at 5.2 mi. the Mount Eisenhower Trail diverges sharp left and descends the steep bank on a former section of the Dry River Trail. Now back on the older route, the trail continues along the east bank, passing at 5.4 mi. a side path (sign) that leads down left 40 yd. to the pool at the foot of Dry River Falls, a very attractive spot. The top of the falls, with an interesting pothole, can also be reached from here. At 5.6 mi. the trail crosses the river to the west side; the crossing is fairly easy, but could be a problem at high water. At 6.3 mi. Dry River Shelter #3 is passed; it will be removed when major maintenance is required. In 60 yd. the trail crosses a major tributary of Dry River at the confluence, and continues along the bank, gradually rising higher above the river.

At 7.4 mi. it begins to swing away from the river, which has been at least audible to this point, and gradually climbs into Oakes Gulf. After crossing a small ridge and descending sharply on the other side, views begin to appear, although the trail remains well sheltered in the scrub. At 8.7 mi. there is a good outlook perch just right of the trail. The trail climbs out of the scrub, turns left and crosses a small brook at a right angle. At 9.1 mi. the trail turns sharp right from its former route, where signs forbid public entry into the area formerly crossed by the trail. The closed area is the habitat of an endangered plant species. The trail continues to climb, passing the Wilderness Area boundary sign in a patch of scrub, and reaches the height-of-land on the southwest ridge of Mt. Washington at 9.4 mi. It then descends to the larger of the Lakes of the Clouds, follows its south edge, and ends at Lakes of the Clouds Hut.

Dry River Trail (map 6:H8-F9)
Distances from US 302
> *to* suspension bridge: 1.7 mi., 1 hr. 5 min.
> *to* Mount Clinton Trail: 2.9 mi., 1 hr. 50 min.
> *to* Isolation Trail: 4.9 mi., 3 hr. 15 min.
> *to* Mount Eisenhower Trail: 5.2 mi., 3 hr. 25 min.
> *to* Dry River Shelter #3: 6.3 mi., 4 hr. 15 min.
> *to* Lakes of the Clouds Hut: 9.6 mi. (15.5 km.), 7 hr.

Mount Clinton Trail (WMNF)
This trail connects the lower part of the Dry River to Mizpah Hut and the southern part of the Southern Peaks. The crossing of Dry River near its junction with the Dry River Trail can be impassable in high water. This trail is almost entirely within the Presidential Range-Dry River Wilderness.

The trail diverges left from the Dry River Trail 2.9 mi. from US 302, and immediately crosses the Dry River. This crossing can vary from an easy skip over the stones to a waist-high ford in a torrent, and there may be no safe way across. On the west side of the river it follows a short stretch of old railroad grade, then swings left up the bank of a major tributary, following an old logging road at a moderate grade much of the way. At 0.5 mi the trail crosses this brook for the first of seven times, and scrambles up a washed-out area on the other bank. At 1.2 mi. the trail turns sharp left off the road and descends to the brook, crosses at a ledgy spot, and soon regains the road on the other side. It follows close to the brook, crossing many tributaries as well as the main brook, to the seventh crossing at 1.8 mi. Above an eroded section where a small brook has taken over the road, the walking on the old road becomes very pleasant, and the Dry River Cutoff Trail enters on the right at 2.5 mi. From here the trail ascends past a large boulder to the Wilderness Area boundary at 2.9 mi., and soon enters the clearing of Mizpah Spring Hut, where it joins the Webster Cliff Trail.

Mount Clinton Trail (map 6:G8)
Distances from Dry River Trail
   to Dry River Cutoff: 2.5 mi., 2 hr.
   to Mizpah Spring Hut: 3.0 mi. (4.8 km.), 2 hr. 35 min.

Mount Eisenhower Trail (WMNF)
This trail connects the middle part of the Dry River valley to the Crawford Path at the Eisenhower-Franklin col. Its grades are mostly easy to moderate and it is only above treeline for a short distance on the ridge top. This trail is almost entirely within the Presidential Range–Dry River Wilderness.

The trail diverges left from the Dry River Trail about 5.2 mi. from US 302, and descends rather steeply on a former route of the Dry River Trail through an area with many side paths; care must be used to stay on the proper trail. The trail crosses Dry River (may be difficult or impassable at high water), and follows the bank downstream. At 0.2 mi. it joins its former route, and bears right up a rather steep logging road. The Dry River Cutoff Trail diverges left at 0.3 mi., and soon the grade eases. The Mount Eisenhower Trail generally leads north, keeping a bit to the west of the crest of the long ridge that runs south from a point midway between Franklin and Eisenhower. At 1.3 mi. it passes through a blowdown patch with views of Mt. Pierce, and from here on there are occasional views from the edge of the ravine to the west. At 1.8 mi. it turns sharp right, then left, and soon ascends more steeply for a while. At 2.4 mi. the trail finally gains the crest of the ridge, and winds among rocks and scrub, passing the Wilderness Area boundary 50 yd. before reaching the Crawford Path, 0.1 mi. north of the upper terminus of the Edmands Path in the Eisenhower-Franklin col.

Mount Eisenhower Trail (map 6:G8)
Distances from Dry River Trail
to Dry River Cutoff Trail: 0.3 mi., 15 min.
to Crawford Path: 2.7 mi. (4.3 km.), 2 hr. 15 min.

Dry River Cutoff Trail (AMC)
This trail connects the middle part of the Dry River valley to Mizpah Spring Hut and the southern section of the Southern Peaks. Grades are mostly easy with some moderate sections. This trail is almost entirely within the Presidential Range–Dry River Wilderness.

The trail diverges left from the Mount Eisenhower Trail 0.3 mi. from the latter trail's junction with the Dry River Trail. In 0.1 mi. it crosses a substantial brook after a slight descent, then turns sharply left and climbs the bank, crosses a tributary, then swings back and climbs above the bank of the tributary. It crosses several branches of the tributary and gains the height-of-land on the southeast ridge of Mt. Pierce at 1.3 mi., then runs almost on the level to its junction with the Mount Clinton Trail at 1.7 mi. Mizpah Spring Hut is 0.5 mi. to the right from this junction via the Mount Clinton Trail.

Dry River Cutoff Trail (map 6:G8)
Distance from Mount Eisenhower Trail
   to Mount Clinton Trail: 1.7 mi. (2.8 km.), 1 hr. 15 min.

Davis Path (AMC)

The Davis Path, constructed by Nathaniel P. T. Davis in 1844, was the third bridle path leading up Mt. Washington. It was in use until 1853 or 1854, but soon after became impassable, and eventually went out of existence. It was reopened as a foot trail in 1910. The sections leading up Mt. Crawford and Stairs Mtn. give some idea of the magnitude of the task Davis performed. The resolution that enabled Davis to push forward with this apparently hopeless task was the inspiration for the naming of Mt. Resolution. This trail is almost entirely within the Presidential Range–Dry River Wilderness.

This path leaves US 302 on the west side of the Saco River at a paved parking lot, and follows the bank of the river about 100 yd. upstream to the suspension footbridge (Bemis Bridge). Beyond the east end of the bridge, the trail passes through private land. Continue straight east across an overgrown field and a small brook and turn southeast on an embankment. Ignore other branching paths and blazes, which relate to new housing. At about 0.3 mi. the path turns east and enters the woods (WMNF and Wilderness Area) on a logging road. It then crosses a dry brook and, leaving the logging road at the foot of a steep hill 0.8 mi. from US 302, soon enters the old, carefully graded bridle path and begins to ascend the steep ridge connecting Mt. Crawford with Mt. Hope. Attaining the crest, the Davis Path follows this ridge north, mounting over bare ledges with good outlooks.

At 2.3 mi. from US 302, at the foot of a large, sloping ledge, a side trail diverges left and climbs to the bare, peaked summit of Mt. Crawford, from which there is an magnificent view of Crawford Notch, the Dry River Valley, and the surrounding ridges and peaks, at 0.3 mi. (15 min.).

From this junction the path turns northeast, descends slightly to the col between the peak of Mt. Crawford and its ledgy, domelike east knob (sometimes called Crawford Dome), and resumes the ascent. It soon passes over the ledgy shoulder of Crawford Dome and dips to the Crawford–Resolution col. Leaving this col, the path runs north, rises slightly, and keeps close to the same level along the steep west side of Mt. Resolution. The Mount Parker Trail, which diverges right (east) at 3.8 mi., leads in about 0.6 mi. to open ledges near the summit of Mt. Resolution. A trail that branches left at this junction descends a short distance to the AMC Resolution Shelter, an open camp with room for eight, situated on a small branch of Sleeper Brook. (WMNF policies call for removal of this shelter whenever major maintenance is required.) Ordinarily there is water just behind the shelter, but in dry seasons it may be necessary to go down the brook a short distance. In most seasons, this is the first water after starting up the grade of Crawford and the last before the site of the former Isolation Shelter.

At 4.1 mi. the path passes just west of Stairs Col, the col between Mt. Resolution and Stairs Mtn. Here the Stairs Col Trail to the Rocky Branch diverges right. The path now veers northwest, passing west of the precipitous Giant Stairs, ascending gradually along a steep mountainside, then zigzagging boldly northeast toward the flat top of

Stairs Mtn. Shortly before the path reaches the top of the slope, a branch trail leads right a few steps to the "Down-look," a good viewpoint. At the top of the climb, 4.5 mi. from US 302, a branch trail leads right (southeast) 0.2 mi. past the summit to the top of the Giant Stairs, where there is an inspiring view.

The Davis Path continues down the north ridge of Stairs Mtn. for about 1 mi., then runs east in a col for about 0.1 mi. Turning north again (watch for this turn), it passes over a small rise and descends into another col. The path next begins to ascend the long north and south ridge of Mt. Davis, keeping to the west slopes. At 8.5 mi. a branch trail diverges right (east) 0.2 mi. to the summit of Mt. Davis, with the finest view on the Montalban Ridge, and one of the best in the mountains.

The main path now descends to the col between Mt. Davis and Mt. Isolation, then ascends the latter. At 9.8 mi. a spur path (which is signed, but easily missed) diverges left, leading in 125 yd. to the summit of Mt. Isolation. The open summit provides magnificent views in all directions.

At 10.6 mi. the path leads past the site of the former Isolation Shelter and at 10.7 mi. the east branch of the Isolation Trail enters right from the Rocky Branch valley. Water can be obtained by going down the Isolation Trail to the right (east); decent water (which is nevertheless unsafe to drink without treatment) may be some distance down. The path continues to climb steadily, and the west branch of the Isolation Trail descends left to the Dry River valley at 11.0 mi. The trail passes over a hump and runs through a sag at 11.6 mi., then ascends steadily to treeline at 12.2 mi. From here the trail is above treeline and completely exposed to the weather. At 12.6 mi. the Glen Boulder Trail joins on the right just below a small crag, and at 13.1 mi. the path passes just west of the summit of Boott Spur (5500 ft.), and the Boott Spur Trail to AMC Pinkham Notch Camp diverges right (east).

Turning northwest, the path leads along the almost level ridges of Boott Spur and crosses Bigelow Lawn. At 13.7 mi. the Lawn Cutoff diverges right to Tuckerman Junction, and a short distance farther on, the Camel Trail diverges left (west) to the Lakes of the Clouds Hut. At 14.1 mi. the Davis Path begins to follow the original location of the Crawford Path, crosses the Tuckerman Crossover, and in about 0.3 mi. is joined on the right by the Southside Trail. Soon the Davis Path enters the present Crawford Path, which climbs to the summit of Mt. Washington.

Davis Path (map 6:H8-F9)
Distances (est.) from US 302
to Mt. Crawford spur path: 2.3 mi., 2 hr. 5 min.
to Mount Parker Trail: 3.8 mi., 3 hr.
to Stairs Col Trail: 4.1 mi., 3 hr. 10 min.
to Giant Stairs spur path: 4.5 mi., 3 hr. 35 min.
to Mt. Davis spur path: 8.5 mi., 6 hr.
to Mt. Isolation spur path: 9.8 mi., 6 hr. 40 min.
to Isolation Trail, east branch: 10.7 mi., 7 hr. 20 min.
to Isolation Trail, west branch: 11.0 mi., 7 hr. 45 min.
to Glen Boulder Trail: 12.6 mi., 8 hr. 55 min.
to Boott Spur Trail: 13.1 mi., 9 hr. 20 min.
to Lawn Cutoff: 13.7 mi., 9 hr. 35 min.
to Crawford Path: 14.6 mi. (23.5 km.), 10 hr. 10 min.
to Lakes of the Clouds Hut (via Camel Trail): 14.6 mi., 10 hr.
to Mt. Washington summit (via Crawford Path): 15.1 mi. (24.1 km.), 10 hr. 45 min.

Stairs Col Trail (AMC)
This trail connects the Rocky Branch valley with Stairs Col on the Davis Path, providing, in particular, the easiest

route to the Giant Stairs. Note that there is water along this trail, but very little on the Davis Path. This trail is almost entirely within the Presidential Range–Dry River Wilderness.

It leaves the Rocky Branch Trail left opposite the Rocky Branch Shelter #1 area, and follows an old railroad siding 50 yd. It then turns sharp left, crosses a swampy area, and climbs briefly to a logging road where it enters the Dry River Wilderness Area. From here nearly to Stairs Col, the trail follows a logging road along the ravine of a brook, crossing it about halfway up the valley. The last part is rather steep. The trail crosses Stairs Col and continues down the west side a short distance to meet the Davis Path. For the Giant Stairs turn right.

Stairs Col Trail (map 6:H9)
Distance from Rocky Branch Trail
  to Davis Path junction: 1.9 mi. (3.1 km.), 1 hr. 45 min.

Rocky Branch Trail (WMNF)
The valley of the Rocky Branch of the Saco River lies between the two longest subsidiary ridges of Mt. Washington: the Montalban Ridge to the west and the Rocky Branch Ridge to the east. In the upper part of the valley the forest is still recovering from fires which swept the slopes in 1914–16. The lack of mature trees, particularly conifers, is evident in many areas. The northeast terminus of the trail is at a paved parking lot on NH 16 about 5 mi. north of Jackson, just north of the highway bridge over the Ellis River. The Jericho (south) trailhead is reached by following the Jericho Rd. (FR 27), which leaves US 302 just east of the bridge over the Rocky Branch, 1 mi. west of the junction of US 302 and NH 16. The Jericho Rd. is asphalt for about 1 mi., then a good gravel road for another 3.4 mi. to the beginning of the trail. From NH 16, the trail ascends

moderately, mostly on old logging roads, to a pass in the Rocky Branch Ridge, then descends easily to the old logging railroad grade in the valley, and follows the railroad grade on its gradual descent to the south terminus. After reaching the valley, the trail crosses the Rocky Branch several times; these crossings are wide, and are difficult and possibly dangerous at high water.

At the northeast terminus, the trail leaves the north end of the parking lot (avoid a gravel road that branches left just below the parking lot) and climbs moderately on an old logging road. At about 0.5 mi. a ski-touring trail enters from the left and shortly leaves right. At 1.3 mi. the trail swings left away from the bank of a small brook, and continues to ascend, then turns sharp left and follows an old, very straight road on a slight downhill grade. After about 0.5 mi. on this road, it swings gradually right and climbs moderately, following a brook part way, and reaches the Dry River Wilderness Area boundary just east of the ridge top. Passing the almost imperceptible height-of-land at 2.8 mi., the trail follows a short bypass left of a very wet area and runs almost level, then descends easily, with small brooks running in and out of the trail. At 3.5 mi. the trail begins to swing left, descends to the Rocky Branch, follows it downstream for a short distance, then crosses it at 3.7 mi. This crossing may be very difficult. (*Note.* If you are climbing to Mt. Isolation from NH 16, and the river is high, you can avoid two crossings by bushwhacking along the east side of the river upstream for 0.4 mi., since the Isolation Trail soon crosses back to the east bank.) On the west bank is the junction with the Isolation Trail, which diverges right (north), following the river bank on the old railroad grade.

The Rocky Branch Trail follows the old railroad grade left at this junction, and passes Rocky Branch Shelter #2 in 60 yd. (USFS Wilderness policies call for removal of this shelter whenever major maintenance is required.) The trail then runs generally south along the west bank for about 2.0 mi., at times on the old railroad grade, then follows the grade, crossing the river four times. These crossings are difficult at high water, but it may be possible to avoid some or all by bushwhacking along the west bank. Passing out of the Wilderness Area, the trail reaches a junction at 8.1 mi. with the Stairs Col Trail right and a spur path 60 yd. left to WMNF Rocky Branch Shelter #1 and tentsite. Continuing south along the river and railroad grade, it crosses the river on a logging road bridge just before reaching the south terminus.

Rocky Branch Trail (map 6)
Distances from parking lot off NH 16
    to height-of-land: 2.8 mi., 2 hr. 20 min.
    to Isolation Trail: 3.7 mi., 2 hr. 50 min.
    to Stairs Col Trail: 8.1 mi., 5 hr.
    to Jericho Rd.: 9.8 mi. (15.8 km.), 5 hr. 50 min.

Isolation Trail (WMNF)

This trail links the Dry River valley (Dry River Trail), the Montalban Ridge (Davis Path), and the Rocky Branch valley (Rocky Branch Trail). It is entirely within the Presidential Range-Dry River Wilderness.

The trail diverges from the Rocky Branch Trail just north of Rocky Branch Shelter #2 (which will be removed when major maintenance is required), at the point where the Rocky Branch Trail swings east to cross the river. The Isolation Trail follows the river north on what is left of the old railroad grade, crossing the river at 0.4 mi. At 0.7 mi. the trail turns sharp right off the railroad grade, climbs briefly, then follows a logging road that runs high above the river. The trail crosses the river three more times; the next two are only 70 yd. apart. The last crossing comes at 1.7 mi., after which the trail climbs easily along a tributary, reaching the Davis Path at 2.6 mi. after passing through an area of confusing side paths where the trail must be followed with care.

Coinciding with the Davis Path, it climbs steadily north for about 0.3 mi., then turns left off the Davis Path, runs level for 0.2 mi., then descends moderately southwest into the Dry River valley. At 4.3 mi. the trail reaches a branch of the Dry River and follows its northwest bank on an old logging road, ending at the Dry River Trail, 4.9 mi. from US 302.

Isolation Trail (map 6:G9-G8)
Distances from Rocky Branch Trail

> *to* fourth crossing of the Rocky Branch: 1.7 mi., 1 hr. 10 min.

> *to* Davis Path, south junction: 2.6 mi., 1 hr. 50 min.

> *to* Davis Path, north junction: 2.9 mi., 2 hr. 10 min.

> *to* branch of Dry River: 4.3 mi., 2 hr. 50 min.

> *to* Dry River Trail: 5.3 mi. (8.6 km.), 3 hr. 20 min.

Distances from Rocky Branch Trail at parking area on NH 16

> *to* Isolation Trail: 3.8 mi., 2 hr. 50 min.

> *to* Davis Path, south junction: 6.4 mi., 4 hr. 40 min.

> *to* Mt. Isolation (via Davis Path): 7.3 mi. (11.8 km.), 5 hr. 15 min.

Mount Langdon Trail (WMNF)

This trail runs from Bartlett village to the Mt. Langdon Shelter, meeting both the Mount Parker Trail and the Mount Stanton Trail, and thus giving access to both the higher and lower sections of the Montalban Ridge. It should be noted that this trail does not get particularly close to the summit of Mt. Langdon, which is crossed by the Mount Stanton Trail.

From the four corners of the junction of US 302 and the Bear Notch Rd. in Bartlett village, follow the road that

leads north across a bridge over the Saco to an intersection
at 0.4 mi. The trail begins almost straight ahead; there are
two entrances which very soon converge (no sign). The trail
follows a fairly recent gravel logging road, and at 0.3 mi.
the path to Cave Mtn. diverges left, marked by the word
"cave" painted on a rock, which is hard to see unless you
are looking for it. The road gradually becomes older and
less evident. The trail crosses a good-sized brook at 1.0 mi.
and climbs more steadily, bearing sharp right twice as the
road fades away.

The Mount Langdon Trail crosses Oak Ridge at 2.2 mi.
and descends, sharply at times, to the Oak Ridge–Mt.
Parker col, where it bears right at 2.5 mi. at the junction
with the Mount Parker Trail. The Mount Langdon Trail
then descends gradually to the WMNF Mt. Langdon Shelter, capacity eight, where this trail and the Mount Stanton
Trail both end. Some care is required to follow the trail
near the shelter. Water may be found in a brook 60 yd.
from the shelter on the Mount Stanton Trail, although in
dry weather the brook may have to be followed downhill.

Mount Langdon Trail (map 6:H9)
Distances from the road on the north bank of the Saco River

> to Mount Parker Trail: 2.5 mi., 2 hr.
>
> to Mt. Langdon Shelter: 2.9 mi. (4.7 km.), 2 hr. 15 min.
>
> to Mt. Langdon (via Mount Stanton Trail): 3.7 mi., 2 hr. 55 min.

Mount Parker Trail (SSOC)

This trail passes some excellent viewpoints, and provides
access from Bartlett to Mt. Parker, Mt. Resolution, the
Stairs Col area, and the upper Montalban Ridge. There is
no sure water.

This trail begins in the Oak Ridge–Mt. Parker col 2.5 mi. from Bartlett, continuing straight ahead to the north where the Mount Langdon Trail turns right (east). It swings right, then sharp left as it joins an old graded path at a switch-back. It follows this, climbing easily with many switch-backs, to an open spot with good views to the southwest. It then slabs to the east of the ridge through beech and oak woods until it reaches the base of some cliffs, where a side path leads left up through a gully to a good viewpoint. Continuing, the trail descends right with a switchback before turning left and climbing steeply onto the main ridge. Heading generally northwest, the trail climbs easily to an outlook to the southwest, then turns right and levels off before the last short, steep climb to the open summit of Mt. Parker, where there are excellent views.

Continuing north, the trail descends to the long ridge between Mt. Parker and Mt. Resolution and passes over three bumps, alternating between spruce woods and open ledges with good views. It then slabs the west and south sides of the remainder of the ridge until it reaches the southeast corner of Mt. Resolution, where it turns sharp right and zigzags steeply up to the col between the main summit ridge and a southerly knob. Here a short branch trail leads left over this open knob, where there are fine views, and rejoins the main trail in about 100 yd. Beyond this junction the trail winds along the flat top of Mt. Reso-lution until it reaches a large cairn on an open ledge with excellent views. The true summit is about 0.1 mi. east-northeast, very slightly higher, with excellent views north but no path. From the cairn the trail descends sharply into a gully where it crosses a brook (water unreliable), then leads northwest down past several ledges, and finally drops steeply to the Davis Path, opposite the branch trail to Reso-lution Shelter.

Mount Parker Trail (map 6:H9)
Distances (est.) from Mount Langdon Trail

- *to* summit of Mt. Parker: 1.3 mi., 1 hr. 15 min.
- *to* branch trail to open southerly knob: 3.0 mi., 2 hr. 20 min.
- *to* high point on Mt. Resolution: 3.5 mi., 2 hr. 40 min.
- *to* Davis Path junction: 4.2 mi. (6.8 km.), 3 hr.

Mount Stanton Trail (SSOC)

This trail passes over the low eastern summits of the Montalban Ridge, and affords many views from ledges. For the east trailhead (the west trailhead is at Mt. Langdon Shelter), leave the north side of US 302, 1.8 mi. west of its junction with NH 16 in Glen, and a short distance east of the bridge over the Saco River. Follow a paved road west about 0.2 mi., then bear right on Oak Ridge Dr., and almost immediately turn sharp right on Hemlock Dr. At a crossroads 0.6 mi. from US 302 turn right, and trailhead is on left of this road (limited parking). This is an area of new home construction; the turns at road junctions are well marked with unobtrusive signs. In 100 yd. it passes a red-blazed WMNF boundary corner to the left of the trail, and at 0.3 mi. turns sharp left with yellow blazes where the red-blazed WMNF boundary continues straight ahead. The trail climbs steeply at times, but there are gentler sections, and the outlooks from White's Ledge begin at 0.8 mi. The trail climbs steeply again after passing a large boulder on the right of the trail, and at 1.2 mi. the trail turns sharp right on a ledge as climbing becomes easier. At 1.4 mi. the trail passes within 15 yd. of the summit of Mt. Stanton. The summit area is covered with a fine stand of red (norway) pines and there are good views from scattered ledges near the summit.

The trail descends to the Stanton–Pickering col, ascends steadily, crosses a ledgy ridge and descends slightly, then climbs again and at 2.1 mi. passes 30 yd. to the right of the summit of Mt. Pickering. The trail then leads to ledges on a slightly lower knob, where there are excellent views. The trail descends to a minor col, then crosses over several interesting small humps sometimes called the Crippies. These humps have scattered outlook ledges, and the best view is from the fourth and last Crippie, which is crossed at 3.3 mi.

From the last Crippie the trail descends somewhat along the north side of the ridge toward Mt. Langdon, then climbs north moderately with a few steep pitches, passing an outlook to Carter Dome, Carter Notch, and Wildcat. At 4.5 mi. the trail passes about 35 yd. to the right of the summit, which is wooded and viewless, then descends easily to a gravel slope, turns right and descends to a brook that is crossed 60 yd. east of Mt. Langdon Shelter, where the Mount Stanton Trail ends.

Mount Stanton Trail (map 6:H10-H9)
Distances from the trailhead off Hemlock Drive
to Mt. Stanton summit: 1.4 mi., 1 hr. 15 min.
to Mt. Pickering summit: 2.1 mi., 1 hr. 50 min.
to fourth Crippie: 3.3 mi., 2 hr. 35 min.
to Mt. Langdon summit: 4.5 mi., 3 hr. 35 min.
to Mount Langdon Trail at Mt. Langdon Shelter: 5.3 mi. (8.5 km.), 4 hr.

Cave Mountain Path

This mountain, remarkable for the shallow cave near its wooded summit, is easily reached from Bartlett via a path that leaves the Mount Langdon Trail for 0.3 mi. to a left fork signed only by a rock with the word "cave" painted on it (watch carefully). In less than 0.5 mi. this branch trail leads up a steep gravel slope to the cave. A faint trail to the right of the cave leads, after a short scramble, to the top of the cliff in which the cave is located, where there is an excellent view of Bartlett.

Cave Mountain Path (map 6:H9)
Distances (est.) from Mount Langdon Trail
to cave: 0.5 mi., 25 min.

to Cave Mtn. summit: 0.8 mi. (1.3 km.), 45 min.

Winniweta Falls Trail (WMNF)

This trail provides easy access to an interesting waterfall. It leaves the west side of NH 16, 3 mi. north of the bridge over the Ellis River in Jackson. It fords the wide bed of the Ellis River, normally a rather shallow stream but difficult to cross at high water, turns right, and follows a logging road up the north bank of Miles Brook. At an arrow, the path turns left from the road and soon reaches the falls.

Winniweta Falls Trail (map 6:G10)
Distance (est.) from NH 16
to Winniweta Falls: 1.0 mi. (1.6 km.), 40 min.

Iron Mountain Trail (JCC)

The summit of this mountain is wooded, with somewhat restricted views, but an outlook on the north side and the fine south cliffs provide very attractive views for relatively little effort. A prominent easterly ridge, on which there was once a trail, descends almost to NH 16, ending in a cliff called Duck's Head, near the Iron Mtn. House. To the east of the cliffs are some abandoned iron mines. The trail is reached by leaving NH 16 in Jackson, next to the golf links and nearly opposite the red covered bridge, and following a road prominently signed Green Hill Rd. At 1.2 mi. the pavement ends, and at 1.4 mi. FR 325 bears right. Bear left here, as the road (FR 119) becomes fairly steep, a bit rough, and very narrow (be prepared to back up if required for other cars to pass). At 2.7 mi. from NH 16, swing left at a sign as the road ahead becomes very poor, and park in a small designated field behind the house of the Hayes Farm (now a summer residence).

The trail crosses the field, passes through a narrow band of trees, and crosses a second field, entering the woods at the top edge. The path climbs steadily and the footing is good. At 0.6 mi. there is a side path right 20 yd. to a fine outlook up the Rocky Branch valley to Mt. Washington, with the Southern Presidentials visible over the Montalban Ridge. The main trail continues to the summit at 0.8 mi., where there are remains of the former fire tower and a rickety wooden tower. The trail descends steadily along a rocky ridge, dropping about 300 ft., then crosses several humps in thick woods. At 1.5 mi. a side path descends left 0.2 mi. and 250 ft. to the old mines (tailings, water-filled shaft), and the main trail ascends shortly to ledges and the edge of the cliffs, where wide views to the south and west are obtained.

Iron Mountain Trail (map 6:H10)
Distances from Hayes Farm
to summit of Iron Mtn.: 0.8 mi., 50 min.
to south cliffs: 1.6 mi. (2.6 km.), 1 hr. 15 min.

The Northern Peaks and the Great Gulf

This section covers the high peaks of Mt. Washington's massive northern ridge, which curves north and then northeast like a great arm embracing the magnificent glacial cirque called the Great Gulf. This ridge runs for 5 mi. with only slight dips below the 5000 ft. elevation, and each of the three main peaks rises at least 500 ft. above the cols. The AMC Mt. Washington Range map (map 6) covers the entire area. The RMC map of the Randolph Valley and Northern Peaks, with a larger scale useful for the dense trail network on the north slopes, is available on plastic-coated paper for $2; the guidebook *Randolph Paths*, 1977 edition, is available for $1.50 (map not included) from the Randolph Mountain Club, Randolph, NH 03570.

In this section, the Appalachian Trail follows the Gulf-side Trail, from its junction with the Trinity Heights Connector near the summit of Mt. Washington, to Madison Hut. It then follows the Osgood Trail over Mt. Madison and down into the Great Gulf, proceeding to the Auto Rd. via the Osgood Cutoff and Madison Gulf Trail.

GEOGRAPHY

Mt. Clay (5541 ft.) is the first peak on the ridge north of Mt. Washington. Strictly speaking it is only a shoulder, comparable to Boott Spur on the southeast ridge of its great neighbor, since it rises barely 150 ft. above the connecting ridge. But it offers superb views from the cliffs, which drop away practically at the summit to form the west side of the Great Gulf headwall.

Mt. Jefferson (5712 ft.) has three summits a short distance apart, in line northwest and southeast, with the highest in the middle. Perhaps the most striking view is down the Great Gulf with the Carter Range beyond; the best views of the gulf are obtained from points on the Gulfside Trail to the north of the summit. There are other fine views, most notably those to Mt. Washington and the other Northern Peaks, to the Fabyan Plain on the southwest, and down the broad valley of the Israel on the northwest. The Castellated Ridge, sharpest and most salient of the White Mtn. ridges, extends northwest, forming the southwest wall of Castle Ravine. The view of the "Castles" from US 2 near the village of Bowman is unforgettable. The Ridge of the Caps, similar in formation but less striking, extends to the west. The two eastern ridges—Jefferson's "knees"—truncated by the Great Gulf, have precipitous wooded slopes and gently sloping tops. South of the peak of Mt. Jefferson is a smooth, grassy plateau called Monticello Lawn (5400 ft.). Jefferson Ravine, a glacial gulf tributary to the Great Gulf on the northeast side of the mountain, and Castle Ravine, a cirque to the north, are divided by the narrow ridge which runs from Jefferson through Edmands Col to Mt. Adams.

Mt. Adams (5774 ft.), second highest of the New England summits, has a greater variety of interesting features than any other New England mountain except Katahdin: its sharp, clean-cut profile; its large area above treeline; its inspiring views, the finest being across the Great Gulf to Mts. Washington, Jefferson, and Clay; its great northern ridges, Durand sharp and narrow, Nowell massive and broad-spreading; its four glacial cirques, King Ravine and the three that it shares with its neighbors, the Great Gulf, Madison Gulf, and Castle Ravine. It has several lesser summits and crags, of which the two most prominent are Mt. Sam Adams (5594 ft.), a flat mass to the west, and Mt. Quincy Adams (5410 ft.), a sharp, narrow shark-fin ridge to the north.

Mt. Madison (5367 ft.) is the farthest northeast of the

high peaks of the Presidential Range, remarkable for the great drop of over 4000 ft. to the river valleys east and northeast from its summit. The drop to the Androscoggin at Gorham (4580 ft. in about 6.5 mi.) is probably the closest approach in New England, except at Katahdin, of a major river to a high mountain. The views of nearby mountains south and southwest, and into the Great Gulf, are very fine. The distant view is cut off in these directions only, though Chocorua can be seen.

Pine Mtn. (2410 ft.) is a small peak lying to the northeast, between Mt. Madison and the great bend of the Androscoggin River at Gorham. Though low compared to its lofty neighbors, it is a rugged mountain with a fine cliff on the southeast side, and offers magnificent, easily attained views of the mountains and of the river valleys to the north and east.

The Great Gulf is the largest cirque in the White Mtns., lying between Mt. Washington and the Northern Peaks and drained by the West Branch of the Peabody River. The headwall, bounded on the south by the slopes of Mt. Washington and on the west by the summit ridge of Mt. Clay, rises from 1100 to 1600 ft. above a bowl-shaped valley that is enclosed by steep walls that extend east for about 3.5 mi. The gulf then continues as a more open valley about 1.5 mi. farther east. The Great Gulf and its tributary gulfs, Madison Gulf and Jefferson Ravine, were hollowed out by the action of glaciers, mainly before the last ice age. The views from its walls and from points on its floor are among the best in New England, and steep slopes and abundant water result in a great number of cascades. The first recorded observation of the Great Gulf was by Darby Field in 1642, and the name probably had its origin in 1823 in a casual statement of Ethan Allen Crawford, who, having lost his way in cloudy weather, came to "the edge of a great gulf." The region was visited in 1829 by J. W. Robbins, a botanist, but was little known until Benjamin F. Osgood blazed the first trail, from the Osgood Trail to the headwall, in 1881.

Caution. The peaks and higher ridges of this range are nearly as exposed to the elements as Mt. Washington, and should be treated with the same degree of respect and caution. Severe wintry storms can occur at any time of the year. Many lives have been lost in this area from failure to observe the basic principles of safety. In addition, all of the major peaks are strenuous climbs by even the easiest routes. The distances quoted may seem short to a novice, but there is only one route to a major peak, the Caps Ridge Trail to Mt. Jefferson, that involves less than 3000 ft. of climbing; and that route is not at all easy, being rather short and steep, with numerous scrambles on ledges which a person unfamiliar with mountain trails might find daunting. Most routes to the summits involve 4000 to 4500 ft. of climbing, roughly equal to the ascent of Mt. Washington, due to the lower elevations of the major trailheads. The substantial amount of effort required to attain these goals, together with the threat of sudden and violent storms, should make the need to avoid overextending oneself quite apparent.

The upper part of the mass of the Northern Peaks is covered with rock fragments. Above 5000 ft. there are no trees and little scrub. Ridges and valleys radiate from this high region on the north and west sides, the most important being, from north to south: on Mt. Madison, the Osgood Ridge, Howker Ridge, Bumpus Basin, Gordon Ridge, and the ravine of Snyder Brook, which is shared with Mt. Adams; on Mt. Adams, Durand Ridge, King Ravine, Nowell Ridge, Cascade Ravine, the Israel Ridge, and Castle Ravine, which is shared with Mt. Jefferson; on Mt. Jefferson, the Castellated Ridge and the Ridge of the Caps; and an unnamed but very salient ridge extending westerly from Mt. Clay. Bumpus Basin, King Ravine, and Castle Ravine are glacial cirques. Two small cirques, Jeffer-

son Ravine and Madison Gulf, branch off from the Great
Gulf, and the two Jefferson knees are prominent ridges,
abruptly truncated by the Great Gulf.

Edmands Col (4930 ft.), between Mt. Adams and Mt.
Jefferson, is named after pioneer trailmaker J. Rayner Ed=
mands. Sphinx Col (4970 ft.) lies between Mt. Jefferson
and Mt. Clay. The col between Mt. Adams and Mt.
Madison has an elevation of 4890 ft. Thus there is a range
of only 80 ft. between the lowest and highest of the three
major cols on this ridge. In the unnamed Adams–Madison
col lies Star Lake, a small, shallow body of water among
jagged rocks with impressive views, particularly up to Mt.
Madison and Mt. Quincy Adams.

The first trail on the Northern Peaks was probably cut
about 1850; in 1860 or 1861 a partial trail was made over the
peaks to Mt. Washington, of which some sections still exist. Lowe's Path was cut in 1875–76, the branch path
through King Ravine was made in 1876, and the Osgood
Path was opened in 1878. Many trails were constructed
between 1878 and the beginning of lumbering in about
1902, but this network was greatly damaged by lumbering,
and some trails were obliterated. The more important ones
have since been restored.

HUTS, SHELTERS, AND CAMPING

HUTS

Madison Hut (AMC)

In 1888, at Madison Spring (4800 ft.), a little north of
the Adams–Madison col, the AMC built a stone hut that
was later demolished. The present hut, rebuilt and improved after a fire in 1940, accommodates fifty guests on a
coed basis and is open to the public from mid-June to mid-

September. It is 6.0 mi. from the summit of Mt. Washington via the Gulfside Trail, and 6.8 mi. from Lakes of the Clouds Hut via the Gulfside Trail, Westside Trail, and Crawford Path. In bad weather the best approach (or exit) is via the Valley Way, which is sheltered to within a short distance of the hut. Nearby points of interest include the Parapet, a crag overlooking Madison Gulf, and Star Lake.

For current information contact Reservation Secretary, Pinkham Notch Camp, Box 298, Gorham, NH 03581 (603-466-2727).

CAMPING

Great Gulf Wilderness

Overnight use will be limited to 75 individuals per night, with a maximum stay of four nights, between 15 June and 15 September. Permits are free and may be reserved no more than thirty days in advance through the Androscoggin District Ranger, Gorham, NH 03581 (603-466-2713). They may be picked up at the WMNF Ranger Station on US 2 near Gorham or at Dolly Copp Campground. Camping is prohibited above treeline, within 200 ft. of any trail except at designated sites, and within one-quarter mile of Spaulding Lake. No campsite may be used by more than ten persons at any one time. All former shelters have been removed.

Restricted Use Areas

The WMNF has established a number of Restricted Use Areas (RUA's) where camping and wood or charcoal fires are prohibited from 1 May to 1 November. The specific areas are under continual review, and areas are added to or subtracted from the list in order to provide the greatest amount of protection to areas subject to damage by excessive camping, while imposing the lowest level of restrictions possible. A general list of RUA's follows, but one should obtain a map of current RUA's from the WMNF.

(1) No camping is permitted above treeline (where trees are less than 8 ft. tall). The point where the restricted area begins is marked on most trails with small signs, but the absence of such signs should not be construed as proof of the legality of a site.

(2) No camping is permitted within one-quarter mile of most facilities such as huts, cabins, shelters, or tentsites, except at the facility itself.

(3) No camping is permitted within 200 ft. of certain trails. In 1986, designated trails included the Valley Way.

Established Trailside Campsites

The Log Cabin (RMC), built about 1890, and totally rebuilt in 1985, is located at a spring at 3300 ft. altitude, beside Lowe's Path at the junction with the Cabin–Cascades Trail. The cabin is partially enclosed, and is open to the public at a charge of $2 per person per night. There is room for about ten. It has no stove, and no wood fires are permitted in the area. Guests are requested to leave the cabin clean and carry out all trash.

The Perch (RMC) is an open log shelter located at about 4300 ft. on the Perch Path between the Randolph Path and Israel Ridge Path, but much closer to the former. It is open to the public and accommodates eight. There are also four tent platforms at the site; the caretaker at Gray Knob often visits to collect the overnight fee—$2 for use of the shelter, $1 for tent platforms.

Crag Camp (RMC) is situated at the edge of King Ravine near the Spur Trail at about 4200 ft. It is open to the public at a charge of $2.50. It is an enclosed cabin, supplied with cooking utensils and a gas stove in the summer, with room for about fourteen. During July and August it is maintained by a caretaker. Wood fires are not allowed in the area. Hikers are required to limit groups to ten and stays to two nights. All trash must be carried out.

Gray Knob (Town of Randolph and RMC) is an enclosed, winterized cabin on Gray Knob Trail at its junction with Hincks Trail, near Lowe's Path, at about 4400 ft. It is open to the public at a charge of $2.50 per person per night. Gray Knob has room for about twelve and is supplied with a gas stove and cooking utensils in the summer. There is a caretaker year round. Rules are the same as for Crag Camp.

These RMC shelters are all Restricted Use Areas, and no camping is allowed within one-quarter mile except at the shelters and tent platforms. Fees should be mailed to the Randolph Mountain Club, Randolph, NH 03570, if not collected by the caretakers. Any infraction of rules or acts of vandalism should be reported to the above address.

Osgood Campsite (WMNF) is located in the Great Gulf Wilderness, near the junction of the Osgood Trail and Osgood Cutoff (which is on the Appalachian Trail). Permits are not required.

Valley Way Campsite (WMNF) is located off the Valley Way above its junction with the Watson Path, 3.1 mi. from US 2 at the Appalachia parking area.

ACCESS ROADS AND PARKING

Important access roads in this section are the Pinkham B Rd. (also called Dolly Copp Rd.), Jefferson Notch Rd., and the Base Rd. Pinkham B Rd. runs from US 2 at the west foot of the great hill between Gorham and Randolph, over the notch between Pine Mtn. and Mt. Madison, to NH 16 about 4.5 mi. south of Gorham. Dolly Copp Campground is on the road near NH 16. Jefferson Notch Rd. runs from the Valley Rd. in Jefferson (which in turn runs between US

2 and NH 115), through the notch between Mt. Jefferson
and the Dartmouth Range, to the Base Rd., which runs
from US 302 at Bretton Woods to the Base Station of the
Cog Railway at Marshfield. Directly across the the Base
Rd. is the Mt. Clinton Rd., which runs south to the Crawford House site. Jefferson Notch Rd., a good gravel road, is
open in summer and early fall, but since it reaches the
highest point of any public through road in NH (3008 ft. at
Jefferson Notch), snow and mud disappear late in the
spring and ice returns early. Drive with care, since it is
winding and narrow in places, and watch out for logging
trucks. The southern half is in better condition than the
north, which is sound but very rough. The high point in the
notch is about 5.5 mi. from the Valley Rd. on the north,
and 3.4 mi. from the Base Rd. on the south.

The most important parking areas are at Pinkham Notch
Camp; at a newly constructed area on NH 16 1.5 mi. south
of Dolly Copp Campground; at Randolph East, on Pink-
ham B (Dolly Copp) Rd. near its junction with US 2; at
Appalachia, on US 2 about 1 mi. west of Pinkham B Rd.; at
Lowe's Store on US 2 (nominal fee charged); and at Bowman, on US 2 about 1 mi. west of Lowe's Store. (Randolph
East, Appalachia, and Bowman owe their names and locations to their former status as stations on the railroad line.)
The highest points from which to climb the Northern Peaks,
not including the summit of Mt. Washington, are Jefferson
Notch Rd. at the Caps Ridge Trail (3008 ft.), the parking lot
on the Base Rd., 1.1 mi. east of the Jefferson Notch Rd. for
the Jewell Trail (2500 ft.); and the Pinkham B Rd., also
called Dolly Copp Rd., at the Pine Link (1650 ft.).

LIST OF TRAILS   MAP

Trails on the Main Ridge

Gulfside Trail   6:F9

THE TRAILS

Gulfside Trail (WMNF)

This trail leads from Madison Hut to the summit of Mt. Washington. It threads the principal cols, avoiding the summits of the Northern Peaks, but offers extensive and ever-changing views. Its altitudes range from about 4800 ft. close to the hut, to 6288 ft. on the summit of Mt. Washington. The name Gulfside was given by J. Rayner Edmands who, starting in 1892, located and made the greater part of the trail, sometimes following trails that had existed before. All but about 0.8 mi. of the trail was once a graded path, and parts were paved with carefully placed stones—a work cut short by Edmands's death in 1910. The whole length is part of the Appalachian Trail, except for a very short segment at the south end.

The trail is well marked with large cairns, each topped with a yellow-painted stone, and, though care must be used, it can often be followed even in dense fog. The trail is continuously exposed to the weather, and dangerously high winds and low temperatures may occur with little warning at any season of the year. If such storms threaten serious trouble on the Gulfside Trail, do not attempt to ascend the cone of Mt. Washington, where conditions are usually far worse. If you are not close to the huts at Madison Spring or at Lakes of the Clouds, descend into one of the ravines on a trail if possible, or without trail if necessary. A night of discomfort in the woods is better than exposure on the heights, which may prove fatal. Slopes on the Great Gulf (southeast) side are more sheltered, but generally steeper and farther from highways. It is particularly important not to head toward Edmands Col in deteriorating conditions; there is no easy trail out in bad weather, and the emergency refuge was removed in 1982. There is no substitute for studying the map carefully before setting out on the ridge.

Part I. Madison Hut–Edmands Col

The trail begins about 30 yd. from Madison Hut, leads southwest through a patch of scrub, then aims to the right (north) of Mt. Quincy Adams and ascends a steep, open slope. At the top of this slope, on the high plateau between King Ravine and Mt. Quincy Adams, it is joined from the right by the Air Line, which has just been joined by the King Ravine Trail. Here there are striking views back to Mt. Madison, and into King Ravine at the "Gateway" a short distance down on the right. The Gulfside and Air Line coincide for a few yards, then the Air Line branches left toward the summit of Mt. Adams. Much of the Gulfside Trail for about the next 0.5 mi. is paved with carefully placed stones. It rises gently southwest, curving a little more south, then steepens, and at 0.9 mi. from the hut reaches a grassy lawn in the saddle (5520 ft.) between Mt. Adams and Mt. Sam Adams.

Here, where several trails intersect at a spot called Thunderstorm Junction, there is a massive cairn about 10 ft. high. Entering the junction right is the Great Gully Trail, coming up across the slope from the southwest corner of King Ravine. Here also, the Gulfside is crossed by Lowe's Path, ascending from Lowe's Store on US 2 to the summit of Mt. Adams. A few yards down Lowe's Path, the Spur Trail branches right for Crag Camp. The summit of Mt. Adams is about 0.3 mi. from the junction (left), via Lowe's Path; a round trip to the summit requires about 25 min.

A cairned trail, known as the "White Trail," runs from Thunderstorm Junction over the summit of Mt. Sam Adams and along its south ridge to the Gulfside at the point where the Israel Ridge Path comes in from Bowman. This is not an official trail, and should not be used in bad weather, since it is more exposed to the wind.

Continuing southwest from Thunderstorm Junction and beginning to descend, the Gulfside Trail passes a junction on the left with the Israel Ridge Path, which ascends a short distance to Lowe's Path and thence to Mt. Adams. For about 0.5 mi. the Gulfside Trail and Israel Ridge Path coincide, passing Peabody Spring (unreliable) just to the right in a small, grassy flat, and more reliable water is just beyond at the base of a conspicuous boulder just to the left of the path. Soon the trail climbs easily across a ridge, then the Israel Ridge Path diverges right at 1.5 mi. from Madison Hut. Near this junction in wet weather there is a small pool called Storm Lake. The Gulfside bears a bit left toward the edge of Jefferson Ravine, and, always leading toward Mt. Jefferson, descends southwest along the narrow ridge that divides Jefferson Ravine from Castle Ravine, near the edge of the cliffs, from which there are fine views into the gulf. This part of the Gulfside was never graded. The trail reaches Edmands Col at 2.2 mi. from the hut, with 3.5 mi. to go to Mt. Washington.

At this col (4930 ft.) is a bronze tablet in memory of J. Rayner Edmands, who made most of the graded paths on the Northern Peaks. The emergency shelter once located here has been dismantled. From Edmands Col the Randolph Path leads north into the Randolph valley. The Edmands Col Cutoff leads south about 0.5 mi. to the Six Husbands Trail, affording the quickest route to shelter in bad weather. Branching from the Randolph Path about 0.1 mi. north of the col are the Cornice, leading west to the Castle Trail, and the Castle Ravine Trail. Gulfside Spring (reliable) is 30 yd. south of the col, and Spaulding Spring (reliable) is about 0.2 mi. north near the Castle Ravine Trail.

Part II. Edmands Col–Sphinx Col

South of Edmands Col the Gulfside Trail ascends steeply southwest over rough rocks, with Jefferson Ravine on the left. It passes flat-topped Dingmaul Rock, from which there is a good view down the ravine, with Mt. Adams on the left. A few yards beyond, the Mount Jefferson Loop branches right, and leads 0.3 mi. to the summit of Mt. Jefferson (5715 ft.). The loop is about the same distance, but involves about 300 ft. of extra climbing and about 10 min. more hiking time than the parallel section of the Gulfside. The views from the summit are excellent, and the extra effort relatively minor.

The path now turns southeast and rises less steeply. It crosses the Six Husbands Trail and soon reaches its greatest height on Mt. Jefferson, 5400 ft. Curving southwest and descending a little, it crosses Monticello Lawn, a comparatively smooth, grassy plateau. Here the Mount Jefferson Loop rejoins the Gulfside in about 0.3 mi. from the summit. A short distance southwest of the lawn the Cornice enters right from the Caps Ridge Trail. The Gulfside continues to descend south and southwest. From one point there is a view of the Sphinx down the slope to the left. A few yards north of the low point in Sphinx Col, the Sphinx Trail branches left (east) into the Great Gulf, through a grassy passage between ledges.

Part III. Sphinx Col–Mount Washington

From Sphinx Col the path leads toward Mt. Washington, and soon the Mount Clay Loop (a rough trail) diverges left to climb over the summits of Mt. Clay, with impressive views into the Great Gulf. It adds about 300 ft. of climbing and 10 min.; the distance is about the same. The Gulfside Trail is easier and passes close to water, but misses the most impressive views. It bears right from the junction with the Mount Clay Loop, runs south and rises gradually, slabbing the west side of Mt. Clay. In about 0.3 mi. a loop leads to water a few steps down to the right. The side path continues about 30 yd. farther to Greenough Spring (more reliable), then rejoins the Gulfside farther up. The Gulfside continues its slabbing ascent, and the Jewell Trail enters from the right, ascending from the Base Rd. From this junction the ridge crest of Mt. Clay is a short scramble up the rocks without trail. The Gulfside swings southeast and descends slightly to the Clay–Washington col (5380 ft.), where the Mount Clay Loop rejoins it from the left. A little to the east is the edge of the Great Gulf, with fine views, especially of the east cliffs of Mt. Clay.

The path continues southeast, rising gradually on Mt. Washington. About 0.1 mi. above the col, the Westside Trail branches right, crosses the Cog Railway, and leads to the Crawford Path and Lakes of the Clouds Hut. The Gulfside continues southeast between the Cog Railway on the right and the edge of the gulf on the left. If the path is lost, follow the railway to the summit. At the extreme south corner of the gulf, the Great Gulf Trail joins the Gulfside from the left, 5.4 mi. from Madison Hut. The Gulfside turns sharp right, crosses the railway, and continues west. It passes a junction with the Trinity Heights Connector, a link in the Appalachian Trail, which branches left and climbs for 0.2 mi. to the true summit of Mt. Washington. In a short distance past this junction the Gulfside joins the Crawford Path just below (north) of the old corral, and the two trails turn left and coincide to the summit. (Descending from the summit, the Gulfside Trail turns sharp right from the Crawford Path just below the old corral.)

Gulfside Trail (map 6:F9)
Distances from Madison Hut
to Air Line: 0.3 mi., 20 min.
to Thunderstorm Junction: 0.9 mi., 50 min.
to Israel Ridge Path, north junction: 1.0 mi., 55 min.
to Israel Ridge Path, south junction: 1.5 mi., 1 hr. 5 min.

to Edmands Col: 2.2 mi., 1 hr. 30 min.

to north end, Mount Jefferson Loop: 2.4 mi., 1 hr. 40 min.

to Six Husbands Trail: 2.6 mi., 1 hr. 50 min

to south end, Mount Jefferson Loop: 3.0 mi., 2 hr. 5 min.

to Cornice: 3.1 mi., 2 hr. 10 min.

to Sphinx Trail: 3.7 mi., 2 hr. 25 min.

to north end, Mount Clay Loop: 3.8 mi., 2 hr. 30 min.

to Jewell Trail: 4.5 mi., 3 hr.

to south end, Mount Clay Loop: 4.8 mi., 3 hr. 15 min.

to Westside Trail: 5.0 mi., 3 hr. 25 min.

to Great Gulf Trail: 5.4 mi., 3 hr. 50 min.

to Trinity Heights Connector: 5.7 mi., 4 hr. 5 min.

to Crawford Path: 5.7 mi. (9.2 km.), 4 hr. 5 min.

to Mt. Washington summit (via Crawford Path): 6.0 mi. (9.7 km.), 4 hr. 20 min.

to Lakes of the Clouds Hut (via Westside Trail and Crawford Path): 6.8 mi., 4 hr. 25 min.

Mount Jefferson Loop (AMC)

This trail diverges right (west) from the Gulfside Trail about 0.2 mi. south of Edmands Col, and climbs steeply. Just below the summit, the Six Husbands Trail enters on the left, then the Castle Trail enters on the right, and soon the junction with Caps Ridge Trail is reached at the base of the summit crag. The high point is a few yards right (west) on the Caps Ridge Trail. The Mount Jefferson Loop then descends to rejoin the Gulfside Trail on Monticello Lawn.

Mount Jefferson Loop (map 6:F9)
Distances (est.) from north junction with Gulfside Trail

to summit of Mt. Jefferson: 0.3 mi., 25 min.

to south junction with Gulfside Trail: 0.6 mi. (1.0 km.), 35 min.

Mount Clay Loop (AMC)

This trail diverges left (east) from the Gulfside Trail about 0.1 mi. south of Sphinx Col, and ascends a steep, rough slope to the ragged ridge crest. The views into the Great Gulf from the brink of the east cliffs are very fine. After crossing the summit, and passing over several slightly lower knobs, the trail descends easily to the flat col between Mt. Clay and Mt. Washington, where it rejoins the Gulfside Trail.

Mount Clay Loop (map 6:F9)
Distances (est.) from north junction with Gulfside Trail
  to summit of Mt. Clay: 0.5 mi., 35 min.
  to north junction with Gulfside Trail: 1.0 mi. (1.6 km.), 55 min.

Edmands Col Cutoff (RMC)

This important link, connecting the Gulfside Trail and Randolph Path at Edmands Col with the Six Husbands Trail, makes a quick descent possible from Edmands Col into the Great Gulf, the fastest way to shelter in bad weather. It is on the lee side of Mt. Jefferson, and scrub provides plentiful shelter. It is almost entirely within the Great Gulf Wilderness.

Leaving Edmands Col, the trail shortly passes a fine spring, then rises slightly and begins a rough scramble of about 0.5 mi. over rocks and through scrub, marked by cairns. The trail is mostly level, with only a few rises and falls over gullies, and good views to the south and the Great Gulf. It ends at the Six Husbands Trail about 0.5 mi. below that trail's junction with the Gulfside Trail.

Edmands Col Cutoff (map 6:F9)
Distances from Edmands Col
  to Six Husbands Trail: 0.5 mi. (0.8 km.), 20 min.

Cornice (RMC)

This trail leads west from the Randolph Path in Edmands Col, 0.1 mi. north of the Gulfside Trail, crosses the Castle Trail and the Caps Ridge Trail, and returns to the Gulfside at Monticello Lawn. From Edmands Col to the Caps Ridge Trail it is extremely rough, with a large amount of tedious and strenuous rock hopping. It is very hard on knees and ankles. It may take considerably more time than the estimates below. As a route from Edmands Col to the Caps Ridge Trail, it saves a little climbing compared to the route over the summit of Jefferson, but is much longer, requires more exertion, and is just as exposed to the weather. This makes its value as a bad weather route very questionable. It does offer some interesting views, and it does provide a good shortcut from the Caps Ridge Trail to the Gulfside south of Mt. Jefferson.

The Cornice leaves the Randolph Path and climbs moderately over large rocks, slabbing around the north and west sides of Mt. Jefferson. It crosses the Castle Trail above the Upper Castle and enters the Caps Ridge Trail above the Upper Cap. It then turns left (east) up the Caps Ridge Trail about 20 yd., diverges right (south), and climbs gradually with improved footing to the Gulfside Trail on Monticello Lawn.

Cornice (map 6:F9)
Distances (est.) from Randolph Path

- *to* Castle Trail: 0.5 mi., 30 min.
- *to* Caps Ridge Trail: 1.5 mi., 1 hr. 5 min.
- *to* Gulfside Trail junction: 2.0 mi. (3.2 km.), 1 hr. 30 min

Randolph Path (RMC)

This graded path extends southwest, from the Pinkham B (Dolly Copp) Rd. near Randolph Village, over the slopes of Mt. Madison and Mt. Adams, to the Gulfside Trail in Edmands Col between Mt. Adams and Mt. Jefferson. In addition to providing a route from Randolph to Edmands Col, it crosses numerous other trails along the way, and thus constitutes an important linking trail between them. It was made by J. Rayner Edmands from 1893 to 1899; parts of it were reconstructed in 1978 as a memorial to Christopher Goetze, active RMC member and former editor of *Appalachia*, a journal published by the AMC.

The path begins at the parking space known as Randolph East, 0.2 mi. south of US 2 on the Pinkham B Rd. and 0.3 mi. west of the Boston and Maine Railroad crossing. It coincides with the Howker Ridge Trail for approximately 80 yd. west, turns south, crosses the railroad, and 30 yd. beyond diverges right (west); the Howker Ridge Trail continues left (southeast). The Randolph Path keeps south of the power line for about 0.3 mi., where it enters the old location. It then turns southwest, crosses the Sylvan Way in about 0.5 mi., and in about another 0.8 mi. reaches Snyder Brook, where the Inlook Trail and Brookside diverge left. The Brookside and the Randolph Path cross the brook at the same place, then the Brookside diverges right and leads down to the Valley Way. A few yards beyond the brook it is crossed by the Valley Way, coming up from Appalachia. The Randolph Path soon joins the Air Line, coincides with it for 20 yd., then branches right. At 2.0 mi. the Short Line, a shortcut (1.3 mi.) from Appalachia, comes in on the right.

The Short Line coincides with the Randolph Path for 0.4 mi., then branches left for King Ravine. The Randolph Path descends slightly and crosses Cold Brook on Sanders Bridge, where the Cliffway diverges right. At 3.0 mi. it crosses the King Ravine Trail at its junction with the Amphibrach, a junction called the "Pentodoi." The Randolph Path crosses Spur Brook and in about 100 yd. the Spur

Trail leads left and the Randolph Path climbs around the nose of the ridge. Soon two short side paths descend right to the RMC Log Cabin. At about 3.9 mi. from Pinkham B Rd., Lowe's Path is crossed.

The grade on the Randolph Path now moderates. Slabbing the steep west side of Nowell Ridge for about 0.8 mi., the path passes Franconia Spring, where there is a view of Mt. Lafayette. At about 4.9 mi. the Perch Path crosses, leading right (southwest) to The Perch and Israel Ridge Path and left (east) to the Gray Knob Trail. There is water on the Perch Path a few yards west of the Randolph Path.

Above this junction the Randolph Path rises due south through scrub. Water is usually found at a spring left. In about 0.5 mi. the scrub ends, and the Gray Knob Trail from Crag Camp and Gray Knob enters left. In a short distance the Israel Ridge Path enters right (west), ascending from Bowman. For a few yards the paths coincide, then the Israel Ridge Path branches left for Mt. Adams. From this point the Randolph Path is nearly level to its end at Edmands Col, curving around the head of Castle Ravine. The path is above treeline, much exposed to the weather, and visible for a long distance ahead. Near the col, right, is Spaulding Spring (reliable water). The Castle Ravine Trail comes in from the right (northwest) and the Cornice leads west to Castle Trail. In about 0.1 mi. more the Randolph Path joins the Gulfside Trail in Edmands Col.

Randolph Path (map 6:E9-F9)
Distances (est.) from Randolph East (parking area)
- *to* Short Line: 2.0 mi., 1 hr. 30 min.
- *to* King Ravine Trail: 3.0 mi., 2 hr. 20 min.
- *to* Lowe's Path: 3.9 mi., 3 hr. 5 min.
- *to* Perch Path: 4.9 mi., 4 hr.
- *to* Israel Ridge Path: 5.4 mi., 4 hr. 30 min.

to Edmands Col and Gulfside Trail: 6.0 mi. (9.7 km.), 4 hr. 50 min.

to Mt. Washington summit (via Gulfside Trail and Crawford Path): 9.8 mi., 7 hr. 45 min.

The Link (RMC)

This path "links" the Appalachia parking area and the trails to Mt. Madison with the trails ascending Mt. Adams and Mt. Jefferson. It connects with the Amphibrach, Cliffway, Lowe's Path, and Israel Ridge Path, and the Castle Ravine, Emerald, Castle, and Caps Ridge trails. The section between the Caps Ridge and Castle trails, although rough, makes possible a circuit of the Caps and the Castles from Jefferson Notch Rd. It is graded as far as Cascade Brook.

The Link, with the Amphibrach, diverges right from the Air Line about 40 yd. south of the junction of the Air Line and Valley Way and 100 yd. south of Appalachia. It runs west about 0.6 mi. to where the Beechwood Way diverges left, and just east of Cold Brook, Sylvan Way enters left. Cold Brook is crossed on the Memorial Bridge, where there is a fine view of Cold Brook Fall, which is reached by Sylvan Way. West of the brook, after 50 yd., the Link diverges right from the Amphibrach.

The Link then follows old logging roads southwest for about 1.5 mi. It enters the WMNF 1.2 mi. from Appalachia, and at 2.0 mi. the Cliffway leads east to viewpoints on Nowell Ridge. At about 2.1 mi. the Link turns left and runs south to Lowe's Path, which it crosses at about 2.8 mi. Continuing south about 0.4 mi., it crosses the north branch of the Mystic, and, turning a little to the right, crosses the main Mystic Stream at 3.3 mi. It soon curves left, rounds the western buttress of Nowell Ridge, and running southeast nearly level, enters Cascade Ravine on the mountainside high above the stream. It crosses a slide and keeps the same general direction at nearly the same altitude until it approaches Cascade Brook.

The Israel Ridge Path comes up right from Bowman and, just above its junction with the Cabin–Cascades Trail, unites with the Link at 4.0 mi. from Appalachia. The trails coincide for 30 yd., then the Israel Ridge Path branches left for Gulfside Trail and Mt. Adams, and the Link crosses Cascade Brook, at 4.1 mi. On the stream, a little below and a little above the Link, are the first and second cascades. The Link continues southeast for 30 yd., then crosses a slide, rounds the tip of Israel Ridge, and turns south and southeast into Castle Ravine, uniting at 5.1 mi. with the Castle Ravine Trail, with which it coincides for about 0.3 mi. The two trails pass Emerald Trail and cross Castle Brook. Then, at 5.4 mi., the Link turns right and ascends west, slabbing the southwest wall of Castle Ravine. In about 0.6 mi. it crosses the Castle Trail below the first Castle at about 4050 ft. It then descends slightly, crosses three small brooks and continues southwest over sections of treacherous roots and hollows for 2.0 mi., slabbing a rough slope, then ascends somewhat to the Caps Ridge Trail, which it enters 1.0 mi. above the Jefferson Notch Rd., just above a ledge with potholes and a fine view up to Jefferson.

The Link (map 6:E9-F8)
Distances (est.) from Appalachia parking area

to Cold Brook Fall: 0.8 mi., 25 min.

to Cliffway: 2.0 mi., 1 hr. 25 min.

to Lowe's Path: 2.8 mi., 2 hr.

to Cascade Brook: 4.1 mi., 2 hr. 50 min.

to Castle Ravine Trail, lower junction: 5.1 mi., 3 hr. 25 min.

to Emerald Trail: 5.3 mi., 3 hr. 40 min.

to Castle Trail: 5.9 mi., 4 hr. 20 min.

to Caps Ridge Trail: 7.9 mi. (12.7 km.), 5 hr. 30 min.

Great Gulf Trail (WMNF)

This trail runs from the new parking area on NH 16 (1.5 mi. south of Dolly Copp Campground), follows the West Branch of the Peabody River through the Great Gulf, climbs up the headwall, and ends at a junction with the Gulfside Trail 0.6 mi. below the summit of Mt. Washington. Ascent on the headwall is steep and rough. Except for approximately the first mile it is in the Great Gulf Wilderness.

Leaving the new parking lot, the trail descends slightly to cross the Peabody River on a bridge, then ascends to a junction at 0.1 mi. with the former route from Dolly Copp Campground—now called the Great Gulf Link Trail. The Great Gulf Trail turns left and follows a logging road south on the west bank of the Peabody River until the West Branch forks from the main river, then continues northwest of the West Branch. At 1.7 mi. the Osgood Trail diverges right; Osgood Campsite is about 0.8 mi. from here via the Osgood Trail. The Great Gulf Trail soon approaches the West Branch and runs for about 0.3 mi. close to the north bank. Then, diverging from the stream, it ascends to the Bluff, where there is a good view of the gulf and the mountains around it. The trail follows the edge of the Bluff, and descends sharply left to Parapet Brook, where the Madison Gulf Trail enters right. The trails cross Parapet Brook on a bridge, continue over the crest of the little ridge that separates Parapet Brook from the West Branch, and descend to cross the West Branch on a suspension bridge. After ascending the steep bank, the Madison Gulf Trail branches left, while the Great Gulf Trail branches right, up the south bank of the river.

At 3.8 mi. the Great Gulf Trail crosses Chandler Brook, and on the far bank the Chandler Brook Trail diverges left and ascends to the Mt. Washington Auto Rd. The Great Gulf Trail continues close to the river for more than 0.5

mi., passing in sight of the mouth of the stream that issues from Jefferson Ravine on the north, to join the Six Husbands (right) and Wamsutta (left) trails at 4.5 mi. The Great Gulf Trail continues on the southeast bank, then in the bed of the stream, to the foot of a waterfall. Scrambling up to the left of this fall, it crosses a large branch brook and passes left of a beautiful cascade on the main stream. The trail soon crosses to the northwest bank, and in a short distance crosses the brook that descends from the Clay–Jefferson col. At this point the Sphinx Trail, leading to the Gulfside Trail, diverges right. The Great Gulf Trail soon crosses again to the southeast bank of the West Branch, passing waterfalls, including Weetamoo, the finest in the gulf. There are remarkable views down the gulf to Mt. Adams and Mt. Madison. The trail crosses an eastern tributary and, after a slight ascent, reaches Spaulding Lake (4250 ft.) at 6.4 mi. from NH 16 and about 1.4 mi. by trail from the summit of Mt. Washington.

The Great Gulf Trail continues on the east side of the lake, and a little beyond begins to ascend the steep headwall. The trail runs south and southeast, rising 1600 ft. in about 0.5 mi., over fragments of stone, many of which are loose. The way may be poorly marked, because snow slides may sweep away cairns, but paint blazes probably will be visible on the rocks. The trail curves a little left until within a few yards of the top of the headwall, then, bearing slightly right, emerges from the gulf and ends at the Gulfside Trail near the Cog Railway. It is 0.6 mi. to the summit of Mt. Washington by the Gulfside Trail and Crawford Path.

Great Gulf Trail (map 6:F10-F9)
Distances (est.) from new parking area on NH 16
to Osgood Trail: 1.7 mi., 1 hr. 10 min.
to Madison Gulf Trail: 2.8 mi., 1 hr. 55 min.

to Six Husbands and Wamsutta trails: 4.5 mi., 3 hr. 10 min.

to Sphinx Trail: 5.5 mi., 3 hr. 55 min.

to Spaulding Lake: 6.4 mi., 4 hr. 40 min.

to Gulfside Trail junction: 7.2 mi., 6 hr.

to Mt. Washington summit (via Gulfside Trail and Crawford Path): 7.8 mi. (12.6 km.), 6 hr. 25 min.

Great Gulf Link Trail (WMNF)

This trail was formerly a segment of the Great Gulf Trail. It leaves Dolly Copp Campground at the south end of the main camp road, just before reaching the site of the old bridge crossing. The trail follows a logging road south, on the west bank of the Peabody River, to its junction with the Great Gulf Trail, which comes in from the new parking lot on NH 16.

Great Gulf Link Trail (map 6:F10)
Distance (est.) from Dolly Copp Campground

to Great Gulf Trail: 0.7 mi., 20 min.

Madison Gulf Trail (AMC)

Caution. The section of this trail on the headwall of Madison Gulf is one of the most difficult in the White Mtns., going over several ledge outcrops, bouldery areas, and a chimney with loose rock. The steep slabs may be slippery when wet, and several ledges require scrambling and the use of handholds—hikers with a short reach may have a particular problem. Stream crossings may be very difficult in wet weather. The trail is not recommended for the descent, in wet weather, or for hikers with heavy packs. Allow extra time, and do not start up the headwall late in the day. The ascent of the headwall may require several hours more than the estimated time; parties frequently fail to reach the hut before dark on account of slowness on the headwall.

This trail begins on the Mt. Washington Auto Rd. a little

more than 2 mi. from the Glen House site, opposite the Old Jackson Road, and descends gently to the West Branch, where it meets the Great Gulf Trail. It then ascends along Parapet Brook to the Parapet, a point 0.3 mi. from Madison Hut. With the Old Jackson Road, it provides the shortest—but far from the easiest—route from Pinkham Notch Camp to Madison Hut. It is well marked, well protected from storms, and has plenty of water. For most people, particularly those with heavy packs, the routes via the Osgood Trail (in good weather) or the Buttress Trail (which is almost as well sheltered), though longer, are a better choice. From the Auto Rd. to Osgood Cutoff the Madison Gulf Trail is part of the Appalachian Trail, and therefore blazed in white; the rest is blazed in blue. It is almost entirely within the Great Gulf Wilderness.

The trail leaves the Auto Rd. above the 2-mi. mark, opposite the Old Jackson Road junction. In a short distance, a side path branches right in a little pass west of Lowe's Bald Spot and climbs to this summit, an excellent viewpoint, in 0.1 mi. The Madison Gulf Trail bears left and ascends about 75 ft. over a ledge with a limited view, descends rapidly for a short distance, then gently, crossing several water courses. The trail comes within sound of the West Branch of the Peabody River and continues along on contour until it meets the Great Gulf Trail on the south bank at 2.3 mi. The Madison Gulf Trail turns sharp right and, coinciding with the Great Gulf Trail, descends the steep bank to the West Branch.

Both trails cross a suspension bridge to the north bank, pass over the crest of the little ridge that divides Parapet Brook from the West Branch, and cross a bridge to the northeast side of Parapet Brook. Here the Madison Gulf Trail turns left up the stream, as the Great Gulf Trail diverges right. Soon the Osgood Cutoff continues ahead, leading in 0.5 mi. to the Osgood Trail for Mt. Madison and

Madison Hut. The Madison Gulf Trail swings left and continues up the stream, soon crosses to the southwest side, and diverges from the brook, to which it later returns, crossing a small branch brook and turning sharp left just before it reaches the main stream. It soon crosses again to the northeast bank, follows that for a little way, then turns right, ascending steeply with good views. The trail next turns left, slabbing the mountainside high above the brook, which it approaches again at the mouth of the branch stream from Osgood Ridge. It ascends rapidly between the two brooks, crosses to the west bank of the main stream, then recrosses, and, climbing more gradually, gains the lower floor of the gulf, crosses again, and soon reaches Sylvan Cascade, a fine fall.

The Madison Gulf Trail then ascends to the upper floor of the gulf, where it crosses four brooks. From the floor it rises gradually to Mossy Slide at the foot of the headwall, then ascends very rapidly by a stream. The trail now turns left, continues near a brook partly hidden among the rocks, then ascends very steeply on the headwall of the gulf. Ultimately it reaches the scrub, emerges on the rocks, and ends at the Parapet Trail. Turn left for the Parapet (0.1 mi.) and Madison Hut (0.3 mi.), and right for the Osgood Trail.

Madison Gulf Trail (map 6:F9)
Distances (est.) from Mt. Washington Auto Rd.
   to Great Gulf Trail: 2.3 mi., 1 hr. 10 min.
   to foot of Madison Gulf headwall: 4.0 mi., 2 hr. 50 min.
   to Parapet Trail: 4.5 mi., 3 hr. 30 min.
   to Madison Hut (via Parapet and Star Lake trails): 4.8 mi. (7.7 km.), 3 hr. 40 min.
Distance (est.) from Pinkham Notch Camp
   to Madison Hut (via Old Jackson Road and Madison Gulf, Parapet, and Star Lake trails): 6.8 mi. (10.9 km.), 5 hr.

Chandler Brook Trail (AMC)

This trail runs from the Great Gulf Trail 3.8 mi. from NH 16 to the Auto Rd. above the Halfway House site. It is almost entirely within the Great Gulf Wilderness. It diverges south from the Great Gulf Trail just west of Chandler Brook, and follows the brook rather closely, crossing three times. Fine waterfalls can be seen from the trail. From the last crossing the course is southeast, rising over a confused mass of stones and keeping west of interesting rock formations. The trail enters the Auto Rd. near a ledge of white quartz slightly less than 0.5 mi. above the 4-mi. post, at the bend above the Halfway House. (Descending, look for this white ledge, which is close to the Auto Rd. The trail is marked by cairns here and is visible from the road.)

Chandler Brook Trail (map 6:F9)
Distance (est.) from Great Gulf Trail
   to Mt. Washington Auto Rd.: 1.0 mi. (1.6 km.), 1 hr. 10 min.

Wamsutta Trail (AMC)

This trail begins on the Great Gulf Trail opposite the Six Husbands Trail, 4.5 mi. from NH 16, and ascends to the Auto Rd. just above the 6-mi. mark, opposite the Alpine Garden Trail, with which it provides routes to Tuckerman Junction, Lakes of the Clouds Hut, and other points to the south. It is almost entirely within the Great Gulf Wilderness. The trail got its name from Wamsutta, the first of six successive husbands of Weetamoo, a queen of the Pocasset Indians, for whom a beautiful waterfall in the Great Gulf is named.

Leaving the Great Gulf Trail, the trail runs southwest to a small stream, then ascends gradually. Soon it climbs the very steep and rough northerly spur of Chandler Ridge. Passing a quartz ledge on the right, the trail continues steeply to a small, open knob on the crest of the spur, which offers a good view. It then ascends gradually through woods, passing a spring on the right. Continuing along the crest, the trail emerges at treeline and climbs to the top end of the winter shortcut of the Auto Rd. After turning right, it ends in a few yards at the Auto Rd.

Wamsutta Trail (map 6:F9)
Distance from Great Gulf Trail

to Mt. Washington Auto Rd.: 1.7 mi. (2.7 km.), 1 hr. 55 min.

Sphinx Trail (AMC)

This trail runs from the Great Gulf Trail below Spaulding Lake to the Gulfside Trail in Sphinx Col, between Mt. Jefferson and Mt. Clay. The trail is important because it affords the quickest escape route for anyone overtaken by storm on Mt. Clay or on the south part of Mt. Jefferson. It diverges east from the Gulfside Trail 40 yd. north of the Clay–Jefferson col, through a grassy rock-walled corridor, and descends to the Great Gulf Trail. Once below the col, the hiker is protected quickly from the rigor of west and northwest winds. The trail's name is derived from the profile of a rock formation seen from just below the meadow where water is found. It is almost entirely within the Great Gulf Wilderness.

The trail branches northwest from the Great Gulf Trail near the crossing of the brook that descends from between Mt. Clay and Mt. Jefferson, 5.5 mi. from NH 16. It ascends through forest, first gradually, then very steeply. It follows the brook rather closely, using the bed for about 0.3 mi., and passes several small cascades. At 0.6 mi. the trail turns southwest, leaves the brook, and scrambles to a sloping shelf or plateau, partly covered with scrub, through which the trail is cut. It crosses a small meadow, where there is usually water under a rock north of the trail. After ascending slightly farther, the Sphinx Trail joins the Gulfside Trail on a level area a little north of the col.

Sphinx Trail (map 6:F9)
Distance (est.) from Great Gulf Trail
   to Gulfside Trail: 1.0 mi. (1.6 km.), 1 hr. 10 min.

Six Husbands Trail (AMC)

This spectacular trail diverges from the Great Gulf Trail at 4.5 mi. from NH 16, opposite the Wamsutta Trail, and climbs up the north knee of Jefferson, crosses the Gulfside, and ends at the Mount Jefferson Loop a short distance northeast of the summit. It is very steep and is not recommended for descent except to escape bad conditions above treeline. Up to the Gulfside Trail junction, it is entirely within the Great Gulf Wilderness. The name honors the six successive husbands of Weetamoo, queen of the Pocasset Indians.

Leaving the Great Gulf Trail, it descends northwest for a few yards, and crosses the West Branch; in times of high water go upstream to a better crossing. The trail bears right away from the West Branch, then ascends gently north until it comes close to the stream that flows from Jefferson Ravine, which it ascends on its southwest bank. At 0.6 mi. the Buttress Trail branches right and crosses the stream. The Six Husbands Trail continues a little farther beside the brook (last sure water), turns west and leads under two huge boulders. It ascends by ladders made of two-by-fours and passes near a cavern (10 yd. to the left), where snow and ice may be found even in August. The trail soon comes to an overhanging ledge and leads along under its edge for a short distance, ascending again by ladders. It then leads to a crag affording a good view up the gulf, continues to ascend steeply, and keeps close to the crest of the ridge until it comes out on the north knee of Jefferson (view), where the ascent becomes easier. Across the bare stretches the trail is marked by cairns. The Edmands Col Cutoff branches right, leading in 0.5 mi. to Edmands Col. Beyond, the trail becomes steeper, begins to climb the cone of Mt. Jefferson, and leads past a snowbank that often lasts well into July. Marked by cairns, the trail crosses the Gulfside Trail and continues west toward the summit of Mt. Jefferson, joining the Mount Jefferson Loop 100 yd. below the summit.

Six Husbands Trail (map 6:F9)
Distances from Great Gulf Trail junction
- *to* Buttress Trail: 0.6 mi., 25 min.
- *to* Gulfside Trail: 1.9 mi., 2 hr. 5 min.
- *to* Mount Jefferson Loop: 2.2 mi. (3.5 km.), 2 hr. 25 min.

Buttress Trail (AMC)
This trail leads from the Six Husbands Trail to the Star Lake Trail near Madison Hut. It is the most direct route from the upper part of the Great Gulf to Madison Hut, as well as the easiest route from the gulf to the hut. It is well sheltered until it nears the hut, and grades are moderate. In bad weather, or for hikers with heavy packs, or for descending, it is probably the best route from the gulf to the hut, in spite of the greater length. It is almost entirely within the Great Gulf Wilderness.

The trail begins in the ravine between Mt. Adams and Mt. Jefferson, leaving the north side of the Six Husbands Trail at a point 0.6 mi. northwest of the Great Gulf Trail. It immediately crosses the brook (last sure water) flowing out of Jefferson Ravine, bears right (east) in 0.1 mi., and climbs diagonally across a steep slope of large, loose, angular fragments of rock—some are easily dislodged, so care must be taken. The trail continues in the same direction, rising gradually along a steep, wooded slope. At the top of this slope, 0.6 mi. from the start, the trail turns north across a gently sloping upland covered with trees. There is a spring (reliable water) on the left, at about 1.0 mi. As the trail nears treeline, it passes under a large boulder. At about 1.3 mi. the trail reaches the foot of the steep, rock-covered peak of Mt. Adams. Here, a little left of the trail, a small, ledgy summit provides a fine view.

The trail runs nearly level northwest and then north, passing through patches of scrub, across patches of rock fragments, and crossing two brooks. Then, rising slightly through scrub, it passes through a gap between the Parapet and Mt. Quincy Adams and enters Star Lake Trail just southwest of Star Lake, 0.2 mi. from Madison Hut.

Buttress Trail (map 6:F9)
Distances from Six Husbands Trail junction
  to Parapet: 1.9 mi. (3.1 km.), 1 hr. 45 min.
  to Madison Hut (via Star Lake Trail): 2.1 mi. (3.4 km.),
    1 hr. 50 min.

Osgood Trail (AMC)

This trail runs from the Great Gulf Trail, 1.7 mi. from the new Great Gulf Wilderness parking area on NH 16, up the southeast ridge to the summit of Mt. Madison, then down to Madison Hut. Made by B. F. Osgood in 1878, this is the oldest trail now in use to the summit of Mt. Madison. Above the Osgood Cutoff it is part of the Appalachian Trail. The section of the trail that formerly ran from the Great Gulf Trail to the Mt. Washington Auto Rd. has been abandoned. The Osgood Trail begins in the Great Gulf Wilderness, but for most of its length it is just outside the boundary (in fact, it constitutes the northern section of the eastern boundary of the Great Gulf Wilderness).

The trail leaves the Great Gulf Trail about 0.2 mi. west

of the previous intersection of the two trails, 1.7 mi. from the new parking lot, and proceeds at an easy to moderate grade, rejoining the old route at 0.3 mi. It continues a moderate climb, crosses a small brook, and soon begins a steeper ascent. At 0.8 mi. the Osgood Cutoff comes in from the left, and a spur path leads right about 100 yd. to Osgood Campsite and to a spring which is the last sure water. From this junction to Madison Hut the Osgood Trail is part of the Appalachian Trail. (The former Madison Gulf Cutoff has been abandoned.)

The steep ascent continues to treeline at 2.3 mi., where the trail emerges on the crest of Osgood Ridge. Ahead, on the crest of the ridge, ten or twelve small, rocky peaks curve to the left in a crescent toward the summit of Mt. Madison. Cairns mark the trail over these peaks; keep on the crest of the ridge. The Daniel Webster–Scout Trail enters right at Osgood Junction, ascending from Dolly Copp Campground. Here, at 2.8 mi. from the Great Gulf Trail, the Parapet Trail diverges left, slabbing the south side of the cone of Madison, a rough but sheltered route to Madison Hut. As the Osgood Trail nears the last prominent hump below the summit and bears more west, it is joined on the right by the Howker Ridge Trail. It continues west over the summit of Mt. Madison, where the Watson Path enters, follows the crest of the ridge past several large cairns, drops off to the left (south) and continues west just below the ridge crest—above steep slopes falling off into Madison Gulf on the left. Soon it recrosses to the north side of the ridge and descends steeply, meeting the Pine Link, which enters right 30 yd. before the Osgood Trail reaches Madison Hut.

Osgood Trail (map 6:F10-F9)
Distances (est.) from Great Gulf Trail
 to Osgood Cutoff: 0.8 mi., 40 min.

   to Osgood Junction: 2.8 mi., 2 hr. 55 min.
   to Mt. Madison summit: 3.3 mi., 3 hr. 25 min.
   to Madison Hut: 3.8 mi. (6.1 km.), 3 hr. 40 min.

Osgood Cutoff (AMC)

This link runs nearly on contour east from the Madison Gulf Trail to the Osgood Trail at its junction with the spur path to the Osgood Campsite. It is entirely within the Great Gulf Wilderness. The cutoff is part of the Appalachian Trail, and provides a convenient shortcut from Pinkham Notch Camp to the summit of Mt. Madison via the Osgood Trail.

Osgood Cutoff (map 6:F9)
Distance from Madison Gulf Trail
   to Osgood Trail: 0.5 mi. (0.8 km.), 15 min.

Daniel Webster–Scout Trail (WMNF)

This trail, cut in 1933 by the Boy Scouts, leads from Dolly Copp Campground to Osgood Junction on the Osgood Trail, about halfway between the timberline and the summit of Mt. Madison. It begins on the main campground road about 0.8 mi. south of the campground entrance on the Pinkham B (Dolly Copp) Rd. It makes several zigzags not apparent on the map, though the approximate location is correct. The trail is steep and quite rough through the scrub and above timberline.

Daniel Webster–Scout Trail (map 6:F10-F9)
Distances (est.) from Dolly Copp Campground
   to Osgood Junction: 3.5 mi., 3 hr. 30 min.
   to Mt. Madison summit (via Osgood Trail): 4.0 mi., 4 hr.

Parapet Trail (AMC)

This trail, marked with blue paint, starts from Osgood Junction, where the Daniel Webster–Scout Trail joins the

Osgood Trail, and leads west to Madison Hut, running nearly on a contour on the south side of the cone of Madison. It meets the Madison Gulf Trail where the latter leaves the scrub at the head of the gulf, and continues beside the Parapet to join the Star Lake Trail to Madison Hut. Although above timberline and extremely rough in its eastern one-third, in bad weather the Parapet Trail is sheltered from the northwest winds. The rocks can be very slippery, the trail may be hard to follow if visibility is poor, and the extra effort of rock-hopping more than expends the energy saved by avoiding the climb of about 500 ft. over the summit of Mt. Madison. Therefore it is probably a useful bad-weather route only if strong northwest or west winds are the problem.

Parapet Trail (map 6:F9)
Distances (est.) from Osgood Junction
> *to* Madison Gulf Trail: 0.7 mi., 30 min.
> *to* Star Lake Trail: 0.9 mi. (1.4 km.), 35 min.
> *to* Madison Hut (via Star Lake Trail): 1.0 mi., 40 min.

Pine Link (AMC)

The Pine Link begins near the highest point of the Pinkham B (Dolly Copp) Rd. on the west side, directly opposite the private road to Pine Mtn., 2.4 mi. from US 2 and 1.9 mi. from NH 16. Near it are a spring and a small parking space.

The trail generally follows the crest of a northeast spur of Howker Ridge. In 1968 a fire below the outlook burned close to the south side of the trail, opening fine views east and south. Above the outlook the trail unites with Howker Ridge Trail at the spring south of the second Howk. For about 0.3 mi. the two trails coincide, running southwest through a group of small Howks. At the foot of the highest Howk the trails diverge, Howker Ridge Trail leading left for Mt. Madison summit. Pine Link, leading right, skirts the upper slopes of Bumpus Basin and crosses the Watson Path high on Gordon Ridge. It then contours around the cone of Mt. Madison, running nearly level—with fine views and great weather exposure—and joins the Osgood Trail, which descends on the left from Mt. Madison 30 yd. from Madison Hut.

Pine Link (map 6:E10-F9)
Distances (est.) from Pinkham B (Dolly Copp) Rd.
  to Howker Ridge Trail, lower junction: 2.3 mi., 2 hr. 20 min.
  to Watson Path: 3.2 mi., 3 hr. 15 min.
  to Madison Hut: 3.8 mi., 3 hr. 35 min.

Howker Ridge Trail (RMC)
This wild, rough trail leads from the Pinkham B (Dolly Copp) Rd. at the Randolph East parking area, 0.2 mi. south of US 2, to the Osgood Trail near the summit of Mt. Madison. It has good outlooks at different altitudes and passes three fine cascades.

Coinciding with the Randolph Path, it runs approximately 80 yd. west, turns south, crosses the railroad, and 30 yd. beyond diverges left (southeast) and leads to the west bank of Bumpus Brook, which it follows. The trail passes a cascade (Stairs Fall) that falls into the brook from the east, and at 0.7 mi. it passes Coosauk Fall, where Sylvan Way enters from the right. The trail continues a little west of the brook, and the Kelton Trail diverges right. About 1 mi. from the highway the Howker Ridge Trail turns east and crosses the brook at the foot of Hitchcock Fall, then rises steeply southeast. Howker Ridge curves right, partly enclosing the deep bowl-shaped valley called Bumpus Basin. The trail follows the crest of the ridge, on which there are several little peaks called the "Howks." The first is a long, narrow ridge covered with woods. In the col south of the first Howk is a spring (unreliable). From the second Howk there is a fine view in all directions, especially into Bumpus Basin. South of this Howk the Pine Link enters left (there is a spring on the Pine Link about 50 ft. to the east). The two trails coincide for about 0.3 mi., ascend among several Howks in a group, and separate again at the foot of the highest Howk, where Pine Link branches right. The Howker Ridge Trail climbs over the highest Howk (4311 ft.), descends a little southwest, then ascends steeply to the crest of Osgood Ridge, where it enters the Osgood Trail 0.3 mi. below the summit of Mt. Madison.

Howker Ridge Trail (map 6:E9-F9)
Distances (est.) from Pinkham B (Dolly Copp) Rd.
- *to* Sylvan Way: 0.7 mi., 30 min.
- *to* Hitchcock Fall: 1.0 mi., 50 min.
- *to* first Howk: 2.3 mi., 2 hr. 15 min.
- *to* second Howk: 3.0 mi., 2 hr. 55 min.
- *to* Pine Link, lower junction: 3.1 mi., 3 hr.
- *to* Osgood Trail: 4.1 mi. (6.6 km.), 4 hr. 10 min.
- *to* Mt. Madison summit (via Osgood Trail): 4.4 mi., 4 hr. 25 min.

Kelton Trail (RMC)

This path links the Howker Ridge Trail to the Valley Way, running nearly from Coosauk Fall to Salmacis Fall, and passing several outlooks.

It branches right from the Howker Ridge Trail about 0.8 mi. from the Pinkham B (Dolly Copp) Rd. It climbs to Kelton Crag, with some steep, slippery sections, then ascends near the northwest arete of the fingerlike north spur of Gordon Ridge, reaching an upper crag at the edge of a very old burn. From both crags there are restricted views; there is usually water between them on the right. Ascending, with good views east, the trail reaches the Overlook at the edge of the old burn, and runs west to the Upper

Inlook where the Inlook Trail enters right from Dome
Rock. The Kelton Trail then runs south, nearly level but
rough in places, through dense woods. It crosses Gordon
Rill (reliable water) and Snyder Brook, and enters the
Brookside 100 yd. below the foot of Salmacis Fall.

Kelton Trail (map 6:E9)
Distances (est.) from Howker Ridge Trail
   to Kelton Crag: 0.3 mi., 20 min.
   to Inlook Trail: 0.8 mi., 55 min.
   to the Brookside: 1.5 mi. (2.4 km.), 1 hr. 20 min.

Inlook Trail (RMC)
This steep path starts at the junction of the Randolph
Path and the Brookside east of Snyder Brook, and leads up
to the Kelton Trail at the Upper Inlook near the crest of the
finger of Gordon Ridge. There are good outlooks west,
north, and east, and several "inlooks" up the valley of
Snyder Brook to Mt. John Quincy Adams and Mt. Adams.
The best outlook is at Dome Rock at the tip of the finger.

Inlook Trail (map 6:E9)
Distances from Randolph Path
   to Dome Rock: 0.5 mi., 40 min.
   to Kelton Trail: 0.7 mi. (1.1 km.), 45 min.

The Brookside (RMC)
This trail follows Snyder Brook, from the point where
the Valley Way leaves the brook at 0.9 mi. from the Ap-
palachia parking lot to the Watson Path 100 yd. south of
Bruin Rock, and offers views of many cascades and pools.
It branches left from the Valley Way about 30 yd. above the
Beechwood Way, and crosses Snyder Brook on a wooden
bridge in common with the Randolph Path. East of the
brook the Randolph Path and the Inlook Trail diverge left.
In 0.3 mi. the Brookside recrosses the brook, and climbs

along the west bank at a moderate grade to its junction with the Kelton Trail, which enters from the left. The trail becomes steeper and rougher, passes Salmacis Fall, and ends at the Watson Path south of Bruin Rock. The brook between Salmacis and Bruin Rock is wild and beautiful, with cascades, mossy rocks, and fine forest.

The Brookside (map 6:E9)
Distance (est.) from the Valley Way
   to Watson Path: 1.3 mi. (2.1 km.), 1 hr. 20 min.

Watson Path (RMC)
The old Watson Path, completed by L. M. Watson in 1882, originally led from the Ravine House to the summit of Mt. Madison. The present path begins at the Scar Trail, leads across the Valley Way to Bruin Rock, and then follows the original route to the summit. It is an interesting route to Mt. Madison, but is steep, rough, and, on the northwest slopes above treeline, exposed to the weather. The cairns above treeline are not very prominent, and the trail may be hard to follow when visibility is poor.

Branching from the Scar Trail 0.3 mi. from Valley Way, it runs level about 0.2 mi. and crosses the Valley Way 2.4 mi. from the Appalachia parking area, then continues at an easy grade to Bruin Rock—a large, flat-topped boulder on the west bank of Snyder Brook. Here the Brookside enters, coming up the west bank of the stream. After the Lower Bruin branches to the right toward the Valley Way, the Watson Path crosses the brook at the foot of Duck Fall at 0.4 mi. East of the stream, the Watson Path soon attacks the steep flank of Gordon Ridge on a very steep and rough footway. At 1.0 mi. the trail emerges from the scrub onto the grassy, stony back of the ridge. It crosses Pine Link at 1.4 mi. and ascends to the summit of Mt. Madison over rough and shelving stones.

Watson Path (map 6:E9-F9)

Distances from Scar Trail

to Valley Way: 0.2 mi., 5 min.

to Pine Link: 1.4 mi., 1 hr. 30 min.

to Mt. Madison summit: 1.7 mi. (2.7 km.), 2 hr.

Distance from Appalachia parking area

to Mt. Madison summit (via Valley Way and Watson Path): 4.1 mi. (6.6 km.), 4 hr. 10 min.

Valley Way (WMNF)

This is the direct route from the Appalachia parking area to Madison Hut, well sheltered almost to the door of the hut. In bad weather it is the safest and easiest route to or from the hut. Portions of its upper section have washed, becoming rocky and rough. Signs for several of the trails that branch from the Valley Way are set so far back from the junctions that they are easy to miss.

The trail, in common with the Air Line, begins at the Appalachia, and crosses the railroad to a fork. The Valley Way leads left and the Air Line right across the power line location. In a few yards, the Maple Walk diverges left, and at 0.2 mi. Sylvan Way crosses. The trail enters the WMNF at 0.3 mi., and at 0.5 mi. the Fallsway comes in on the left, soon leaving left for Tama Fall and the Brookbank, then reentering the Valley Way in a few yards—it is a short but worthwhile loop.

The Valley Way leads nearer Snyder Brook and is soon joined from the right by Beechwood Way. About 30 yd. above this junction the Brookside diverges left, and the Valley Way turns right and climbs 100 yd. to the crossing of the Randolph Path at 0.9 mi. It then climbs at a comfortable grade high above Snyder Brook. At 2.2 mi. Scar Trail branches right, and at 2.4 mi. the Watson Path crosses, leading left to the summit of Mt. Madison. The Valley Way slabs the rather steep slopes of Durand Ridge considerably above the stream. At 2.7 mi. the Lower Bruin enters left, coming up from Bruin Rock and Duck Fall. At 3.1 mi. a path leads 0.1 mi. right to Valley Way Campsite (tent platforms), and soon the main trail passes a spring to the right of the trail. At 3.2 mi. the Upper Bruin branches steeply right, leading in 0.2 mi. to the Air Line at the lower end of the Knife-edge.

Now the Valley Way steepens and approaches nearer to Snyder Brook. High up in the scrub, the path swings right away from the brook, then swings back toward the stream and emerges from the scrub close to the stream, reaching a junction with the Air Line Cutoff 50 yd. below the hut.

Valley Way (map 6:E9-F9)
Distances (est.) from Appalachia parking area

- *to* Randolph Path crossing: 0.9 mi., 45 min.
- *to* Watson Path crossing: 2.4 mi., 2 hr. 10 min.
- *to* Upper Bruin junction: 3.2 mi., 3 hr. 5 min.
- *to* Madison Hut: 3.7 mi. (6.0 km.), 3 hr. 40 min.
- *to* Mt. Madison summit (via Osgood Trail): 4.2 mi. (6.8 km.), 4 hr. 10 min.

Lower Bruin (RMC)

This short trail branches right from the Watson Path on the west bank of Snyder Brook, near Bruin Rock, and climbs at a moderate grade to the Valley Way.

Lower Bruin (map 6:E9)
Distance (est.) from Watson Path

- *to* Valley Way: 0.3 mi. (0.5 km.), 20 min.

Upper Bruin (RMC)

This short but steep trail branches right from the Valley Way 3.2 mi. from Appalachia (sign very hard to see from Valley Way) and climbs to the Air Line above treeline, 3.1 mi. from Appalachia.

Upper Bruin (map 6:E9)
Distance (est.) from Valley Way
   to Air Line: 0.1 mi. (0.2 km.), 10 min.

Air Line (AMC)

This trail, completed in 1885, is the shortest route to Mt. Adams from a highway. It runs from the Appalachia parking area up Durand Ridge to the summit. The middle section is rather steep, and the section on the knife-edged crest of Durand Ridge is very exposed to weather but affords magnificent views.

The trail, in common with the Valley Way, begins at Appalachia and crosses the railroad to the power line clearing, where the Air Line leads right and Valley Way left. In 40 yd. the Link and the Amphibrach diverge right. The Air Line soon crosses Sylvan Way and, 0.6 mi. from the Appalachia parking area, crosses Beechwood Way and Beechwood Brook. At 0.8 mi. from Appalachia the Short Line diverges right, and at 0.9 mi. it enters the Randolph Path, coincides with it for 15 yd., then diverges left uphill. At 1.6 mi. there may be water in a spring 30 yd. left (east) of the path (sign). From here the path becomes very steep for 0.5 mi., then eases up and reaches an old clearing known as Camp Placid Stream (water unreliable) at 2.4 mi., where the Scar Trail enters left, coming up from the Valley Way.

At 3.0 mi. the Air Line emerges from the scrub, and at 3.1 mi. the Upper Bruin comes up left from the Valley Way. The Air Line now ascends over the bare, ledgy crest of Durand Ridge known as the "Knife-edge," passing over crags that drop off sharply into King Ravine on the right, and descend steeply but not precipitously into Snyder Glen on the left. At 3.2 mi., just south of the little peak called Needle Rock, the Chemin des Dames comes up from King Ravine. From several outlooks along the upper part of this ridge, one can look back down the ridge for a fine demonstration of the difference between the U-shaped glacial cirque of King Ravine on the left (west), and the ordinary V-shaped brook valley of Snyder Brook on the right (east). At 3.5 mi. the Air Line Cutoff leads left (southeast) 0.2 mi. through the scrub to Madison Hut, which is visible from this junction in clear weather. Water is found on this branch not far from the main path.

The Air Line now departs a little from the edge of the ravine, going left of the jutting crags at the ravine's southeast corner, and rises steeply. At 3.7 mi. it passes the Gateway of King Ravine, and the King Ravine Trail diverges right and plunges between two crags into that gulf. Here there is a striking view of Mt. Madison. In a few steps the path enters the Gulfside Trail, turns right, and coincides with it for a few yards, attaining the high plateau at the head of the ravine. Then the Air Line diverges to the left (southwest), passing west of Mt. John Quincy Adams, up a rough way over large, angular stones to the summit of Mt. Adams.

Air Line (map 6:E9-F9)
Distances from Appalachia parking area
  to Randolph Path: 0.9 mi., 50 min.
  to Scar Trail: 2.4 mi., 2 hr. 25 min.
  to Chemin des Dames: 3.2 mi., 3 hr. 10 min.
  to Air Line Cutoff: 3.5 mi., 3 hr. 30 min.
  to Gulfside Trail: 3.7 mi., 3 hr. 45 min.
  to Mt. Adams summit: 4.5 mi. (7.2 km.), 4 hr. 20 min.
  to Madison Hut (via Air Line Cutoff): 3.7 mi. (6.0 km.),
    3 hr. 40 min.

Scar Trail (RMC)
This trail runs from the Valley Way 2.0 mi. from Appalachia to the Air Line at Camp Placid Stream, an old clearing 2.4 mi. from Appalachia. It provides a route to Mt. Adams which includes the spectacular views from

Durand Ridge while avoiding the steepest section of the Air Line, and also has good outlooks of its own.

It diverges from the Valley Way, and in 0.2 mi. it divides. The Scar Loop, an alternative route to the right, goes over Durand Scar and another viewpoint, while the main trail leads left to the beginning of Watson Path, ascends to rejoin the loop, and continues to the Air Line.

Scar Trail (map 6:E9)
Distances (est.) from Valley Way
   to Durand Scar (via Scar Loop): 0.3 mi., 20 min.
   to Watson Path (via main trail): 0.4 mi., 25 min.
   to Air Line (via either route): 1.0 mi. (1.6 km.), 1 hr.
Distance (est.) from Appalachia parking area
   to Mt. Adams summit (via Valley Way, Scar Trail or Scar Loop, and Air Line): 5.1 mi., 4 hr. 50 min.

Air Line Cutoff (AMC)
This short trail provides a direct route, sheltered by scrub, from the Air Line high on Durand Ridge to the Valley Way just below Madison Hut.

Air Line Cutoff (map 6:F9)
Distance from Air Line
   to Madison Hut: 0.2 mi. (0.3 km.), 10 min.

Star Lake Trail (AMC)
This trail leads from Madison Hut to the summit of Mt. Adams, slabbing the southeast side of Mt. John Quincy Adams. It is often more sheltered from the wind than the Air Line, but is steep and rough, especially in the upper part, and may be difficult to follow on descent. It runs south from the hut, in common with the Parapet Trail, rising gently. In about 0.1 mi. the Parapet Trail branches to the left, passing east of Star Lake. The Star Lake Trail passes west of the lake and reaches the Adams–Madison col

about 0.3 mi. from the hut. Here the Buttress Trail diverges left and descends. The Star Lake Trail continues southwest on the steep southeast slope of John Quincy. There is usually water issuing from the rocks on the right. The trail continues to slab up the steep east slope of Mt. Adams to the crest of a minor easterly ridge, then turns right and follows that ridge to the summit.

Star Lake Trail (map 6:F9)
Distances (est.) from Madison Hut
   to Buttress Trail: 0.3 mi., 15 min.
   to Mt. Adams summit: 0.9 mi. (1.4 km.), 1 hr.

Short Line (RMC)
This graded path, leading from the Air Line to the King Ravine Trail below Mossy Fall, was made in 1899–1901 by J. Rayner Edmands. It offers easy access to the Randolph Path and to King Ravine from the Appalachia parking area.

The Short Line branches right from the Air Line 0.8 mi. from Appalachia. At 0.5 mi. it unites with the Randolph Path, coincides with it for 0.4 mi., then branches left and leads south up the valley of Cold Brook toward King Ravine, keeping a short distance east of the stream. At 2.8 mi. from Appalachia, the path joins the King Ravine Trail just below Mossy Fall.

Short Line (map 6:E9)
Distances (est.) from Air Line Junction
   to Randolph Path, lower junction: 0.5 mi., 30 min.
   to Randolph Path, upper junction: 0.9 mi., 50 min.
   to King Ravine Trail: 1.5 mi. (2.4 km.), 1 hr. 30 min.

King Ravine Trail (RMC)
This branch from Lowe's Path through King Ravine was made by Charles E. Lowe in 1876. It is very steep and

rough on the headwall of the ravine, but is one of the most spectacular trails in the White Mtns., offering an overwhelming variety of wild and magnificent scenery. It is not a good trail to descend, on account of steep, rough, slippery footing, and extra time should be allowed for the roughness and the views. The trip to the floor of the ravine is worthwhile even if you do not ascend the headwall.

King Ravine Trail diverges left from Lowe's Path 1.8 mi. from US 2, and rises over a low swell of Nowell Ridge. At 0.8 mi. it crosses Spur Brook below some cascades, and in a few yards more it crosses the Randolph Path at its junction with the Amphibrach, a spot called the "Pentodoi." Skirting the east spur of Nowell Ridge, it enters the ravine and descends slightly, crosses a western branch of Cold Brook, goes across the lower floor of the ravine, and crosses the main stream. In 0.2 mi. more it is joined by the Short Line, the usual route of access from the Appalachia parking area, near the foot of Mossy Fall (last sure water). Just above this fall Cold Brook, already a good-sized stream, gushes from beneath the boulders that have fallen into the ravine.

So far the path has been fairly level, rising only 400 ft. in 1.5 mi.; but in the next 0.3 mi. it rises about 550 ft. and gains the upper floor of the ravine (3500 ft). The grandeur of the view of the ravine and to the north warrants a trip to the top of a bank of fallen rocks. The Chemin des Dames branches left here. From this point to the foot of the headwall, about 0.4 mi., the path is very strenuous, winding over and under boulders ranging up to the size of a small house. A shortcut called the "Elevated" avoids some of the main boulder-caves. The main trail, the "Subway," 550 ft. long, is more interesting and takes only a few minutes longer. The Great Gully Trail diverges right a little farther south. In a boulder-cave near the foot of the headwall, reached by a wet loop path, there is ice through-

out the year. About 2.6 mi. from Lowe's Path the ascent of
the headwall begins. It is very steep and rough, rising
about 1300 ft. in 0.4 mi., over large blocks of rock, to the
"Gateway"; here the trail issues from the ravine between
two crags, and immediately joins the Air Line close to its
junction with the Gulfside Trail. From the Gateway there is
a striking view of Mt. Madison. Madison Hut is in sight,
and can be reached by the Gulfside Trail, left. The summit
of Mt. Adams is about 0.5 mi. farther, by the Air Line.

King Ravine Trail (map 6:E9-F9)
Distances (est.) from Lowe's Path
  to Randolph Path: 0.9 mi., 40 min.
  to Short Line: 1.6 mi., 1 hr. 10 min.
  to foot of King Ravine headwall: 2.6 mi., 2 hr.
  to Gulfside Trail: 3.0 mi. (4.8 km.), 3 hr.

Chemin des Dames (RMC)
   This trail leads from the floor of King Ravine up its east
wall, and joins the Air Line above treeline. It is the shortest
route out of the ravine, but is very steep and rough, climbing up over large rocks; it is also a difficult trail to descend.
   From the King Ravine Trail, it winds through scrub to
the east side of the ravine, where it climbs steeply over
blocks of talus, alternately through scrub and over slides.
Reaching the foot of a cliff, it angles to the right and climbs
south to join the Air Line in a shallow col.

Chemin des Dames (map 6:E9-F9)
Distance from King Ravine Trail
  to Air Line Trail junction: 0.3 mi. (0.5 km.), 40 min.

Great Gully Trail (RMC)
   This trail provides an alternative route between the floor
of King Ravine and the Gulfside Trail, reaching the latter
at Thunderstorm Junction. It is extremely steep and rough,

and, like the other trails in the ravine, especially difficult to descend. Leaving the King Ravine Trail, it leads up the southwest corner of King Ravine and makes some use of the gully, crossing the brook above a high fall. Near the top of the headwall is a spring (unreliable). After emerging from the ravine the trail runs south to the junction of the Gulfside Trail and Lowe's Path at Thunderstorm Junction.

Great Gully Trail (map 6:F9)
Distance (est.) from King Ravine Trail
   to Gulfside Trail: 1.0 mi. (1.6 km.), 1 hr. 15 min.

Amphibrach (RMC)

This trail runs from the Appalachia parking area to Memorial Bridge, then swings south and parallels Cold Brook to the five-way junction with the Randolph Path and King Ravine Trail known as the "Pentodoi." The trail takes its unusual name from its marking when it was first made, about 1883: three blazes—short, long, and short. It is a good approach to King Ravine, or to any point reached via the Randolph Path or the Link; and also, via the Beechwood Way, to points reached by the Short Line, the Air Line, or the Valley Way. Its moderate grade and relative smoothness make it relatively less difficult for descent after dark. It is, in fact, one of the kindest trails to the feet in this region.

The Amphibrach, in common with the Link, diverges right from the Air Line about 40 yd. south of its junction with the Valley Way and 100 yd. south of the Appalachia parking area. It runs west, and at 0.7 mi. the Beechwood Way diverges left, and the Sylvan Way enters left just east of Cold Brook—which is crossed on Memorial Bridge. Memorial Bridge is a memorial to J. Rayner Edmands, Eugene B. Cook, and other pioneer pathmakers: King, Gordon, Lowe,

Watson, Peek, Hunt, Nowell, and Sargent. Cold Brook Fall is visible from the bridge, a short distance upstream.

In about 50 yd. the Link diverges right, and 30 yd. beyond a side trail branches left to the foot of Cold Brook Fall. The Amphibrach now follows the course of Cold Brook, ascending west of the stream but generally not in sight of the water, and enters the WMNF. At 1.6 mi., near the confluence of Spur Brook and Cold Brook, the Monaway diverges right. The Amphibrach crosses Spur Brook on the rocks, ascends the tongue of land between the two brooks, shortly diverges left (east), and climbs gradually. It crosses the Cliffway and at 2.6 mi. the Amphibrach ends at "Pentodoi."

Amphibrach (map 6:E9)
Distances from Appalachia parking area
   to Memorial Bridge: 0.7 mi., 25 min.
   to Monaway: 1.6 mi., 1 hr. 20 min.
   to Randolph Path and King Ravine Trail: 2.6 mi. (4.2 km.), 2 hr. 10 min.

Cliffway (RMC)

This path runs from the Link 1.9 mi. from the Appalachia parking area, crosses the Amphibrach, and ends at the Randolph Path at the west end of Sanders Bridge over Cold Brook, 2.1 mi. from Appalachia. Gradients are generally easy, and much of the trail is level, but there are several short, steep pitches, and the trail changes direction frequently. Leaving the Link, it crosses some of the overgrown cliffs and ledges of the low swell of Nowell Ridge. The best view is from White Cliff. Here the Ladderback Trail diverges left along the cliff top to the Monaway. A very short and obscure path, Along the Brink, leads from the Cliffway to the Ladderback Trail via the mossy brink of White Cliff. At King Cliff the Monaway diverges left. The

Cliffway then passes Spur Brook Fall, crosses Spur Brook and the Amphibrach, and ends at the Randolph Path.

Cliffway (map 6:E9)
Distances (est.) from the Link
   to White Cliff: 0.7 mi., 30 min,
   to Spur Brook Fall: 1.6 mi., 1 hr.
   to Randolph Path: 2.0 mi. (3.2 km.), 1 hr. 15 min.

Monaway (RMC)

The Monaway leads from the Cliffway near King Cliff, past a junction with the Ladderback Trail, to the Amphibrach 50 yd. below its crossing of Spur Brook. It is a narrow woods path of moderate grade, except for a short, steep pitch between the Ladderback Trail and the Cliffway.

Monaway (map 6:E9)
Distance (est.) from Cliffway
   to Amphibrach: 0.3 mi. (0.5 km.), 10 min.

Ladderback Trail (RMC)

The Ladderback Trail leads from the Cliffway at White Cliff to the Monaway. Fine views of the Randolph Valley can be obtained from the cliff.

Ladderback Trail (map 6:E9)
Distance (est.) from Cliffway
   to Monaway: 0.2 mi. (0.3 km.), 5 min.

Spur Trail (RMC)

This trail leads from the Randolph Path just above its junction with the King Ravine Trail, up the east spur of the Nowell Ridge near the west edge of King Ravine, and ends at Lowe's Path close to Thunderstorm Junction. At several points there are views into King Ravine. The section known as the New Spur proved too steep for the amount of use it received and has been abandoned.

The Spur Trail diverges south from the Randolph Path about 100 yd. west of its junction with the King Ravine Trail, just west of Spur Brook. In 0.3 mi. there is a short branch to Chandler Fall, and 0.3 mi. farther up the Hincks Trail to Gray Knob diverges right and the Spur Trail crosses to the east side of the brook, the last water until Crag Camp. It ascends the spur that forms the west wall of King Ravine and goes over the Lower Crag, giving one of the best views of the ravine and an outlook east and north. A little farther on, a short branch leads to the Upper Crag, near which Crag Camp is situated. Here the Gray Knob Trail leads west 0.4 mi. to Gray Knob.

The trail continues up the spur, but not so near the edge of the ravine. It soon enters the region of scrub and passes a side path that leads east to Knight's Castle, a crag at the edge of the ravine about 0.1 mi. from Spur Trail. Above this junction the trail leaves the scrub, ascends to the east of the crest of Nowell Ridge, and merges with Lowe's Path just below Thunderstorm Junction and the Gulfside Trail, 0.3 mi. below the summit of Mt. Adams.

Spur Trail (map 6:E9-F9)
Distances from Randolph Path
   to Crag Camp: 0.8 mi., 1 hr. 5 min.
   to Lowe's Path: 1.9 mi. (3.1 km.), 2 hr. 10 min.

Hincks Trail (RMC)

The Hincks Trail diverges right from the Spur Trail about 0.3 mi. above the Chandler Fall side path, immediately before the Spur Trail crosses Spur Brook. The trail climbs steeply through blowdown areas and around many washouts to Gray Knob. The trail is rough and may be difficult to follow on descent due to the washouts.

Hincks Trail (map 6:E9-F9)
Distance (est.) from Spur Trail
   to Gray Knob: 0.7 mi. (1.1 km.), 50 min.

Gray Knob Trail (RMC)

The Gray Knob Trail leads from the Spur Trail near Crag Camp to Gray Knob, and continues past Lowe's Path and the Perch Path to the Randolph Path just before its junction with the Israel Ridge Path. It provides a route from Crag Camp and Gray Knob to Edmands Col without loss of elevation, but is rough and offers little protection from the elements. From the Spur Trail it runs almost on contour 0.4 mi. to Gray Knob, and continues a very short distance and crosses Lowe's Path. A very short path called the Quay diverges right just before this junction to a ledge on Lowe's Path a short distance north of the Gray Knob Trail crossing. In another 0.4 mi. the Perch Path diverges right. Ascending slightly, the Gray Knob Trail joins the Randolph Path near its junction with Israel Ridge Path.

Gray Knob Trail (map 6:E9-F9)
Distances (est.) from Spur Trail
   to Gray Knob: 0.4 mi., 15 min.
   to Randolph Path: 1.4 mi. (2.3 km.), 1 hr.

Perch Path (RMC)

This path runs from the Gray Knob Trail across Randolph Path, past the Perch, and ends on Israel Ridge Path. It diverges right from the Gray Knob Trail about 0.3 mi. south of Gray Knob. It descends moderately and crosses the Randolph Path at 0.3 mi., soon passes the Perch and runs nearly level to the Randolph Path.

Perch Path (map 6:F9)
Distances from Gray Knob Trail
   to Randolph Path: 0.3 mi., 10 min.

to the Perch: 0.4 mi., 15 min.
to Randolph Path junction: 0.5 mi. (0.8 km.), 20 min.

Lowe's Path (AMC)

This trail, cut in 1875–76 by Charles E. Lowe and Dr. William G. Nowell from Lowe's house in Randolph to the summit of Mt. Adams, is the oldest of the mountain trails that lead from the Randolph valley.

The trail begins on the south side of US 2, 100 yd. west of Lowe's Store, where cars may be parked (small fee). It follows a broad wood road for 100 yd., then diverges right at a sign giving the history of the trail and passes through a logged area, crosses the railroad track and then the power lines. It ascends through woods at a moderate grade, at first toward the southwest then swinging more south, crosses several small brooks, bears left where it enters the former route, and at 1.7 mi. crosses the Link.

At 1.8 mi. the King Ravine Trail branches left. Lowe's Path continues to ascend, and at 2.5 mi. passes close to the Log Cabin. Here two short spur paths lead left to the Randolph Path, and the Cabin–Cascades Trail to the Israel Ridge Path in Cascade Ravine leaves on the right. Water is always found at the Log Cabin and midway between the cabin and treeline. Very steep climbing begins, and at 2.7 mi. Lowe's Path crosses the Randolph Path. At an outlook at 3.2 mi., the short path called the Quay diverges left to Gray Knob Trail, and 30 yd. farther the Gray Knob Trail crosses. The cabin at Gray Knob is 0.1 mi. left (east). The grade moderates somewhat after these junctions.

The rest of the trail is above treeline and much exposed to wind. Views are very fine. The trail ascends steadily to the summit known as Adams 4 (5348 ft.)—the culminating peak of Nowell Ridge—at 4.1 mi., then descends a little, keeping to the left of Mt. Sam Adams. The Spur Trail enters left 100 yd. before Lowe's Path crosses the Gulfside

Trail at Thunderstorm Junction at 4.5 mi.; the Great Gully Trail also enters at Thunderstorm Junction. It climbs moderately over the jumbled rocks of the cone of Mt. Adams, the Israel Ridge Path enters right at 4.6 mi., and Lowe's Path reaches the summit of Mt. Adams at 4.8 mi.

Lowe's Path (map 6:E9-F9)
Distances from US 2 near Lowe's Store

>   *to* the Link: 1.7 mi., 1 hr. 25 min.
>   *to* King Ravine Trail: 1.8 mi., 1 hr. 30 min.
>   *to* Log Cabin: 2.5 mi., 2 hr. 10 min.
>   *to* Randolph Path: 2.7 mi., 2 hr. 25 min.·
>   *to* Gray Knob Trail: 3.2 mi., 3 hr. 5 min.
>   *to* Adams 4 summit: 4.1 mi., 4 hr.
>   *to* Gulfside Trail: 4.5 mi., 4 hr. 20 min.
>   *to* Mt. Adams summit: 4.8 mi. (7.7 km.), 4 hr. 35 min.

Cabin–Cascades Trail (RMC)

One of the earliest AMC trails (1881), Cabin–Cascades Trail leads from the Log Cabin on Lowe's Path to the Israel Ridge Path near the cascades on Cascade Brook. It links the Log Cabin with the trails in the vicinity of Cascade Ravine, as well as the cascades themselves.

The trail begins at Lowe's Path 2.5 mi. from US 2, opposite the Log Cabin, runs gradually downhill in general, with frequent ups and downs, and is narrow and wet for the first 0.3 mi. It crosses two small streams, then descends gradually to Israel Ridge Path just above its upper junction with the Link, near the first cascade at the Link's crossing of Cascade Brook. Not far from here is the second cascade, which can be visited by taking the Israel Ridge Path uphill.

Cabin–Cascades Trail (map 6:E9-F9)
Distance from Lowe's Path

>   *to* Israel Ridge Path: 1.0 mi., 30 min.

Israel Ridge Path (RMC)

This trail runs from the Castle Trail 1.3 mi. from Bowman (on US 2, 1.0 mi. west of Lowe's Store) to the summit of Mt. Adams. It was constructed as a graded path by J. Rayner Edmands beginning in 1892. Although hurricanes and slides have severely damaged the original trail, and there have been many relocations, the upper part is still one of the finest and most beautiful of the Randolph trails. Some brook crossings may be difficult in high water.

From Bowman follow the Castle Trail for 1.3 mi. Here, the Israel Ridge Path branches left and at 0.1 mi. crosses to the east bank of the Israel River. It follows the river, then turns left up the bank at 0.4 mi., as the Castle Ravine Trail continues along the river. The Israel Ridge Path bears southeast up the slope of Nowell Ridge into Cascade Ravine, and at 1.2 mi. the Link enters left. The trails coincide for 50 yd., and then the Link diverges right to cross Cascade Brook—the cascades can be reached by following this trail for a short distance. In another 60 yd. the Cabin-Cascades Trail enters left from the Log Cabin. The Israel Ridge Path now enters virgin growth. From this point to treeline, the forest has never been disturbed by lumbering, though slides have done much damage.

The path continues to ascend on the north side of Cascade Brook to the head of the second cascade at 1.4 mi., where it crosses the brook, turns right downstream for a short distance, then turns left and climbs. It runs southwest, then southeast, making a large zigzag up the steep slope of Israel Ridge—sometimes known as Emerald Tongue—between Cascade and Castle ravines. Soon the path turns sharply east, and at 2.2 mi. Emerald Trail diverges right for 0.2 mi. to Emerald Bluff, a remarkable outlook, and continues steeply down into Castle Ravine. The Israel Ridge Path zigzags up a rather steep slope, and the Perch Path diverges left (east) at 2.4 mi. The main path turns sharply south and ascends to treeline, where it joins the Randolph Path at 2.8 mi. The junction of the Gray Knob Trail with the Randolph Path is a short distance to the left (north) at this point. For 0.1 mi. the paths coincide, then the Israel Ridge Path branches to the left and, curving east, ascends the southwest ridge of Mt. Adams and joins the Gulfside Trail at 3.3 mi., near Storm Lake. It coincides with the Gulfside for 0.5 mi., running northeast past Peabody Spring and south of Mt. Sam Adams, aiming for the Adams–Sam Adams col. At 3.8 mi., just before and in sight of the col (Thunderstorm Junction), the Israel Ridge Path branches right from the Gulfside Trail, and at 3.9 mi. enters Lowe's Path, which leads to the summit of Mt. Adams at 4.1 mi. The cairns between the Gulfside Trail and Lowe's Path are rather sketchy, so in poor visibility it might be easier to follow Lowe's Path from Thunderstorm Junction to the summit.

Israel Ridge Path (map 6:E8-F9)
Distances from Castle Trail
- *to* Castle Ravine Trail: 0.4 mi., 20 min.
- *to* the Link: 1.2 mi., 1 hr. 5 min.
- *to* Perch Path: 2.4 mi., 2 hr. 25 min.
- *to* Randolph Path, lower junction: 2.8 mi., 2 hr. 55 min.
- *to* Gulfside Trail: 3.3 mi., 3 hr. 20 min.
- *to* Mt. Adams summit: 4.1 mi. (6.6 km.), 4 hr. 5 min.
- *to* Edmands Col (via Randolph Path): 3.4 mi., 3 hr. 15 min.

Emerald Trail (RMC)
This trail begins on the Castle Ravine Trail and the Link, about 0.2 mi. southeast of their lower junction, and climbs a very steep and rough route to Emerald Bluff, a fine viewpoint, then runs about level to Israel Ridge Path. The fine forest above Castle Ravine makes it worth the effort. A

good loop can be made by way of the Castle Ravine Trail, Emerald Trail, and Israel Ridge Path.

The trail leaves the Castle Ravine Trail and the Link, which coincide in this area, and descends slightly, crosses several brooks, then ascends a steep and rough route to Emerald Bluff. Follow blazes carefully. The viewpoint is 25 yd. to the left on a side path, while the main trail bears right and runs level through high scrub for 0.1 mi. to the Israel Ridge Path 0.2 mi. below its junction with the Perch Path.

Emerald Trail (map 6:F9)
Distances (est.) from Castle Ravine Trail and the Link
   to Emerald Bluff: 0.6 mi., 40 min.
   to Israel Ridge Path: 0.7 mi. (1.1 km.), 45 min.

Castle Ravine Trail (RMC)

This trail runs from the Israel Ridge Path, about 1.7 mi. from Bowman on US 2 (via the Castle Trail and Israel Ridge Path), and leads through Castle Ravine to the Randolph Path near Edmands Col. This is a wild and beautiful ravine, but parts of the trail are very rough, and it is a difficult trail to descend. While it is reasonably well sheltered after the first section, it crosses a great deal of unstable talus on the headwall, making footing extremely poor, especially for descending or when the rocks are wet. Still, it must be considered as a potential escape route from Edmands Col. Some of the brook crossings may be very difficult at moderate to high water.

From Bowman follow the Castle Trail and the Israel Ridge Path to a point 1.7 mi. from Bowman. Here the Israel Ridge Path turns left up a slope, while the Castle Ravine Trail leads straight ahead near the river. It crosses to the west bank (difficult at high water, and not easy at other times) and soon reaches a point abreast of the Forks of Israel, where Cascade and Castle brooks unite to form

Israel River. The trail crosses to the east bank, passes a fine cascade, and recrosses to the west bank. In general, it follows the route of an old logging road, now almost imperceptible. After entering Castle Ravine, the trail crosses to the east bank and climbs at a moderate to steep grade high above the brook. At 1.4 mi. the Link enters from the left, and the two trails coincide for about 0.2 mi. to the junction with the Emerald Trail left (north) from Israel Ridge. They continue together for another 0.1 mi., then cross to the southwest side of the brook in a tract of cool virgin forest beloved of musca nigra. The Link then turns right while the Castle Ravine Trail continues up the ravine southwest of the brook. Close to the foot of the headwall it crosses again, and in a few yards reaches the place where Castle Brook emerges from under the mossy boulders that have fallen from the headwall. At the foot of the headwall, the trail turns left and mounts the steep slope to Roof Rock, under which it passes (last water). This is a good shelter from rain.

Rising very steeply southeast, with very rough footing, the trail soon winds up a patch of bare rocks, marked by small cairns and dashes of paint, reentering the scrub at a large cairn. In a few hundred feet it emerges from the scrub at the foot of a steep slide of very loose rock (use extreme care when descending). It ascends, marked by paint, to the top of the headwall, and crosses rocks and grass, marked by cairns, to Spaulding Spring, and joins the Randolph Path (sign) 0.1 mi. north of Edmands Col. Descending, follow Randolph Path north from the col to Spaulding Spring, then follow the line of cairns north.

Castle Ravine Trail (map 6:E8-F9)
Distances (est.) from Israel Ridge Path
   to Forks of Israel: 0.3 mi., 10 min.
   to the Link: 1.4 mi., 1 hr. 10 min.

to Emerald Trail: 1.6 mi., 1 hr. 20 min.
to Roof Rock: 2.0 mi., 1 hr. 40 min.
to Randolph Path: 2.7 mi. (4.3 km.), 2 hr. 40 min.

Castle Trail (AMC)

This trail follows the narrow, serrated ridge that runs northwest from Mt. Jefferson, providing magnificent views in a magnificent setting. In bad weather it can be a dangerous trail due to long and continuous exposure to the northwest winds. It was made in 1883–84 but most of the path has since been relocated.

It begins at Bowman on US 2, 3 mi. west of the Appalachia parking area and 4.2 mi. east of the junction of US 2 and NH 115. Park on the north side of the railroad, cross the track, and follow the right-hand driveway for 150 yd. to where the trail enters woods on the right (signs). The trail circles left, crosses a power line, and at 0.4 mi. crosses the Israel River (may be difficult at high water) at the site of an old footbridge.

At 1.3 mi. the Israel Ridge Path branches left (east) toward the brook. Last sure water is a short distance along this trail. The Castle Trail continues southeast, on the northeast flank of Mt. Bowman, and at 2.3 mi. it passes a very large boulder on the left and becomes much steeper for the next 0.5 mi. At 2.8 mi., near the saddle between Mt. Bowman and the Castellated Ridge, it becomes less steep. The view into the ravine left and toward Jefferson is quite spectacular. The trail dips slightly, then continues level along the ridge through thick growth. At 3.4 mi. it is crossed by the Link coming up left from Castle Ravine and leading right to the Caps Ridge Trail. The ridge becomes very narrow and the trail is steep and rough. After passing over two ledges with an outlook from each, it reaches the first and most prominent Castle (4360 ft.), 3.6 mi. from Bowman. The view is very fine. The trail leads on over several lesser crags and ascends as the Castellated Ridge joins the main mass of Mt. Jefferson. Above, the Cornice crosses, leading northeast to the Randolph Path near Edmands Col and south to the Caps Ridge and Gulfside trails. The Castle Trail continues to within a few yards of the summit of Mt. Jefferson, where it connects with the Mount Jefferson Loop and the Six Husbands and Caps Ridge trails.

Castle Trail (map 6:E8-F9)
Distances (est.) from Bowman
   to Israel Ridge Path: 1.3 mi., 50 min.
   to first Castle: 3.6 mi., 3 hr. 15 min.
   to Mt. Jefferson summit: 4.8 mi. (7.7 km.), 4 hr. 30 min.

Caps Ridge Trail (AMC)
The Caps Ridge Trail makes a direct ascent of Mt. Jefferson from the height-of-land on the Jefferson Notch Rd., at an elevation of 3008 ft. This is the highest trailhead on a public through road in the White Mtns. Because of this high start, it is possible to ascend Mt. Jefferson and Mt. Clay with less climbing than by other routes. (In the ascent of Mt. Washington from the Caps Ridge, the descent from Monticello Lawn to Sphinx Col mostly cancels out the advantage of the higher start in comparison to the Jewell Trail.) However, the trail is steep and rough, the upper part is very exposed to weather, and there are numerous ledges which require rock scrambling and are slippery when wet. Therefore the route is more strenuous than might be inferred from the relatively small distance and elevation gain.

The trail leaves the Jefferson Notch Rd. at a parking area and crosses a wet section on puncheons. The trail then steadily ascends the lower part of the ridge; at 1.0 mi. there is an outcrop of granite on the right which provides a fine view, particularly of the summit of Jefferson and the Caps

Ridge ahead. There are several potholes in this outcrop which are normally formed only by torrential streams. Such streams occur on high ridges like the Ridge of the Caps only during the melting of a glacier, so these potholes indicate to geologists that the continental ice sheet once covered this area.

About 100 yd. beyond this outcrop, the Link enters from the left, providing a link to the Castle Trail. The trail follows the narrow crest of the ridge, becoming steeper and rougher as it climbs up into scrub, and views become more and more frequent. At 1.5 mi. the trail reaches the lowest cap (4400 ft.) after a steep scramble up ledges, and the trail is entirely in the open from here on. The trail continues very steeply up the ridge to the highest cap (4830 ft.) at 1.8 mi., then continues to climb steeply as the ridge blends into the summit mass. At 2.1 mi. the Cornice enters left, providing a very rough route to the Castle Trail and Edmands Col, and then diverges right in 20 yd., providing an easy shortcut to Monticello Lawn and points to the south. The Caps Ridge Trail continues east, keeping a little south of the crest of the ridge, to the summit of Mt. Jefferson, then descends east 40 yd. to the base of the little summit cone, where it meets the Castle and Six Husbands trails and the Mount Jefferson Loop.

Caps Ridge Trail (map 6:F8-F9)
Distances from Jefferson Notch Rd.

   to the Link: 1.1 mi., 55 min.
   to lower Cap: 1.5 mi., 1 hr. 30 min.
   to upper Cap: 1.9 mi., 1 hr. 50 min.
   to Cornice: 2.1 mi., 2 hr. 5 min.
   to Mt. Jefferson summit: 2.5 mi., 2 hr. 40 min.
   to junction with Mount Jefferson Loop: 2.6 mi. (4.2 km.), 2 hr. 45 min.
   to Gulfside Trail (via Cornice): 2.5 mi., 2 hr. 30 min.

to Mt. Washington summit (via Cornice and Gulfside Trail): 5.5 mi., 4 hr. 35 min.

Boundary Line Trail (WMNF)

This trail begins on the Jewell Trail 0.3 mi. from the new parking area on the Base Rd. 1.1 mi. from its junction with the Jefferson Notch Rd., and runs to the Jefferson Notch Rd. 1.5 mi. below the Caps Ridge Trail—providing a shortcut between the base of the Caps Ridge Trail and the Jewell Trail and the Ammonoosuc Ravine Trail (Section 1). It follows the straight boundary line between two unincorporated townships, and is nearly level. Leaving the Jewell Trail, it runs north approximately along a surveyor's line, crosses Clay Brook, and ends at the Jefferson Notch Rd.

Boundary Line Trail (map 6:F8)
Distances from Jewell Trail
to Jefferson Notch Rd.: 0.7 mi. (1.1 km.), 20 min.
to Caps Ridge Trail (via Jefferson Notch Rd.): 2.2 mi., 1 hr. 5 min.

Jewell Trail (WMNF)

This trail begins at the new parking area on the Base Rd., climbs the unnamed ridge that leads west from Mt. Clay, and ends at the Gulfside Trail high on the west slope of Mt. Clay, 0.3 mi. north of the Clay–Washington col. The grade is constant, but seldom steep, there are no rock scrambles, and the footing is generally very good. It provides the easiest route to Mt. Washington from the west, with a great length of ridge above treeline with fine views but full exposure to the weather, and no shelter between the summit and treeline. In bad weather, or if afternoon thunderstorms threaten, it is safer to descend via Lakes of the Clouds Hut and the Ammonoosuc Ravine Trail, despite the steep and slippery footing on the latter trail; descent by the

Jewell Trail is much easier. The trail is named for Sergeant W. S. Jewell, an observer for the Army Signal Corps on Mt. Washington, who perished on the Greeley expedition to the Arctic in 1884.

The trail enters the woods directly across the road from the parking area, crosses the Ammonoosuc River at 0.1 mi., then swings northeast and ascends at an easy grade. At 0.3 mi. the Boundary Line Trail diverges left, while the Jewell Trail continues up the crest of the low ridge between the Ammonoosuc River and Clay Brook, joining the old route of the trail at 0.9 mi. At this point it descends slightly to Clay Brook, crosses on a footbridge, then climbs northeast by switchbacks up the south flank of the ridge and winds around its west end. Avoiding the craggy crest, it slabs the north flank and comes out above treeline on the west slope of Mt. Clay. It zigzags up the slope of Mt. Clay and enters the Gulfside Trail 0.3 mi. northwest of the Clay–Washington col. For Mt. Washington, follow the Gulfside right. For Mt. Clay, scramble up the rocks above the junction.

Jewell Trail (map 6:F8-F9)
Distances from Base Rd. parking area
- *to* Clay Brook crossing: 1.0 mi., 40 min.
- *to* Gulfside Trail: 3.5 mi. (5.6 km.), 3 hr. 10 min.
- *to* Mt. Washington summit (via Gulfside Trail): 5.0 mi., 4 hr. 25 min.

Pine Mountain Road
This private automobile road to the summit of Pine Mtn. begins a little northwest of the highest point of the Pinkham B (Dolly Copp) Rd., 2.4 mi. from US 2 and 1.9 mi. from NH 16, and opposite the foot of Pine Link. It is closed to public vehicular use, but may be used as a foot trail to the summit. Hikers should watch for automobiles descending on this road. The Ledge Trail, a foot trail over the top of the south cliff, diverges from the road and runs

to the summit; it is frequently used to make a loop over the summit. The views from the summit are fine, both to the much higher surrounding peaks and to the valleys of the Androscoggin, Moose, and Peabody rivers. The Douglas Horton Center, a center for renewal and education operated by the New Hampshire Conference of the United Church of Christ (Congregational), occupies a tract of 100 acres on the summit. The center (not open to the public) consists of six buildings and an outdoor chapel on the more precipitous northeast peak. Although camping is not permitted, day hikers are welcome to appreciate the views.

The road runs east from Pinkham B Rd. across the col, and turns northeast and north to ascend along the west flank of the mountain, where the Ledge Trail branches right to climb around the south cliff and so to the summit. About 1.4 mi. from the highway a side trail leads left to a good spring. Opposite this path a shortcut leads right to the summit. The road climbs to the saddle north of the main summit, and turns south to the summit.

Pine Mountain Road (map 6:E10)
Distances (est.) from Pinkham B Rd.
    to Ledge Trail: 1.0 mi., 35 min.
    to summit: 1.8 mi. (2.9 km.), 1 hr. 20 min.
    to Pinkham B Rd. (loop via Ledge Trail with return via Pine Mountain Road): 3.4 mi. (5.5 km.), 2 hr. 5 min.

Ledge Trail (WMNF)
This trail runs to the summit from the Pine Mountain Road (private, closed to public vehicles), 1.0 mi. from the Pinkham B (Dolly Copp) Rd. It runs around the south cliff and gives beautiful views westward.

Ledge Trail (map 6:E10)
Distance (est.) from Pine Mountain Road
    to summit: 0.6 mi. (1.0 km.), 35 min.

Town Line Brook Trail (RMC)

A good but steep path runs from Pinkham B (Dolly Copp) Rd., 1.4 mi. southeast of the railroad crossing, to Triple Falls. These three beautiful cascades on Town Line Brook are named Proteus, Erebus, and Evans. The watershed is steep and the rainwater runs off very rapidly, so the falls should be visited during or immediately after a rain.

Town Line Brook Trail (map 6:E10)
Distance from Pinkham B (Dolly Copp) Rd.
  to Triple Falls: 0.2 mi., 15 min.

Sylvan Way (RMC)

The Sylvan Way leads from the Link at Memorial Bridge, 0.7 mi. from the Appalachia parking area, over Cold Brook to Howker Ridge Trail at Coosauk Fall. Leaving Memorial Bridge it passes Cold Brook Fall in a few yards. At 0.1 mi. Beechwood Way crosses. Sylvan Way crosses Air Line at 0.6 mi. and Valley Way at 0.7. Soon, at 0.8 mi., Fallsway crosses, and Maple Walk enters left. Sylvan Way then crosses Snyder Brook and immediately after, the Brookbank. Randolph Path crosses at 1.1 mi. from Memorial Bridge, and, after a gradual ascent, the Sylvan Way ends at Howker Ridge Trail.

Sylvan Way (map 6:E9)
Distance from Memorial Bridge
  to Howker Ridge Trail: 1.7 mi. (2.7 km.), 1 hr.

Fallsway (RMC)

Fallsway is an alternative route to the first 0.6 mi. of the Valley Way, following close to Snyder Brook and passing several falls. From the east end of the Appalachia parking area it goes east for 60 yd., then turns right on a gravel road and crosses the railroad and power lines. Here the Brookbank diverges left as Fallsway enters the woods. At

0.3 mi. from the Appalachia parking area, the path passes
Gordon Fall, and Gordon Fall Loop diverges right. In a
few yards Sylvan Way crosses and Maple Walk enters.
Lower and Upper Salroc Falls are passed, and soon Fall-
sway enters Valley Way below Tama Fall. In a few yards
Fallsway leaves Valley Way and passes Tama Fall. Brook-
bank then enters, and Fallsway ends in a few yards at
Valley Way, above Tama Fall.

Fallsway (map 6:E9)
Distance from Appalachia parking area
>   *to* Valley Way junction above Tama Fall: 0.6 mi. (1.0
>   km.), 30 min.

Brookbank (RMC)
Brookbank diverges from Fallsway near the railroad and
rejoins Fallsway above Tama Fall. It leaves Fallsway at the
edge of the woods just beyond the power lines, 0.1 mi.
from the Appalachia parking lot, and runs parallel to the
railroad for about 0.1 mi., then crosses Snyder Brook,
turns sharp right (south), and enters the woods. It runs up
the east side of the brook, passing Gordon Fall, Sylvan
Way, Upper and Lower Salroc Falls, and Tama Fall. Above
Tama Fall it recrosses the brook and reenters Fallsway.

Brookbank (map 6:E9)
Distance from lower junction with Fallsway
>   *to* upper junction with Fallsway: 0.6 mi. (1.0 km.), 30
>   min.

Maple Walk (RMC)
The Maple Walk diverges left from Valley Way a few
yards from the Appalachia parking area and runs to the
junction of Fallsway and Sylvan Way. Just before the latter
junction, Gordon Fall Loop diverges left and in 60 yd.
reaches Fallsway at Gordon Fall.

Maple Walk (map 6:E9)
Distance from Valley Way

 to Sylvan Way and Fallsway: 0.2 mi. (0.3 km.), 5 min.

Beechwood Way (RMC)

 This path runs from the Amphibrach 0.5 mi. from the Air Line, to the Valley Way just below its junctions with the Brookside and the Randolph Path. It follows a good logging road with moderate gradients. It leaves the Amphibrach, crosses Sylvan Way at 0.2 mi., then the Air Line at 0.6 mi., and joins the Valley Way just below its junction with the Brookside.

Beechwood Way (map 6:E9)
Distance from Amphibrach

 to Valley Way: 0.8 mi. (1.3 km.), 40 min.

White Mountain History

For more than three centuries Mount Washington has exerted an almost mystical attraction that has brought to its deep ravines and barren, wind-swept summit a great variety of visitors: rock and ice climbers, hikers and wildflower enthusiasts; botanists, meteorologists, and other scientific investigators; writers such as Nathaniel Hawthorne, Ralph Waldo Emerson, Henry David Thoreau, and John Greenleaf Whittier; artists such as Thomas Cole, Frederic Church, Benjamin Champney, Albert Bierstadt, and Winslow Homer; and tourists by the thousand. This section will recount some of the historical events and the next section will describe a number of the natural features that have contributed to this attraction, so strongly felt by so many people with such diverse interests.

Mount Washington is the highest mountain in North America east of Hudson Bay, the Great Lakes, and the Mississippi River, except for a dozen great wooded hills in the southern Appalachians, which exceed its elevation by less than 400 feet and lack its rocky ruggedness and its great expanses of bare, rocky land above the treeline. Its only rivals for eminence in New England are Katahdin in central Maine, rising in splendid solitude from countless lakes and vast forests, and the Franconia Range in the White Mountains, a gothic masterpiece of rock towers and flying buttresses. However, both are about a thousand feet lower and far less massive.

To the dominating size of Mount Washington, add the legendary ferocity of its weather: its record wind of 231 mph, its climate similar to that of northern Labrador, its worst weather conditions comparable to those of Antarctica or of the great mountains of Alaska and the Yukon. And all this is within a day's drive of millions of residents of the temperate zone—"an arctic outpost in the midst of civilization," as F. Allen Burt wrote. Ponder the stories of the dozens of people who have died on the slopes of Mount Washington, so many of them from foolishly challenging the overwhelming natural forces. Consider, in contrast, the tiny, beautiful, rare plants that flourish in a climate whose worst conditions could kill any one of us in a few minutes. Then add in the fabled skiing on the cone and in Tuckerman Ravine, the rock and ice climbing in Huntington Ravine, and such artifacts of human ingenuity as the Cog Railway.

At first the mountain could only be admired at a distance. The native peoples who first lived in the nearby valleys regarded the mountain as the sacred abode of spirits, where a human trespasser would be punished for the act of impiety. To the adventurous sailors who sailed along the northern coast in the cold seasons and were the first Europeans to see Mount Washington, and to the early settlers along the coast, this mountain must have seemed a great mystery, a ghostly white shape that appeared with the approach of winter, looming beyond the coastal hills, and then disappeared with the coming of summer only to appear again in the fall. The mountain was thought to be composed of crystal (quartz) and was thus called the Crystal Hill; later the name White Mountains evolved from the mountain's visibility from great distances when covered with snow.

Even when the mountain was finally ascended, it retained its claim to the visitor's awe. Darby Field, who made the first recorded climb in 1642, reported—clearly under the mountain's influence—the existence of large diamonds and huge sheets of muscovy glass (mica), described an endless lake lying to the north, and provided estimates of distances above treeline far in excess of what dispassionate measurements have since confirmed. John Josselyn wrote in 1772 a description of the view from the summit which, as an example of the power of the wilderness over the first visitors, can scarcely be improved upon: "Beyond these hills —northward is daunting terrible, being full of rocky hills as thick as mole hills in a meadow, and cloathed with infinite thick woods." Even Jeremy Belknap, New Hampshire's first historian and leader of a scientific expedition to Mount Washington in 1784, was led astray by the mountain's influence. On that expedition, Manasseh Cutler attempted a measurement of the mountain's height, but bad weather interfered, and only a crude estimate of 10,000 ft. could be produced. Accurate measurements have since shown that Cutler's estimate was far too high; Belknap, however, had ventured the opinion that Mount Washington would prove to be even higher.

Today—with civilization firmly ensconced on a summit which has had at various times several hotels, a newspaper, a television station, an automobile road, and a railway—most visitors, even those who are comfortably conveyed to the top by cars or trains, can share the awe and reverence with which the Abenaki regarded the mountain when it was still untrodden, and the astonishment that influenced Field, Josselyn, and Belknap when they explored it.

HISTORY

Early Exploration and Settlement

Several names, including "Waumbekket Methna" and "Agiochook" or "Agiocochook," have been suggested as Abenaki names for Mount Washington or the White Mountains, but there is no clear authority for any of them. "Christall hill" was apparently common among early visitors and settlers. The name "White Mountains" was first applied to the range by John Josselyn in his *New England's*

Rarities Discovered (1672). There has been some disagreement about the origin of this name, which tends to appear somewhat inappropriate to those who visit the mountains in summer; some attempts have been made to explain the name by some fancied whitish appearance of the gray rocks when seen from a distance. But to anyone who has seen Mount Washington in winter, when its pure white dome is strikingly visible from many low hills far to the south, the probable origin of the name will be quite apparent.

Far too little is known about the Abenaki, who once inhabited the river valleys and had a major village at Pequawket (near Conway). According to Frederick Kilbourne, they had already been decimated by disease and warfare before the first British settlers moved into the area. The Abenakis, one of the ten major Algonquin nations, occupied most of New Hampshire, including the region around the Presidential Range. Vestiges of their wigwam villages, surrounded by wooden palisades, have been found in the river valleys and intervales. These hunting and fishing people also grew some corn; corn hills and other hints of their agriculture survive, along with earthenware, pipes, and burial mounds. It is generally assumed that none of them attempted to climb Mount Washington; superstitious fears of mountain spirits are often mentioned, but it is perhaps also true that these practical people found sufficient challenge in the daily struggle for existence in this harsh climate, and saw no need to undertake unnecessary risks.

Although John and Sebastian Cabot had probably seen the White Mountains in 1497–98, the Italian explorer Verrazano is credited with being the first European to record a sighting of the White Mountains, in his ship's log, on a coastal exploration in 1524. The mountains were not visited until May or June of 1642, when Darby Field made the first known ascent of Mount Washington, accompanied by two

Abenakis. Based on Field's description of his journey, it is believed that he ascended Mount Washington via Boott Spur. He reported that "within 12 miles of the top was neither tree nor grass, but low savins [shrubs], which they went upon the top of sometimes . . . within four miles of the top they had no clouds, but very cold." Twelve miles is, of course, several times the actual distance from the tree-line to the summit. Field's glowing but wildly inaccurate account of the mineral riches to be had there—the crystals he thought were diamonds—led to several later expeditions, but there were no mineral riches, and the region was left until the turn of the nineteenth century to' other explorers, scientists, and naturalists, who found riches indeed—the plants, animals, insects, weather, and geological phenomena discussed earlier.

"It was not until the latter part of the eighteenth century," Kilbourne states, "that the New England colonies were sufficiently established, and the country secure enough from Indian depredations, for the settlement of the remoter regions to be thought of and attempted." The first town in the region, Fryeburg ME, was chartered in 1762 and settled a year later; Conway NH was founded in 1765. Many of the other towns in the region were first settled in the following decade.

The real frontier drama of the region surrounding the Presidential Range, however, lies in the settlement of the towns and, particularly, the mountain country. In this drama the greatest figure—and perhaps a truly tragic one—was Ethan Allen Crawford. Much of the history of the early settlement of Crawford Notch involves Crawford and his wife, Lucy Howe Crawford, and other relatives such as his father, Abel Crawford, and his grandfather, Eleazar Rosebrook. Lucy Crawford wrote a fine book about their life in Crawford Notch, and thus she preserved many stories and details which would otherwise have been lost.

The notch, which was formerly called the "White Mountain Notch" but now bears Crawford's name, was discovered about 1771 by a settler named Timothy Nash; one common legend has it that he was pursuing a moose on Cherry Mountain and climbed a tree to look for landmarks, and thus discovered the notch by accident, while Lucy Crawford states that Nash and Benjamin Sawyer went deliberately to search for a pass through the mountains. As the settlers in the fertile intervales of the upper Connecticut River around Lancaster were in desperate need of a more convenient route for trade with the coastal towns than what the river itself provided, it seems more than likely that a deliberate search produced the discovery of Crawford Notch. Nash and Sawyer fulfilled Governor John Wentworth's requirement of getting a horse through the notch, and were rewarded with a grant of land. This grant included the area where the present-day Mount Washington Hotel and the Crawford Depot and Hostel are located. It was many years before a good road was built through this notch, but the settlers passed through on foot and even managed to get horses and their loads through.

In 1792 Eleazar Rosebrook bought from his son-in-law Abel Crawford a parcel of land at the north end of the notch that Abel had bought and had lived on for a while before. Both Rosebrook and Crawford had previously lived in Guildhall VT, on the Connecticut River above Lancaster, but they were apparently the kind of men who preferred not to have many neighbors. Rosebrook and his wife Hannah had come to Guildhall from Grafton MA shortly after the birth of their first child, and then, after the birth of their second child, they made an attempt to establish a farm near present-day Colebrook NH on the Connecticut River, 30 miles north from the nearest fellow settler. Rosebrook's service in the Revolutionary War ended this venture, but the urge to pioneer clearly never deserted him.

His son-in-law Abel was of similar temperament; after selling out to Rosebrook, "rather than be crowded by neighbors," he moved twelve miles farther south into the wilderness of the notch, where he built what was to become the first Mount Crawford House.

Conventional history emphasizes the actions and accomplishments of the men who settled these wild regions; the contributions of the women are usually ignored, because it is less exciting to recount the endless, grinding hours of household and farm labor, and the repeated childbearing without adequate rest or nutrition—or effective health care—that sent so many settler women to an early grave. Lucy Crawford follows this tradition to a substantial degree—she wrote her book in the first person, as if spoken by Ethan—but she does provide occasional glimpses into the hardships that her pioneer sisters bore with such great restraint. In these days one can drive from Grafton MA to Guildhall VT in four or five hours; in Hannah Rosebrook's time, with poor transportation and the limited leisure available to farmers in the seasons when such travel was possible, the move from Grafton to Guildhall meant a separation from family and friends practically as final as death. During the time when she and her husband were the lone settlers in Colebrook, they possessed but one cow, which for lack of a fence was allowed to run free; often Hannah, "in the absence of her husband, shut her dear child up in her cabin and taking her infant in her arms, [did] proceed into the woods in search of her cow . . . Sometimes she was under the necessity of wading the river to get where the animal was, and then she would return home and find the deserted child safe, and, with the infant still in her arms, and followed by the other child, did she milk her cow." (The "infant in her arms," Hannah, became the wife of Abel Crawford and the mother of Ethan Allen Crawford, while the "deserted child," Mercy, became the mother of Lucy Crawford.)

Later, Hannah Rosebrook "used frequently to work a whole week, both night and day, without undressing herself. She would only lie down for a short time with her clothes on, while carding and spinning." This was in the relatively civilized Guildhall; how much more burdensome must have been the conditions in the wild notch. After the move to the notch, "as they were dependent on their neighbors for food, they were obliged to go, or send their children that distance [twelve miles] to obtain it, always feeling anxious for their safety when they were gone, fearing some accident might befall them, . . . Many an hour . . . she has spent in meditation of her absent children." On the day that Lucy Crawford gave birth to her first child, attended only by the aged grandmother Hannah Rosebrook, she suffered the loss by fire of her home and almost everything except the bed she gave birth in. Such were the daily hardships and occasional harsh blows dealt by life in the wilderness.

The Rosebrooks and the Crawfords farmed, and they worked on improving the roads, occasionally receiving pay for their road work. In 1803 the New Hampshire legislature chartered the Tenth New Hampshire Turnpike, which would cause the construction of a good road (by the standard of that time) through the Notch. As the roads improved and the traffic on them increased, a growing number of travelers arrived at the Rosebrook and Crawford farms seeking lodging during their journeys. One of these travelers was Timothy Dwight, then president of Yale. For farmers who lived along the roads of the sparsely settled areas, putting up travelers had always been a source of the hard cash which was so rare and so necessary for purchasing what the farmers could not produce for themselves. It is not clear that the settlers of Crawford Notch originally intended to become innkeepers, but the income that fell into their hands from this business was welcome in a region where the severe climate and rocky soil made subsistence farming a precarious way to maintain a family. At first the guests were lodged right with the family, but as this business increased, such an arrangement led to very cramped quarters. Soon after the completion of the turnpike through the notch and the consequent increase in traffic, Rosebrook put up a two-story building and furnished it for the comfort of his guests, no doubt in the somewhat rough style of the times—including the inevitable barroom. This was the first building constructed specifically for lodging guests in the region, and thus the first of the White Mountain hotels, rude though it was. Whether or not he planned it, Eleazar Rosebrook had become the first of the great line of White Mountain innkeepers.

Meanwhile, twelve miles down the notch, his grandson Ethan Allen Crawford was growing to manhood in the harsh life of the wilderness. Used to very hard labor at an early age, inured to pain and cold, he was well prepared for the physical feats which would later be required of him. As a young boy, he chopped trees to clear land until his hands swelled and he required poultices on them to be able to sleep at night; he harnessed horses in light clothing in the coldest weather. He grew to be a large man, over six feet in height, whose great strength was renowned even in a day when most men made their living by hard physical labor. At the age of 19, he enlisted as a soldier, and spent several years in the army at Plattsburgh NY. After this he worked at building roads in New York State. In 1816, when Ethan was 24, Rosebrook contracted cancer of the lower lip, and asked Ethan to come and care for him. He offered to give his property to Ethan if Ethan would care for him and Hannah, and also assume all of Rosebrook's debts, a sum of between $2000 and $3000. With some reluctance, Ethan consented. To help care for his grandfather he brought to the notch a first cousin named Lucy Howe. Thus, in one short space of time, Ethan acquired the property which would become the stage upon which he would earn lasting fame, the woman who would become his wife and record the story of his life, and the debt that he would never be able to repay, which would stalk him all the way to debtor's prison and an early grave.

Two months after Rosebrook died, Lucy and Ethan were married. The next summer Lucy gave birth to a son, attended only by Hannah Rosebrook. Ethan went out, at their grandmother's request, to catch some trout; when he returned, he found his house in flames, and his wife and newborn son lying out in the open in a bed which, in the process of removing it from the burning house, had three times caught fire, requiring Lucy to smother the flames with her hands. The fire apparently started from a lit candle which the old grandmother forgetfully left burning on a chair.

Ethan's loss, uninsured, was about $3000. Although he could not have known it then, this catastrophe sealed his financial doom; never, in spite of all his exertions during the next two decades, would he be able to escape the consequences of the financial burdens that had been placed upon him by his grandfather's death and this ruinous fire. In good years, Crawford was able to repay some of his debt, but fires and floods caused him severe loss in other years. Taken together, the inn, his farming, and his activities as a mountain guide were more than adequate to support his family, but they never generated enough hard cash to reduce his debt; in fact, the requirements of this expanding business, in which he had set out with so little premeditation, forced him to borrow even more. Eventually, when he had proved that an inn could be successfully operated in Crawford Notch, competitors took up the business and cut into Crawford's profits, making it impossible for him to make progress out of debt.

Ethan attempted to sell the property in the winter of

1819, but the deal fell through, so he and Lucy set out to make a go of their projects, and were able to accomplish great things in spite of their financial insecurity. In the summer of 1819, noting that several parties had come to climb Mount Washington, Ethan and Abel Crawford cut a footpath from the notch through the woods to treeline. This was the beginning of the Crawford Path, which is considered to be the oldest continuously maintained mountain footpath in the country. This path was advertised in some newspapers, and visitors began to come to use it, although they were compelled to stay at Abel Crawford's due to Ethan's lack of space. Ethan's patrons at this time consisted mostly of travelers and those transporting goods over the notch road, which had become an important market route; such guests, who traveled by necessity and not for pleasure, demanded less comfort. In 1820, Ethan guided to the summit a party which included Philip Carrigain (who made the first reasonably accurate map of the state of New Hampshire in 1816); these men gave names to Mounts Adams, Jefferson, Madison, and Monroe (although the peaks they named Adams and Jefferson have since had their names interchanged).

In 1824, Ethan Crawford finally constructed a building specifically for lodging guests, although in his circumstances this expense caused him some worry. He also made several unsuccessful attempts to provide a comfortable place to spend the night on the summit of Mount Washington; first he built stone cabins that proved too damp for comfort, then he bought and carried up a tent and an iron stove, but the tent was soon destroyed. During this time, he led many parties to the summit of Mount Washington, and often had to carry out exhausted climbers on his back. He constructed a camp part way up the mountain, as the distance was too great for most parties to make a complete trip in one day. In 1825, Lucy Crawford made her first ascent of Mount Washington.

Near the end of the summer of 1826, heavy rains caused great damage to Ethan Allen Crawford's property, and even greater damage to Abel Crawford's property down in the deep valley in the southern portion of the notch area. At the latter place, Ethan's mother stood at a window with a pole, pushing away stream-borne debris which was collecting at the corner of the house and might have caused the house to be swept away, occasionally hearing the bleating of their drowning sheep that were carried past the house in the swift current. But the most famous disaster produced by this storm was the destruction of the Willey family, which became the inspiration for Nathaniel Hawthorne's well-known story, "The Ambitious Guest."

Midway between the Rosebrook and Crawford farms, in the heart of Crawford Notch, the Willey House was a lonely refuge for travelers in the wilderness. When the flood occurred, there was naturally great concern for the family, which consisted of the parents, five children, and two hired men. The following day a traveler found the Willey house deserted, as if the family had left in great haste. Over the next several days the bodies of the husband, wife, two children, and the two hired hands were discovered among the debris of a huge landslide. The bodies of three other children were never found. Although it will always be uncertain exactly what happened, it is believed that the family, which had seen smaller slides earlier in the storm and had made plans to escape, fled the house when they heard the landslide amid the storm. But a ledge between the house and the mountain slope protected the dwelling from the slide, which split into two parts that cascaded down on either side; thus, ironically, they ran away from safety directly into the path of the slide. The scar left by the slide is still visible on the face of Mount

Willey, which was named for the family; there is a monument at the Willey House Site in Crawford Notch State Park.

The flood left Ethan Crawford and his family intact, but it swept away the fruits of several years of hard labor, and made the prospect of his paying off his debts even more remote, since he lost his entire cash crop. It also nearly totally destroyed the turnpike which was the very reason for the existence of Crawford's establishment, but with the help of a donation of $1500, raised by the people of Portland ME, the road was rebuilt. Still Ethan persevered, rebuilt, and even worked on constructing a new road toward the base of Mount Washington, near the present location of the Cog Railway Base Station, which would make ascents of the mountain in a single day more practical for the average visitor. In 1828, another heavy rain struck, from which the floods again caused great damage to Crawford's property and destroyed the turnpike. At first the directors of the turnpike declined to rebuild, which would have left Crawford isolated, with little business and unable to obtain food without great difficulty, but he was able to secure enough support in the turnpike corporation to proceed with the reconstruction. Still, he was forced to advance $400 of his own money and only got it back four years later. A man who was himself deeply in debt could ill afford to make what was in effect an interest-free loan to the turnpike corporation, but Crawford did what seemed to be required for his own and the public's benefit. Still, he managed to construct with his father a new lodging at the top of the notch, near the present-day Crawford Depot information center, and his brother Thomas was installed as manager. This was a great service to travelers, and became a popular stopping-place, but again it was a drain on Ethan's financial resources.

By this time Ethan Crawford had begun to find routine ascents of Mount Washington rather tiresome; however, he still led botanists and others with scientific purposes to the mountain. In fact, he became so familiar with the rare mountain plants, and the places to find them, that he was occasionally asked to collect plants himself and send them off to botanists or museums. In 1831 he guided his most famous guest, Daniel Webster, to the summit. Webster was a native of Franklin NH; he was perhaps the most famous native son of New Hampshire (although he was elected to the Senate from Massachusetts), and the most spellbinding speaker in the country at a time when political oratory was one of the highest forms of public entertainment. Reaching the summit in the clouds, he addressed the mountain thus: "Mount Washington, I have come a long distance, have toiled hard to arrive at your summit, and now you seem to give me a cold reception."

In 1832 Crawford enlarged his guest lodgings. The expense of building and furnishing this addition was great, but his existing lodgings were frequently overcrowded—even to the point of filling up the family's own quarters—the prospect for increased business seemed promising, and the owners of the stage line put considerable pressure on him to enlarge his accommodations, as their business depended in part on having adequate lodgings for their patrons. However, the increase in business convinced others that a good living might be made in this line of service. A competitor set up an inn within a mile of Crawford's, and offered stage drivers free feed and stabling in order to induce the drivers to bring their passengers to his establishment. The horses that Crawford kept to carry guests to the foot of Mount Washington, so that they could climb it in a day, were also a constant drain on his resources, as they had to be fed and cared for throughout the year though they were only used for a few short months. Crawford had made it a point of great pride that he always conducted his business openly and honestly and with a strong concern for the public good, and that he had always paid his hired workers fully and on time, no matter what other obligations he might have to leave unpaid. The traditional Yankee sharp practices he forswore might have paid his debts more effectively, but Crawford was a man ruled by public spirit and a stern conscience, and an honesty and a trust in the honesty of others which was sometimes almost naive.

Through all the years of hardship and hard labor, Ethan and Lucy had been fortunate in having good health; Ethan had occasional rheumatism from having frequently worked in water during his road-building days in New York State, and in 1821 he had suffered an axe wound to his heel that lamed him for some time, but neither he nor Lucy lost more than a few days of work to sickness. This good fortune came to an end in 1834. First, Lucy became ill soon after the birth of her ninth child, was unable to nurse it, and decided to give the child over to her brother and sister-in-law, who had recently lost their own infant. Knowing that the sister-in-law, having nursed the child, would be reluctant to give it back, Lucy consoled herself with the knowledge that the child would be comfortably taken care of. Lucy's illness continued and appeared to be threatening her life. By great fortune, one of their guests that summer was Dr. John Collins Warren, the eminent Boston physician who twelve years later performed the first public operation in the world in which ether was used as an anaesthetic. Dr. Warren treated her, without charge, and apparently effected a cure that local doctors had failed to accomplish.

Next, in the fall of 1834, Ethan suffered an painful injury while riding a horse. This injury, severe in itself, was no doubt exacerbated by the toll taken on his body by the long years of hardship, overwork, and the frequent feats of strength and endurance for which he was famous. Never again would the "Giant of the White Hills" enjoy the physical and mental vigor of which the legends were written, since his ailments, together with the mental strain from his financial troubles, affected his mind as well as his body; Lucy Crawford later described his condition as "a premature decay of mind [which] caused him to wander from his native mind more and more rapidly." During this period he made an unwise agreement to sell his property to a land speculator, and was thus forced to pass up even better deals; by the time the agreement expired, and the sale fell through, the better terms were no longer available. An operation performed by a generous doctor in 1836 finally relieved some of his suffering and improved his condition somewhat, but some creditors had heard of his illnesses and feared that he would die without paying what he owed them; he was therefore put in the Lancaster jail for 25 days, while still in a weakened condition recuperating from his ordeals. Within the year he departed from the notch, leaving his property in the hands of his creditors to be sold. For six years he farmed in Guildhall VT, with the help of his large family, on land once occupied by his grandmother, Hannah Rosebrook.

In 1843 Ethan and Lucy Crawford returned to Crawford Notch, renting a house within a mile of their former mountain home. They still entertained hopes of returning to that scene of their many years of toil and service; in fact, one of Lucy's motives in writing her History was the hope that the book would produce enough profits and public goodwill to restore them to their old home. But it was not to be; Ethan contracted typhoid fever in the fall of 1845 and gradually declined. He died on June 22, 1846, at the age of 54. William Oakes, the botanist that Crawford had guided over the hills to the rare plants, had a marble tombstone placed on Crawford's grave on a knoll overlooking the region where his great deeds had taken place. Lucy Crawford lived for another 23 years.

Ethan and Lucy Crawford had been great pioneers; they had accepted endless labor and hardship. Ethan's services to botanists, mountain climbers, and travelers were great and can be appreciated even today, particularly since the path he and his father built still exists, and is for much of its distance part of the Appalachian Trail. Perhaps less obvious is the service the Crawfords provided to the people of the settlements of the upper Connecticut River valley; by helping to keep the road through Crawford Notch open and making travel along that route relatively comfortable and safe, they made a tremendous contribution to the economy of the region, undoubtedly making the difference between prosperity and poverty, and perhaps even between survival and failure for many settlers in that fertile but remote area. They broke ground and made the way smoother for many that followed, but they never fully enjoyed the fruits of their labors; in some sense, Ethan was repaid for his great services by a constant burden of debt ending in prison, and died in circumstances in which he must have thought himself to a great degree a failure. Except for his good fortune in marrying a woman who, against all odds, proved to have significant literary ability, his deeds might have faded into the obscurity which has claimed the stories of most of the brave people who settled this wilderness. Thus the Crawfords also stand as examples of the men and women who built the settlements of the New England wilderness, and who are now remembered, if at all, mostly by names, dates, and verses on weathered gravestones. The innkeepers who succeeded the Crawfords within a very short period of time created a little world of luxury which far exceeded anything that the Crawfords could have imagined, but which seems almost tawdry in comparison to the simple and steadfast virtues that governed the lives and works of Ethan and Lucy Crawford.

The Era of the Grand Hotels

By the latter part of the nineteenth century, resort hotels dotted the White Mountain landscape, served by a rail network bringing vacationers from all over the East. Both a railway and a carriage road climbed Mount Washington, and there was a thriving seasonal community on the summit to serve the whims of the visiting travelers. In its heyday, the region attracted artists and writers as well as other distinguished visitors, and was considered a chic and opulent watering place.

Early access to the Presidential Range depended, naturally, on the available transportation. The first main road in the region, as mentioned earlier, was the turnpike from the seacoast at Portland ME through Crawford Notch to the upper Connecticut River valley. The earliest settlers, most notably the Crawfords, did much to keep this road open in spite of floods, landslides, and blizzards, for their livelihoods depended on it. The earliest traffic was commercial, farm produce from the settlements exchanged for finished goods from the long-established towns nearer the coast. Noncommercial visitors tended to be scientists and explorers, not tourists.

Catering to this trade were a half-dozen inns in Crawford Notch. The first, as noted previously, was built by Eleazar Rosebrook on the site of his decade-old homestead at the north end of the Notch in 1803. In 1816 Ethan Allen Crawford and his wife Lucy came to take care of Rosebrook, and, after his death the following year they ran an inn on the spot until forced out of the notch by illness and debt in 1837. At about the same time that Rosebrook opened his inn, a second waystation was opened by Henry Hill at the Willey House site, halfway through the Notch, and a third was begun by Abel Crawford, Rosebrook's son-in-law and Ethan Allen Crawford's father, at the south end of the Notch. These early inns were not always planned to be such; in many cases, they started with farmers offering lodging to travelers in exchange for scarce hard cash, and gradually developed into full-scale inns as this business increased.

In 1819, Abel and Ethan Crawford cut their first path—now the Crawford Path—over the Southern Peaks, and in 1821 Ethan cut another path in roughly the location used today by the Cog Railway. This ushered in a new era, attracting tourists who came in increasing numbers, not for business but for pleasure, to see the mountains. By 1825 tourists had begun to come to North Conway, which then had five hotels, the first having been opened in 1812. The town was the terminus of a stagecoach line from Center Harbor on Lake Winnipesaukee, which brought travelers from southern New Hampshire and beyond. Business increased steadily in Crawford Notch. Ethan Allen Crawford constructed a new building for lodging guests in 1824, and enlarged it in 1832. With his father he built a new inn between the present Crawford Hostel and the Gate of the Notch, in 1828, which was managed by his brother T. J. Crawford for almost 25 years.

Soon the area began to attract notable visitors whose interests were not directed toward exploration or science. Daniel Webster, as previously mentioned, ascended Mount Washington with Ethan Allen Crawford in 1831. Nathaniel Hawthorne, who wrote several stories with White Mountain settings, including "The Ambitious Guest," first visited the area in 1832. He was only one of many famous writers to visit these mountains; others were Henry Wadsworth Longfellow, Henry David Thoreau, Ralph Waldo Emerson, Francis Parkman, John Greenleaf Whittier, and William Cullen Bryant. Many artists of national importance also came to the mountains—but for work rather than play—including Thomas Cole and Asher B. Durand of the Hudson River School, and Albert Bierstadt, Benjamin Champney, and John Kensett; many of these painters did important work in the White Mountains. Soon the region was established as a true resort, and people came to the White Mountains summer after summer, staying for several weeks in their favorite hotels, visiting with summertime friends and amusing themselves with the grand mountain scenery.

It would be a great era for the region, an era that would bring a new generation of entrepreneurs, but at first the pattern of hard work with great financial risk and frequent failure persisted. In 1837, after Ethan Allen Crawford had been forced to give up his property, Horace Fabyan purchased it, renamed it as the Mount Washington House, and ran it for 15 years. In 1845 he built another hotel at the Willey House site, and in 1851 took over management of the Conway House, but in 1853 the Mount Washington House burned and Fabyan was financially ruined. Abel Crawford's son-in-law, Nathaniel P. T. Davis, assumed the management of Abel's Mount Crawford House, but went heavily in debt to Dr. Samuel A. Bemis, a long-time summer visitor to the region; Bemis finally took over this hotel. All this activity in the hotel business spurred major changes in the routes to Mount Washington's summit, as the new visitors had to be given the opportunity to enjoy the region's chief natural attraction. In 1839 and 1840 the original Crawford path over the Southern Peaks was rebuilt as a bridle path, and Abel Crawford, at the age of 75, rode the first horse to the summit in 1840. Fabyan improved Ethan Crawford's 1821 path along the present-day Cog Railway route so that it could also be used by horses, and in 1845 Davis built his own bridle path, which what was perhaps the most arduous construction project of all the Presidential bridle paths. This last path was abandoned around 1853 but was reopened in 1910, and still exists as one of the longest and most strenuous routes to Mount Washington.

Around mid-century the hotel business started to spread

more widely through the region. In Crawford Notch, hotels continued to be built and renovated; they periodically burned down and were rebuilt. Destruction by fire was the almost inevitable fate of these huge wooden buildings. In 1852 the railway was completed from Portland ME to Gorham NH, at the head of Pinkham Notch on the eastern side of the Presidentials, and the Alpine House was built in Gorham. In the same year, the first real hotel in Pinkham Notch—the Glen House—was constructed near where the present Auto Road begins its ascent of Mount Washington. For many years before this Dolly Copp had put up travelers at the Copp farm several miles to the north of the Glen House site, and had built a thriving business similar to those in Crawford Notch. The railroad also reached Conway from the south at about that time, and as the much more comfortable railroads replaced stagecoaches and horseback rides, many more visitors found the trip to the mountains enjoyable.

Commercial interest was also growing in the summit of Mount Washington. Until 1852 no permanent building was successfully constructed in that weather-whipped and rocky place, but in that year the first Summit House was built of stones blasted from the mountain top. The following year the Tip-Top House opened, and this building still stands in spite of a fire in 1915. With two hotels, it is not surprising that a road to the summit was considered desirable, thus the Mount Washington Road Company was chartered in 1853, with General David O. Macomber as president. The project proved more difficult and expensive than expected, and the company failed in 1855–6 after four miles had been completed. In 1861 the Mount Washington Summit Road Company finished the road, the world's first mountain toll road, which rises 4700 feet in 8 miles. The route of that road was substantially the same as the one that the Mount Washington Auto Road uses today, a testimony to the surveying and engineering skill of the earlier era. (For a good description of what can be seen from the Auto Road, which leaves NH 16 opposite the Glen House site, see Peter Randall's *Mount Washington*.)

On the other side of the mountain an even more daring engineering project was under way. Its principal sponsor was Sylvester Marsh, who in 1833 had moved from Boston to Chicago, then a village of about 300 people. He sold beef, then invented meat-packing machinery which made him rich. After losing everything in the financial panics during the 1830s, he went into the grain business and became rich again. Retiring from business at the age of 52, he came to the White Mountains looking for a new outlet for his genius and fortune, and thus decided to build the world's first mountain cog railway, to the summit of Mount Washington.

The engineering and planning skill for this project, and possibly even the original idea, came from Herrick Aiken of Franklin NH and his son Walter. Herrick Aiken, a manufacturer of knitting needles, invented the first circular knitting machine for making seamless stockings, and was considered by many to be almost a genius because of his inventions. He looked over a route and made a model for a cog railway, but railroad people dissuaded him from the project. Marsh's financial and promotional ability finally made the project a reality, and Aiken later built several of the early engines at his factory in Franklin. Many years later, after acrimonious struggles for authority, Walter Aiken took control of the enterprise and made it a profitable business.

When Marsh went to the New Hampshire legislature in 1858 for a charter for his cog railway, the idea was considered so preposterous that he was offered a charter to build a "railway to the moon" if he desired it. Undaunted, in 1866 he began construction, and two years later his railway was open as far as Jacob's Ladder. On July 3, 1869, the first train reached the summit, and a turnpike had been built from Fabyan to the Base Station. However, until 1874, when the main railway line was extended to Fabyan, Crawford Notch was still accessible only by a long and uncomfortable stagecoach ride. "Old Peppersass," Marsh's first locomotive, is still on display at the Base Station. (For a good description of what can be seen from the cog railway, see, again, Randall's *Mount Washington*.)

New development occurred rapidly on the summit of Mount Washington. In 1862 Col. John R. Hitchcock leased both summit hotels, and when his Alpine House in Gorham burned a decade later, he connected the two summit hotels and at the same time began construction of a new Summit House. In 1870 a train shed was built on the summit, and in 1874 the Signal Station was constructed to house the world's first mountain weather station, which had operated in borrowed buildings since 1870. When the new Summit House was completed in 1873, the old Tip-Top House was turned into a dormitory and later became the first office of "Among the Clouds," the first newspaper printed on top of a mountain. A stage office was constructed in 1878, so that by 1880 there were six buildings on the summit of Mount Washington. In 1908, fire destroyed the Summit House and all other buildings on the summit of Mount Washington except the old Tip-Top House. In 1915, a new Summit House opened, after five years in the building, but by then the twentieth century—and a new era in the Presidentials—was well underway.

The 1870s saw the advent of the last great era of hotel-building in the White Mountains, resulting from increasing numbers of visitors brought to the area by an improved transportation system; it lasted until the turn of the century, when the motor car ushered in a new age. In 1876, there was much activity in Crawford Notch: the railway was extended from Fabyan to the Cog Railway Base Station, and two new hotels were built in the vicinity. The harbinger of the end of this era came in 1899, when the first automobile ascended the carriage road; by 1904 an annual automobile race, "The Climb to the Clouds," was being run. The huge and sumptuous Mount Washington Hotel, built on virgin ground a mile from Fabyan, was completed in 1901–2. So visible from the road and from many summits, this last survivor of an era of grandeur may seem the epitome of the White Mountain hotel, but in fact the era had already come near its end when the Mount Washington Hotel was built. It gained its greatest fame when, in 1944, it was the site of the international financial conference which set up the World Bank and the International Monetary Fund. Today, it is the last of the great hotels of the region, the only one that has not been torn down or burned to the ground. In recent years, it has been the region's greatest white elephant, and there has been talk of turning it into a gambling casino, but nothing has come of this, and it survives as a monument to a short but opulent period in the region's history.

The Era of the Logging

The history of the logging in the White Mountains begins in 1867, when the New Hampshire legislature passed a law permitting the governor to sell all of the state's public lands to pay for school maintenance. The governor quickly did so, at very low prices, and much of this land was later bought up by a half-dozen lumber barons who systematically clear-cut large forested areas in the White Mountains between 1875 and 1915, stripping the mountain slopes and starting forest fires with their spark-spewing steam locomotives. A fascinating account of this era is contained in C. F. Belcher's *Logging Railroads of the White Mountains*. It was the wanton destruction of the forests, more than anything else, that caused the sense of outrage among White Mountain visitors and residents that inspired the movement toward conservation and preservation in the twentieth century.

By 1907, 650 million board feet were being cut in the region each year to satisfy the demand caused by the building boom in New England. Also, techniques for making paper from spruce pulpwood by the sulphite process became reasonably sophisticated near the end of the nineteenth century, so trees that would otherwise have been regarded as having little economic value—particularly those typical of higher slopes—were now enthusiastically cut. A forestry study of the period indicates that New Hampshire was "the most intensively lumbered state, per acre of wooded area, of any of the states. . . ."

River driving was tried as a method of getting logs to the mill; this had been successful in the lowlands where rivers were large, but the mountain rivers and streams were generally too small and rocky, and were useful for only a short time in the spring. The railroad, then, became the principal mode of transportation for the lumber companies. Each laid its own tracks into the wilderness it had purchased, until most of the White Mountain region bore a network of active and abandoned rail lines. When an area was logged out, the tracks were usually taken up and moved to the next area to be stripped of timber. When the trains were not hauling out logs, they sometimes took excursion parties in on their flat-cars. The ruins of old lumber camps, now mostly clearings, are still visible in many parts of the region, and many of the abandoned railroad beds and logging roads are used for hiking trails.

Compared to other areas of the White Mountains, the Presidential Range was relatively unscathed by timber harvesting, probably because its slopes rose so quickly from the valley that they lacked the fine stands of large trees that grew on lower, gentler slopes. One railroad line ran from

Whitefield up the south branch of the Israel River to service the logging in the area northwest of the Northern Peaks, where the gentler terrain produced finer stands of timber. This operation reached into the great northwest ravines of the Presidential Range. From the south, lines ran from the Saco valley below Crawford Notch up the Rocky Branch and the Dry River, the long valleys south and southeast of Mount Washington.

However, the damage caused by lumbering was still sufficient to provoke determined criticism throughout New England. The devastation in the Zealand valley, just west of Crawford Notch and within a few miles of the site of Ethan Allen Crawford's inn, was described as follows in an editorial titled "The Trail of the Sawmill" in the *Boston Transcript* of July 20, 1892:

> The beautiful Zealand Valley is one vast scene of waste and desolation; immense heaps of sawdust roll down the slopes to choke the stream and, by the destructive acids distilled from their decaying substance, to poison the fish; smoke rises night and day from fires which are maintained to destroy the still accumulating piles of slabs and other mill debris.

Other criticisms of the timber industry in New Hampshire at the time were even more strident, with one account comparing the destruction to that of the Holy Land around Jerusalem.

Completing the devastation of many areas were forest fires, mostly caused by lightning or the timber harvesters' spark-belching locomotives, which ignited dry slash left after lumbering. In 1903 such fires destroyed more than 10% of the White Mountain forests. Altogether 554 serious fires were reported to the authorities during the first eight

months of that year. The most notorious fire occurred in
this same Zealand valley in 1907, leaving a devastation that
was described by Ernest Russell in *Collier's*:

> Today, however, it is a dull brown waste of
> lifeless, fire-eaten soil and stark white boulders.
> All about lie the great blackened stumps and
> tangled roots of what were once majestic trees. It
> is as if the contents of some vast cemetery had
> been unearthed in that little valley.

An observant visitor today can detect the traces of these
fires in many places, including the Rocky Branch valley,
which suffered fires in three successive years, the last in
1914. However, most of these areas are well on their way to
recovery; in some places, particularly around Zealand Valley, beautiful stands of white birch have grown up on slopes
that were once left hideous by the fires.

Such events were obviously a grave threat to the White
Mountains as a summer resort area, since its appeal to
visitors depended on its scenic beauty. In 1888 the historian
Francis Parkman had made an early plea for the preservation of White Mountain forests because of their importance to the beauty of the mountains sought by visitors.
Writing in the February 1893 issue of *Atlantic Monthly*,
Julius H. Ward proclaimed his view that the White Mountains were "worth infinitely more for the purpose of a great
national park than for the temporary supply of lumber
which they furnish to the market."

The Twentieth Century

By the turn of the century there was a strong public
sentiment in favor of a forest preserve maintained by the
US government where conservation, through selective timber harvesting, would be practiced. The Society for the

Protection of New Hampshire Forests was founded in 1901 to pursue this aim, and in 1903 the New Hampshire legislature passed a bill favoring such a preserve. That same year the New Hampshire resolution was introduced into Congress as a bill, but it met with intense political opposition; many in Congress felt that the government had no constitutional authority to spend money for such a purpose. Much legislative maneuvering during several congressional sessions was needed to get what came to be known as the Weeks Act finally passed in 1911. It had started as a specific bill to protect the White Mountains, introduced by and named after Massachusetts Congressman (later US Senator and then Secretary of War under President Harding) John Wingate Weeks, a native of Lancaster NH; it ended up, because of the legislative compromises needed to get it enacted, as a general doctrine in which the government asserted its right to protect the headwaters of navigable rivers and to acquire watersheds for that purpose. In 1912 the commission empowered to apply the new law purchased more than 30,000 acres on the northern slopes of the Presidentials. By 1914 the total acreage exceeded 224,000, approximately one-third of the area within the purchase boundary; acquisitions included the all-important Mount Washington, except for the summit area. In 1912 the state of New Hampshire purchased a 6000 acre tract in the heart of Crawford Notch and made it into a state park.

A strong force behind passage of the Weeks Act was the Appalachian Mountain Club, an organization founded in 1876 by a Massachusetts Institute of Technology professor (and later director of the Harvard Observatory), E. C. Pickering, "for the advancement of the interests of those who visit the mountains of New England and adjacent regions, whether for the purpose of scientific research or summer recreation." One of its first efforts had been to take over maintenance of some of the footpaths that had been cut in the Presidentials and nearby ranges over the past half-century by guides and explorers. In the 1920s the AMC hired a professional trail crew, the first of its kind in the country. Now made up of seasonal and fulltime employees, the AMC crew continues to maintain about 375 miles of trail in the White Mountains, as well as about twenty backcountry shelters and campsites. An important part of the trail system in New Hampshire is the Appalachian Trail (AT), a long-distance hiking trail from Maine to Georgia first conceived in the 1920s and completed in the 1930s; in the White Mountains (east of Kinsman Notch) the AT was made up from existing trails of the AMC. The AT is now administered by the Department of the Interior, and maintained principally by a number of volunteer organizations coordinated by the Appalachian Trail Conference. The AMC and its various New England chapters are responsible for more than 275 miles of the AT in the northeast.

Along the AT in New Hampshire are eight mountain huts, the only alpine-style hut system in this country. The system began with a shelter constructed on Mount Madison by the AMC in 1888 to provide protection for hikers caught in inclement weather. This hut was later enlarged, and a second was built on the flank of Mount Washington in 1915 at Lakes of the Clouds. Today a string of eight, each a day's hike from the next, traverses the White Mountains, running from Carter Notch to Lonesome Lake, west of Franconia Notch. There is also a base camp at Pinkham Notch, at the foot of Mount Washington. The original intent of the hut system was to enable hikers, in a time before lightweight backpacking equipment was available, to walk this entire scenic area with only a knapsack on their backs, thus making it accessible to many who could not otherwise enjoy its beauty. At first only shelters from the weather, the huts are now equipped with bunks and serve meals; a large part of the huts' supplies is packed in on the backs of young hut crew members. The huts also dispense information, provide educational programs, and serve as a base for search-and rescue-operations.

Shortly after the turn of the century, the new mobility provided to the average person by the automobile brought an end to the era of the grand hotels, although many of them managed to stay in operation until after World War II. New patterns of tourism were arriving. As Frederick Kilbourne described it in 1916:

> The advent of the automobile, with its almost immediate leap into general use for touring, greatly to the regret of many, including some landlords, has largely transformed in character the summer hotel and tourist business in the White Mountains, as well as elsewhere. While the volume of travel has increased, the majority of the visitors to the region are now of the transient variety, making in most cases but a fleeting stay at any one place and consisting largely of those who are "doing" the Mountains in their "motor-car."

Now motorists stopped at the resort hotels for a meal, or perhaps to stay overnight; at most they stayed a few days, using the hotel as a jumping-off point for visiting nearby sights. The summer-long sojourn, when people returned year after year to spend weeks or even months at the same hotel, gradually became less and less common, and the large establishments suffered, especially those off the major scenic highway routes. Today the visitors backpack, or stay in motels or campgrounds, or own condominiums or vacation homes in the mountains. The volume of passenger traffic on trains also declined steadily, until shortly after World War II the railroads began to drop passenger service; one or two now remain as scenic attractions. With the new modes of transporting and sheltering visitors have come new tourist attractions: "theme" parks and ski areas that now try to stay open all year with gondola rides or alpine slides.

One serious effect of these changes in vacation patterns, from the hiker's point of view, is the decline of some of the local trail systems, which depended greatly on the pride and attachment felt for "our trails" by people who returned to the same place year after year; they came to regard these trails, in a sense, as a part of themselves. The conditions created by this process are acute and very obvious today, as some of the fine trail networks that once provided varied walks, without the crowds that the major trunkline trails draw, are now sinking into oblivion.

Skiing came to the mountains in the 1920s, at first practiced by a few hardy individuals who were looking for a winter sport more thrilling than snowshoeing—a sport that most of them also practiced. When mechanized tows were invented, and skiers no longer had to climb up the mountain in order to enjoy the exhilarating swoop down the slopes, the sport's popularity increased very rapidly. Perhaps the last important role of the railroads in recreational passenger transportation was played by the ski trains that once left Boston every weekend. One important twentieth century trend in the region, which owed much to the boom in alpine skiing, was its use by visitors throughout the year. Kilbourne noted that in the nineteenth century only the hardy inhabitants and a few intrepid mountaineering enthusiasts could be found anywhere near the Presidential Range in winter. However, the phenomenal growth of downhill skiing in New England, and more recently of ski touring, has made the region a four-season resort area today. For this reason the AMC now keeps two of its huts open on a caretaker basis throughout the winter, and Pinkham Notch Camp is an important base for winter ice climbers, snowshoers, and ski tourers, as well as summer hikers and rock climbers.

The most renowned winter sport in the Presidentials is the spring skiing in Tuckerman Ravine. There, skiable snow often lasts well into May; once winter avalanche danger has subsided, ambitious skiers hike up the two miles from Pinkham, then climb the precipitous headwall for each run, since there is no lift. A few places are safe for average skiers, but the headwall has sections that can severely challenge the most expert skier. The acme of this tradition was the three Inferno Races from the summit of Mount Washington to Pinkham, sponsored by the Dartmouth Outing Club in the 1930s.

The growth of tourism and developed recreation, along with increased use of the backcountry, has often brought pressure for kinds of development that are viewed as destructive by those who want to preserve the wild and scenic values of the woods and mountains. As early as 1915, plans were made for a second scenic railway to the summit of Mount Washington; as surveyed, this railroad would have required a tunnel through the Castellated Ridge and one and a half loops around the summit cone. Fortunately (or so most people probably feel today), the promoters ran into financial problems unrelated to this project and were unable to get it started. In the 1930s the Works Progress Administration drew up plans for a scenic highway crossing all the Presidential peaks, similar to those that now exist in the southern Appalachians, and got as far as sending surveying crews into the field. This plan met bitter opposition and died. Today, controversies come from ski areas that want to expand both in area and in summer activities, and housing developments, particularly for condos and other vacation homes. Southwest of the Presidential Range, in Franconia Notch, a parkway is now nearing completion after more than a decade of struggle and compromise between those who wanted a superhighway and those who wanted to protect the scenic values of New England's most famous notch.

During the modern era the White Mountain National Forest has become the dominant institution in the White Mountain region. Organized under the authority of the Weeks Act of 1911, the WMNF grew steadily as lands were acquired from lumber companies and other private owners, and it now totals about 750,000 acres. Approximately 85% of the land within the designated purchase boundary is now part of the forest, a very high percentage among national forests. Because it is situated so close to the east coast population centers, the WMNF is one of the ten most heavily used national forests in the country. It is estimated that 200,000 people visit the summit of Mount Washington each year, on foot or by the Cog Railway or auto road.

This great and rather sudden popularity has led to much concern about overcrowding and the degradation of the backcountry. The development of lightweight backpacking equipment in the 1960s and 1970s contributed to a tremendous increase in the use of the backcountry; efforts to educate hikers and campers in the means of preserving the natural values of the wild country, including the development of the "clean camping" ethic, have helped to minimize campers' impact on the land, but it has still been necessary to prohibit or limit camping in some areas (see Restricted Use Areas). Tent platforms are provided at several backcountry sites to limit the areas where the ground cover will be damaged by the pitching of tents. In the Great Gulf Wilderness the old shelters were removed because their sites had been overused and abused, and permits are now required for camping during the summer; by limiting the number of campers in the region on any night, forest managers hope to keep the level of wear and tear within the ability of the land to recuperate. Careful backcountry users have helped to make possible a relatively low level of restriction on camping throughout the WMNF.

A major recent development has been the designation of areas as Wilderness, which is done by Congress on the recommendation of the Forest Service with advice from other groups. This process started when the Great Gulf area was officially designated a Wild Area by the WMNF in 1959, and was then included in the new Wilderness system when Congress passed the Wilderness Act in 1964. The Presidential Range–Dry River Wilderness was added in 1974, and in 1984 this Wilderness was expanded and the Pemigewasset Wilderness and Sandwich Range Wilderness were established. Several other areas of the Forest have been proposed for Wilderness designation, including the Caribou–Speckled Mountain area in the WMNF in Maine, which has been recommended for Wilderness designation by the WMNF. The Wilderness program has engendered a lively debate, which is likely to retain its vigor for some time, between those who would like to see the areas kept available for a wider variety of uses and those who support as much Wilderness as possible because they fear lumbering, road-building, and other development detrimental to the present wild character of the lands.

It is safe to predict that Mount Washington will continue to attract large numbers of people with very diverse interests to this region, and that problems will arise that will require imaginative solutions in order to preserve, as far as possible, the variety and the quality of the experiences that these people come in search of.

SECTION 4

Natural History

The Presidential Range lies somewhat north of the center of the White Mountains. The main ridge extends for more than 14 miles from northeast to southwest and consists of eleven peaks, with Mount Washington, the highest at 6288 ft., roughly in the center. To the north of Mount Washington are the Northern Peaks—Mounts Clay (5541 ft.), Jefferson (5712 ft.), Adams (5774 ft.), and Madison (5367 ft.). The Southern Peaks consist of Mounts Monroe (5384 ft.), Franklin (5004 ft.), Eisenhower (4761 ft.), Pierce (or Clinton) (4310 ft.), Jackson (4052 ft.), and Webster (3910 ft.). The five highest peaks in the range—Washington, Adams, Jefferson, Monroe, and Madison (Clay being generally regarded as a shoulder of Washington)—are the five highest in the northeastern United States. There are several subsidiary ridges, of which the longest, the Montalban Ridge, extends southward from Mount Washington over Boott Spur (5502 ft.) for about 15 miles. Several of the peaks on this ridge offer exceptional views, including Mount Isolation (4005 ft.), Mount Davis (3840 ft.), Stairs Mountain (3460 ft.), Mount Crawford (3129 ft.), Mount Resolution (3428 ft.), Mount Parker (3015 ft.), Mount Pickering (1942 ft.), and Mount Stanton (1748 ft.).

There are many interesting features of the range other than the peaks, of which perhaps the most striking are the great ravines, technically called glacial cirques, that cut into the sides of the range. The largest of these, the Great Gulf, lies to the northeast of Mount Washington and is enclosed by Mounts Washington, Clay, Jefferson, Adams, and Madison. There are several cirques on the Northern Peaks, the most prominent of which is King Ravine, which lies on the north side of Mount Adams. On Mount Washington's east face lie Tuckerman Ravine and Huntington

Ravine, famous respectively for alpine skiing and rock and ice climbing. To the south are the Gulf of Slides, also a skiers' attraction, and Oakes Gulf at the head of Dry River. There are numerous waterfalls on the steep mountain brooks that drain the slopes of the range.

The Presidential Range is supplied with an extensive network of trails, described in Sections 1 and 2 of this guide. The Appalachian Trail, running between Georgia and Maine, makes use of this network to cross the range (although it misses several of the summits), passing the AMC Mizpah, Lakes of the Clouds, and Madison huts.

Deep valleys and lower mountain ranges surround the Presidential Range. Across Pinkham Notch to the east lies the Carter–Moriah Range; to the south and southwest is Crawford Notch, with the Willey Range lying on the opposite side; to the west, across Jefferson Notch, is the Cherry–Dartmouth Range; to the north, across the valleys of the Israel and Moose rivers, lie the Pliny and Pilot ranges.

The range is encircled by several main roads. To the north, US 2 runs from the Connecticut River at Lancaster up the valley of the Israel River and down the valley of the Moose River to NH 16 at Gorham, passing through Jefferson and Randolph along the way. To the east, NH 16 ascends the valley of the Peabody River to Pinkham Notch, passing the Mount Washington Auto Rd., Wildcat Ski Area, and the AMC's Pinkham Notch Camp, and descends the valley of the Ellis River, passing through Jackson, to US 302 at the small village of Glen. From Glen, US 302 runs along the valley of the Saco through Bartlett, then ascends through Crawford Notch, and runs along the Ammonoosuc River past Bretton Woods to Twin Mountain where it meets US 3. US 3 runs north to Lancaster; in two miles NH 115 diverges and skirts the west end of Cherry Mountain to connect with US 2 near Jefferson. In addition to the main roads, there are several lesser roads, normally open in summer only, that provide access to some trails. On the northeast side of the range, the Pinkham B (Dolly Copp) Rd. makes a shortcut between US 2 and NH 16. On the southwest, the Base Rd. runs from US 302 at Fabyan to the Base Station of the Cog Railway at Marshfield. The Mount Clinton Rd. leads to the Base Rd. from US 302 at a point near the top of Crawford Notch. Directly across from the junction of the Base Rd. and Mount Clinton Rd., the Jefferson Notch Rd. begins and climbs through Jefferson Notch (3008 ft.) to the Valley Rd. in Jefferson, which in turn connects US 2 and NH 115.

More detailed descriptions of the geography of the range will be found in Sections 1 and 2.

GEOLOGY

Viewing this massive range, with its broad plateaus and deeply-carved cirques, many visitors have been moved to wonder how all this came to be. Although the mountains are a common symbol of permanence—by the standard of a human lifetime they are indeed virtually unchanging—like people they are born, flourish, and then die, eventually to be replaced by new mountains. What mountains may someday stand where Washington now rises we cannot know, but the past history of the Presidential Range lies encrypted in the kinds of rocks and their arrangement.

Any explanation of geological history is subject to modification or even complete replacement as new methods of research are devised and new discoveries are made. Thus, all accounts of the formation of the Presidential Range are based on theories that are subject to change as knowledge advances. The discussion that follows is primarily based on a geological booklet, *The Geology of the Mount Washington Quadrangle*, which presents the most widely accepted accounts of the development of the Presidential Range. (*The Geology of the Mount Washington Quadrangle* and *The Geology of the Crawford Notch Quadrangle* provide very useful and detailed discussions of the geology of the Presidential Range area, written for readers without geological training. They are available from the NH Department of Resources and Economic Development, PO Box 856, Concord NH 03301—at $2.50 and $2.00, respectively, in 1987.) Also presented is an alternative and somewhat iconoclastic theory of recent geological history drawn from Will F. Thompson's three-part article "The Shape of New England Mountains," which was published in the AMC's magazine *Appalachia* in 1960 and 1961.

The history of the bedrock of the Presidential Range, inferred from the known patterns of the rock that can be studied today, is thought to have begun about 500 million years ago in a shallow inland sea that is believed to have covered this region. Over countless centuries, due to erosion of land to the east, a sheet of mud and sand many thousands of feet thick accumulated at the bottom of the sea, which continued to exist because its floor gradually sank as the sediment layers grew thicker and heavier. The rock that was formed from these sediments is no longer part of the Presidential Range, having been converted to quartzite and forced out of the area by subsequent activity, and is found today only to the northwest of the Presidentials.

Next came a period of volcanic activity in the land to the east; great quantities of volcanic ash and debris were carried into the sea and probably filled it completely. The depth of this sheet of volcanic material eventually amounted to about a mile; subsequently altered by heat and pressure, this material, called the Ammonoosuc volcanics, now crops out along the lower northern edge of the Presidentials and presumably underlies much of the range.

Then, about 400 million years ago, seas once again covered the region, depositing many more layers of sediment on top of the previous ones. About 390 million years ago, these sediments (known as the Littleton Formation) were squeezed and folded under great heat and pressure, metamorphosing the shale and sandstone of the sea floor into gneiss, schist, and quartzite. The latter two rocks, which have proved relatively resistant to weathering, are the primary components of the crest of the Presidential Range today—as well as such lower but locally prominent peaks as Moosilauke, Stinson, the southern Kearsarge, and Grand Monadnock. Granite, which is often thought of as the principal component of the White Mountains, is often much less durable than the schists and quartzites; some varieties of granite, particularly those found around Mount Chocorua and Mount Osceola, become so "rotten" after exposure to weathering that they can be crumbled in the hand. Many of the rocks found at the higher elevations of the Presidential Range exhibit definite layering and folding which discloses the nature of their development. Recent chemical analysis, which attempts to deduce the temperature and pressure at which rocks were formed by studying their constituent minerals, indicates that the squeezing and folding of the Littleton Formation probably occurred about seven miles below the surface.

Then, about 360 million years ago, molten rock welled up into the region; the resulting granite rocks are found to the west, around Jefferson Notch, and to the north, around Randolph Station (near the Randolph East trailhead). Since then the rocks that form the bedrock of the Presidential Range have changed little—although other rocks were probably deposited by volcanic action on top of them and then worn away—but glaciers, wind, frost, and running water have greatly changed the surface, breaking down and removing great amounts of rock. At the estimated rate of about 2 feet per 10,000 years, the 7 miles of rock which is thought to have overlain the present Presidential ridge crest could have been eroded in 200 million years. It is believed that some of this eroded rock was recycled into the formation of the Catskill Mountains in New York.

The Presidential Range may never have been substantially higher than now, since the land tended to rise as erosion lightened the overlayer of rocks. The generally accepted theory is that the land was eroded to a rolling plain surmounted by a number of hills that are now the Presidential peaks. Then the land rose gradually, and as it did streams carved deep valleys in the rocks around the peaks, sparing the region of the peaks themselves because of its resistant schist and quartzite cap. This remnant of a once extensive plain is called the Presidential upland. This explanation is suggested by the relatively gentle slopes above treeline, so much in contrast to the steep slopes that descend from the treeline down; as its proponents point out, it takes little effort for a visitor on the upper slopes of the Presidentials to imagine a vast plain continuing outward.

However, in the series of articles on "The Shape of New England Mountains," Will F. Thompson challenged the eroded-plain theory and advanced a far different explanation for the contrast in the steepness of slopes above and below treeline. The area above treeline was commonly thought to be geologically inactive, for large rocks observed above treeline were almost without exception covered by lichens on all their exposed surfaces; thus it was concluded that these boulders could not have moved in recent times. But Thompson argued that all this proved was that the rocks were not rolling along the ground; he advanced the theory that they were being borne along downhill on a mantle of soil where frost action was very vigorous. This process tended to level the ground wherever it took place, and it occurred primarily above treeline because there the winter winds blew the snow cover away, allowing very cold air to sink deep into the soil through gaps between the boulders. This cold air remained well into the summer, making the temperature below ground much colder than average temperature records suggested, and producing the vigorous frost action required to move the mantle of soil and the rocks resting on top of it.

Glacial action is evident throughout the Presidential Range, which has been completely covered by a glacier at least once, and probably several times. Glacial till—a claylike accumulation bearing fragments of rock different from those normally found on the range—has been found in excavations made near the summit. Erratics—boulders of different composition than local rocks, carried by the glacier from other areas—have been discovered almost on the summit of Mount Washington; rocks from the Pliny Range, several miles to the north, have been found high in the Presidentials. In addition, potholes made by torrential streams have been found on high ridges (for example, the ledge mentioned in the Caps Ridge Trail description), and scratches and grooves made by rocks embedded in the ice can still be seen on many ledges, allowing geologists to plot the direction of flow of the ice. The major notches of the Presidential Range, Crawford and Pinkham, have the distinctive U-shape of a glacier-carved valley, with a flat floor and steep walls, showing that they were gouged out by a continental glacier which was compressed as it passed through these narrow defiles.

Among the most striking features of the Presidential Range are the glacial cirques, such as the Great Gulf and Tuckerman and King ravines, U-shaped gorges with steep walls and a gently sloping floor, which contrast with the V-shaped valleys cut by mountain streams. These cirques were carved by small local glaciers formed from snowdrifts which built up in times of unusual cold on the east side of the range, where prevailing winds deposit the snow which they blow off the upper plateau, and also on the north side, where lesser drifts are sheltered from the sun. The discovery of rounded rocks with glacial scratches high in Tuckerman Ravine, and the lack of moraines—the characteristic tongues of rock debris found in areas where the foot of a glacier melts away—seemed to confirm the commonly held opinion that no local glaciers could have occurred after the retreat of the last continental glacier, about 12,000 years ago.

Thompson, however, argued that the rocks high in Tuckerman Ravine were rounded and scratched by boulders brought to the edge of the ravine from above by frost action and then swept down over the edge by winter avalanches. He also argued that debris that might have formed moraines would have been carried away as quickly as it appeared by processes similar to those which moved the soil and boulders above treeline. Then, on the basis of evidence collected at Katahdin in Maine, nearby and with similar climatic conditions, he argued that it is probable that Presidential Range cirques have borne small glaciers in relatively recent times, and that a relatively small decrease in average annual temperature might convert Tuckerman's famous Snow Arch snowfield—some of which is often present in August—into a real glacier again.

Whether either of these theories accurately explains the present state of the Presidential Range has not been settled, and indeed we can never know with absolute certainty the causes which produced this magnificent scenery.

CLIMATE

The severity of the weather on Mount Washington is legendary, and statistics can be quoted almost without limit to prove that the legend is based on cold numerical fact. A few such items follow.

The year-round average wind velocity is a brisk 35 mph. In winter, hurricane force winds (75 mph or higher) are common; they blow an average of 104 days a year. Gusts of over 100 mph have been recorded in every month of the year, and gusts of over 150 mph in every month from September to May. On April 12, 1934, the wind reached 231 mph on the summit of Mount Washington, the highest wind velocity ever recorded except in tornadoes.

The average annual temperature on the summit of Mount Washington is a chilly 27° F. The summit temperature has never risen above 72° F.; the record low is –47° F. It is below zero 65 days a year on the average, and in June of 1945 a temperature of –8° F. was recorded.

Precipitation on the summit each year usually amounts to the equivalent of more than 70 inches of water. Much of this falls as snow, which averages 195 inches annually. The winter of 1968–1969 saw the heaviest snowfall on record—over 47 feet. More than 4 feet came in one 24-hour period, a record for US weather observatories.

Fog and clouds are also quite common on the summit of Mount Washington, occurring, on the average, on 305 days a year. Visitors can expect the summit to be socked in 55% of the time, according to Weather Observatory records. Occasionally a lenticular (lens-shaped) cloud—formed when moisture in the air condenses as it passes over the peak and then evaporates again as the wind descends the other slope—can be seen directly over the summit.

The combination of low temperature, high wind, and much precipitation creates a unique climate on the Presidential Range summits, an area that has been called an arctic island in the midst of the temperate zone. The mountains lie at the intersection of two major North American storm tracks, one sweeping up the coast from the Gulf of Mexico and the other a polar track traversing central Canada, the Midwest, and the St. Lawrence River valley. The

disturbances created when these two tracks cross are en-
hanced in power by their steep rise over the mountains.

It is no wonder, then, that the mountain has attracted
many scientists. The Mount Washington Weather Observatory, the first of its kind in the world, was initiated in 1870
and has been staffed permanently on a year-round basis
since the 1930s, accumulating the detailed knowledge we
now have of the climate on the summit. During World War
II, all three major military services tested cold-weather
equipment and clothing on Mount Washington, and more
recently the Air Force used the site to perform icing tests
on engines and propellers.

Despite the summit buildings, the road, and the railroad,
Mount Washington is far from domesticated, and the other
Presidential peaks remain mostly uncivilized. The combination of cold, wind, and rain or snow often creates a
chilling effect that can freeze exposed flesh in minutes in
winter and can kill at any time of the year; some claim that
this weather is the equal in severity of any on earth. More
lives have been lost on Mount Washington than on any
other peak in North America, mostly due to hypothermia,
the uncontrolled loss of body heat.

PLANTS AND ANIMALS

Note: No consistent attempt is made here to systematically provide identification information for the species discussed. Several field guides are listed in the bibliography.

The short White Mountain summer, from June through
August, is characterized by variety, color, and abundance
of life. But from September until mid-May quite a different
set of conditions—including shortened days, high winds,
intense cold, rain, snow, and ice—severely challenges those
members of the natural community that do not migrate.
The necessity of surviving the brutal climate on the Presi-

dential Range—and even, to a lesser degree, on its lower slopes—exerts a powerful influence on every species that makes its home there. Adaptation, often to a radical extent, is required in order for them to survive through to yet another summer's growth.

Climbing to the crest of the Presidential Range from the surrounding valleys, one passes through a series of zones whose climate and vegetation are characteristic of regions progressively farther north; on the high lawns, for example, one is in an area ecologically comparable to northern Labrador. The elevations at which these zones begin and end vary in response to a number of climatic factors, including exposure to weather and amount of available sunlight; often past disturbances—such as fires, landslides, or logging—cause local variations. The general pattern, however, is evident throughout the range. Given the wide climatic variation between the base and the summit ridges of the Presidential Range, it would require a very large book to discuss all the plants and animals that live there. One study of the alpine zone alone lists 110 plant and 95 insect species. However, a general description of the various plant and animal communities of the range is possible.

Most trails start in a forest dominated by the northern hardwoods, where the most common large trees are American beech and several birches and maples. The beech and the various types of birch are the easiest to identify. The beech is recognized by its smooth light-gray bark on younger trees or upper limbs. A single large beech is often surrounded by numerous pole-size trees that have sprouted from the older tree's roots, making it almost possible to map the root system by the location of these sprouts. The white (or paper) birch has shiny white bark, which tends to peel off in strips, on its mature trunk and limbs; young trees and limbs are bronze in color. The gray birch is a smaller tree, often growing in clumps of three to five, with prominent black horizontal scars on white bark that does not peel in large strips. The yellow (or silver) birch is a large tree with lustrous silvery yellow bark that peels off in narrow translucent strips. The quaking aspen, best identified by its generally smooth gray-green bark, is a common resident on the borders of marshes and beaver ponds. Birches and aspens are fast growing but cannot tolerate shade; birches in particular are often found in pure stands where a disturbance, such as a fire, has opened up the forest floor to full sunlight.

Maples are a major component of the hardwood forest. The sugar maple is a large tree with gray bark, darker than the beech. The bark of young trees has irregular cracks, while that of older ones is often deeply furrowed. Three smaller maples are also commonly found in the White Mountains. The red maple, recognized by its gray bark (smooth when young and scaled when older) and conspicuous red twigs, grows very well in swampy soil that would be too moist for many other trees. The striped maple (or moosewood) is a small, shrubby tree which grows well beneath a canopy of other hardwoods; its leaves are very large and its furrowed dark-brown or green bark sports vertical white stripes, more obvious on smaller trunks and branches, which give the tree its name. The mountain maple is bushy, often forming thickets; its thin, slightly fissured bark is a light reddish-brown, and its hairy green to red-brown twigs reveal a brown pith when broken.

Conifers are also common in this zone: red spruce is found throughout the zone, hemlocks grow in some of the lower valleys, and a few fine stands of red pines may be seen on some of the lower southern ledges of the range. Perhaps the most unusual tree in the woods is the tamarack, which sheds its needles each fall—the only deciduous conifer in the White Mountains. Tamaracks are slender with reddish, scaly bark, and bear small spherical cones that stand upright on the branch. Tamarack and black spruce commonly grow together in swamps and peat bogs at elevations up to 4000 ft., and a winter hiker coming on a mixed stand of tamarack and black spruce is likely to think that the tamaracks are dead.

There are also numerous smaller trees and shrubs, including the striped and mountain maples discussed above. The American mountain ash—not an ash at all, but a relative of the apple tree—is fairly common above 2000 ft.; it produces clusters of bright red fruits about the size of blueberries, which often remain on the tree until mid-winter unless eaten by birds. The hobblebush, which grows in cool, moist woods up to about 3000 ft., is a straggling shrub less than 10 feet tall with large oval leaves. Its branches often take root where they touch the ground and may trip an unwary traveler—thus the name. In spring it produces showy white flowers—composed of small fertile flowers surrounded by large sterile flowers—which turn into cluster of bright red to purple berries in late summer and fall. Hobblebush buds are favorite deer food and make the shrub simple to identify in winter, since they are brown, furry, and always in pairs, suggesting rabbit ears.

In fact, variety is the primary characteristic of this region, whose gentler weather provides at least a little suitable habitat for a great many species, in contrast to the higher regions where the severity of the weather greatly restricts the number of species that can survive. But the lower-slope forest community must still contend with severe winter conditions. Although protected from the extremes found on exposed ridges, these plants are also subjected to storms, high winds, and cold. Herbaceous or woody, they must remain dormant for seven months a year. Trees in the forest canopy cannot wait winter out beneath a blanket of snow, and almost invariably show scars from the high winds that send limbs crashing into one another and from storms that overload branches with ice and snow. The loss of a limb opens the door to attack by fungus or insects and can permanently weaken the tree. Violent gusts can make the entire tree a victim of windthrow. Smaller trees, particularly birches, may be bowed or snapped off by ice loading.

This type of woodland, with its high, open canopy of trees and its abundance of shrubs growing in the rich humus of the forest floor, covers much of northern New England. In high summer very little sunlight penetrates to the forest floor, so small plants have had to adopt several strategies in order to flourish. Some sprout as soon as the snow is gone—some even start as soon as sunlight begins to filter through the snowdrifts—then flower as quickly as possible, and complete their annual cycle before the leaves of their larger neighbors choke off their access to the sun, the ultimate source of all energy for plant growth. This strategy is adopted by the familiar flowers of the spring woodlands: yellow violet, spring beauty, red and painted trilliums, bellwort, and trout lily (also called dogtooth violet, but it is not a violet).

The trout lily also shows another common strategy: it sends up leaves for several years, carefully hoarding in its root the tiny amounts of extra food that it is able to photosynthesize each year, until it finally has saved enough to flower and manufacture seeds. It is not uncommon to find a small area completely covered by trout lily leaves without a single plant large enough to flower. With such a strategy plants are able to make use of more shady spots, and avoid the risks of late-spring snowfalls and frosts to which the early bloomers expose themselves.

Once leaves fill the upper canopy, the common flowering plants are the perennials and the shade-tolerant species: Canada mayflower, clintonia (whose blue berries in late summer are far more conspicuous than its flowers), twisted stalk, pink lady's slipper (and often its white variant), bunchberry, starflower, wild sarsaparilla, Indian cucumber, foamflower, and false Solomon's Seal. In wet areas Indian poke, jewelweed, and tall meadow-rue are sometimes abundant, and such uncommon but magnificent plants as the purple fringed orchis provide an occasional treat. In late summer, asters, goldenrods, and Joe-pye-weeds are frequently seen. Ferns and mosses, which are not flowering plants, are also shade-tolerant and very common in the deep woods.

It is interesting to note that the common summer flowers of lawns, fields, and roadsides—daisies, dandelions, buttercups, common yarrow, red and yellow hawkweed, black-eyed susans, and most clovers—are not natives to the region but immigrants. Except for black-eyed susan, an invader from the west, they are not even native to North America. These larger, fast-growing species, mostly annuals, are seldom found in the mountains except along logging roads and in overgrown clearings—and sometimes near the AMC huts. Their huge requirements for sunlight make it impossible for them to grow in the deep woods, and they proliferate only where human activities have created openings; prior to large-scale human intervention, there was no ecological niche for such plants in the White Mountains. Fortunately for hikers, poison ivy is likewise intolerant of shade, so this noxious native species is seldom found in the White Mountains.

Flitting among the trees and shrubs of the northern hardwood forest will be warblers, thrushes, vireos, rose-breasted grosbeaks, and redstarts. Chipmunks and red squirrels, the latter frequently heard and seen scolding the intruding hiker from a tree, are the mammals most likely to be encountered. The engineering feats of beaver are visible in many ponds, and sometimes trails are flooded by this energetic animal. Rabbits and deer abound, though their tracks in winter are seen far more often than the animals themselves in any season. Porcupines and raccoons, learning to profit from human presence, often become major pests. Moose have steadily increased their numbers over the last two decades, so hikers have a much improved chance of meeting this huge, ungainly living symbol of the north woods, which has not yet been taught to fear humans. Bears are fairly common, but they make a mostly successful effort to stay out of sight—except for the semi-civilized individuals who have learned that hikers often carry food and can be persuaded to relinquish it, and who sometimes become pests at popular campsites. Bears are normally dangerous only when surprised or threatened. Toads are ubiquitous, and garter snakes, wood frogs, and red-spotted newts are also common. There are many small rodents, but these shy nocturnal beasts are seldom seen, although they are frequently heard at night helping themselves to campers' food.

As the trails attain an elevation of 2500 to 3000 ft., the trees change to those of the boreal forest, which is composed primarily of red spruce, balsam fir, and paper birch. At some of the high trailheads, one begins in this forest. The transition between these zones is often slow, with the boreal species taking over gradually, but occasionally a sharp boundary can be seen. The variety of species decreases markedly with increasing elevation. In the course of evolution, deciduous trees found it more energy-efficient to put out new leaves each spring than to maintain them through the winter. In the fall, they withdraw what nutrients and organic molecules they can from the leaves before letting them go. These chemicals—most notably chlorophyll—are broken down and sent to the roots to be stored. Our spectacular autumn colors result from the predominance of anthocyanin pigments left in the leaves after the chlorophyll is gone. By November the deciduous forest has

lost most of its summer foliage; the loss of leaves deprives
the naturalist of the easiest means of distinguishing one
tree from another, so identifying species in the winter requires attention to bark, twigs, buds, and overall growth
form. As elevation increases and the growing season becomes shorter, most deciduous trees are unable to photosynthesize enough food to replace their full set of leaves
each year. The major exception is the paper birch, whose
fast growth—much faster than the conifers—allows it to
take advantage of any opening. The presence of a stand of
nearly pure white birch at higher elevations is an almost
certain sign of a forest fire many years ago. Eventually the
birches age and the small conifers that have grown up
between them take over; new birches cannot grow in the
shade of the old ones. The conifers, which are adapted to
very slow growth patterns, and whose needles are relatively
resistant to damage by freezing and can therefore be used
for several years, have an overwhelming advantage on the
higher slopes. Since these trees maintain their foliage during the winter, loss of water through the needles is a real
danger; the cold winter winds contain very little moisture
and have a strong drying effect, and surface and ground
water is generally frozen. To protect against moisture loss,
the surfaces of evergreen leaves and stems are covered with
a thick waxy or resinous coating as the tree prepares for
winter; the needlelike leaf form also exposes less surface
area from which water can evaporate.

Under the dense growth of evergreens only shade-tolerant species and the most patient perennials can survive. The
highly acid soils derived from evergreen needles also limit
species diversity. Goldthread, which has evergreen leaves
and thus wastes less hard-earned energy, is one of the principal species of the deep shade. Wood sorrel often covers
large areas; its cloverlike leaves, tart and refreshing, are
often chewed by hikers. Clintonia, bunchberry, Canada

mayflower, and other species take advantage of breaks in forest cover, including trailsides.

Birds include juncos and a number of northern warblers—black-throated blues and greens, Canadas, and magnolias. In addition to the mixed forest species, a number of birds prefer this habitat, among them the winter wren, Swainson's thrush, hermit thrush, myrtle warbler, kinglet, and yellow-bellied sapsucker. Here the white-throated sparrow, calling in its assertive voice for "Old Sam Peabody, Peabody, Peabody," provides the most distinctive of all bird songs. Here also are found two of the species that are most likely to engage a hiker's attention. The spruce grouse, a fairly large bird, lacks natural enemies and is not afraid of humans. The male is slate gray with a red patch over the eye, the female is brown. If you meet one, it will probably watch you curiously until you get to within ten yards of it, and then amble casually off into the woods. In late June or early July a female may well burst out of the woods directly at you, and then hop down the trail ahead as if her wing were broken. Listen for the low cheep of her chicks, and be careful not to step on them! Another friendly bird is the gray jay, also called the Canada jay or whiskey jack. This bird is a northern species, and the high evergreen forests are at its extreme southern limit, but one or two often inhabit peaks of about 4000 ft. elevation where they appear to live off the generosity of passing hikers. They will frequently eat out of one's hand, and they often snatch food left on rocks whether intended for them or not. You need not search for them, since if they are present they will undoubtedly come around to inspect you (and your provisions).

As one ascends and the climate becomes more severe, the average size of the trees tends to decrease fairly steadily until, as treeline—aptly called by ecologists a zone of tension—is approached at 4000 to 4500 ft., they rapidly become smaller and more thickly spaced. Trees growing in exposed areas have their top branches trained by the prevailing winds. The tops of these "flagged" trees show branches pointing downwind in the shape of a pennant. Here some plant species make their final appearance, although most that have survived this high can also grow in sheltered spots above treeline.

At treeline, the last stunted trees—the same ones that grow 50 to 70 feet tall only a thousand feet lower on the slope—are shaped by the increasing rigors of wind and snow into low mats of tangled branches called krummholz (a German word meaning "crooked wood"), which may be a century or more old. They are occasionally found quite high above treeline in sheltered spots, usually where snowdrifts form, or in the lee of boulders or in natural depressions in the terrain. The location of treeline seems to be primarily influenced by climate. On the north-facing slopes exposed to prevailing winter winds from the northwest, treeline is lower; on the eastern and southern slopes, where snow accumulates in the lee of the peaks, it is higher. (Southern slopes also usually receive more sunlight during the growing season.) However, the causes that determine the exact elevation of treeline—which occurs in the Presidential Range at roughly half the elevation of treeline in the Rockies—have yet to be fully explained.

Some of the most severe weather in the world occurs above treeline in the Presidential Range; the combination of frequent fog and cloud cover, cool summer temperatures, heavy precipitation, and high winds create an island of arctic tundra in the temperate zone, with a climate similar to that in Labrador, north of the continental treeline. This area, the largest continuous above-treeline alpine zone in the eastern United States, runs for 8.5 miles from Mount Madison to Mount Eisenhower and has an area of approximately 7.5 square miles. In the alpine zone itself, it is too harsh for full-sized trees, so the plants that predominate are low-lying heaths, grasses, rushes, sedges, lichens, mosses, and the tiny but beautiful mountain wildflowers. Above treeline, there are probably about 110 species of higher plants, of which 75 are true alpine plants that only grow in this zone. The other 35 are native to the boreal forest, but survive at higher elevations in the krummholz mats. Three of the alpine plants are endemics—that is, they only exist in a small geographic area. The dwarf cinquefoil, which only grows in one area in the White Mountains, is the most famous of these; alpine avens and a variety of bluet occur here and on a few islands in the Canadian Atlantic.

Low posture is universal among plants of the alpine zone. Close to the ground, the winter gales are buffered by friction from the land surface. The fact that a given species will grow taller in the lee of a large boulder than on nearby open ground attests to the limitations wind places on growth. Smaller leaf area or loss of leaves in the fall helps to protect against wind damage and desiccation. On plants that retain their leaves through the winter, waxy or hairy surfaces also help to prevent loss of moisture and make leaves more resistant to abrasion by wind-blown snow crystals. Scientists believe that many of the alpine plants migrated south ahead of the advancing continental ice sheet, then, as the climate became milder and the glaciers receded, these plants migrated upslope, were eliminated by competition in gentler climates, and survived only in this climatic island where their competitors could not live. Consequently, these species, and other similarly adapted ones, are found only on other alpine islands in New England and the Adirondacks, and in Labrador far to the north.

Despite common adaptive strategies, there is no single key to survival. Within the alpine zone, local areas differ greatly in their exposure to wind and sun, snow depth, and soil moisture. It is a combination of these and other factors—called a microclimate—that determines what vascular plants can grow in a particular location. Different species that habitually grow under similar conditions may be grouped into plant communities. Let us look at four distinct communities and their adaptations to the severe climate.

The hiker who ascends beyond treeline will first encounter the krummholz community of dwarf black spruce and balsam fir, tightly intergrown mats from 4 inches to 8 feet in height. By growing in this manner, each tree can provide a degree of shelter from the wind for its neighbors; together, they often shelter a considerable community of smaller plants. Snow, which limits the growing season of these evergreens, provides a beneficial service in return. The plants cannot grow while covered with snow, but in the eight-month winter the snow that drifts into the krummholz patches provides a protective blanket, insulating them from the wind, low temperatures, and excessive drying out at a time when their roots cannot take up water from the frozen ground. Beneath the snow it remains at roughly the temperature at which the snow fell, as much as 40° to 50° F. warmer than the outside air. The height of a krummholz patch is directly controlled by the depth of drifted snow which that patch is able to accumulate, since new growth that protrudes above the following winter's snow will be killed. The growth of individual trees is therefore primarily horizontal rather than vertical, often extending only downwind from the original stalk. Different patches vary greatly in height due to variations in local topography. On the lee side of a boulder or other topographic high, trees will grow flush with the height of that obstacle, gradually tapering off as the area downwind becomes more exposed. In a local depression, the krummholz will grow with small trees around the perimeter and taller trees in the center so as to form a roughly level surface with the surrounding slopes. If part of a patch is cut, the bordering trees will likely retain less snow and will die back during the winter; therefore, the cutting of a campsite in krummholz usually has a disastrous effect on the surrounding vegetation, perhaps destroying a hundred years of growth.

A second alpine community that depends upon drifted snow for protection during the winter is the snowbank community, composed of both woody and herbaceous plants, most of which are deciduous. These plants establish themselves at the base of cliffs, in depressions or in the lee of rocks and other windbreaks—particularly krummholz patches—at elevations ranging from 4800 to 5800 ft. Plants common in such communities are heaths, sedges, grasses, goldenrods, alpine bluet, Canada mayflower, Clintonia (bluebead lily), Indian poke, and goldthread. The herbaceous members of the snowbank community are among the last to begin growing in the spring, since they must wait until their winter insulation has melted before they can begin their growing season, although some species—most strikingly Indian poke—may actually begin to push up through the snow when enough light filters through the melting snowdrift.

On moist, gentle slopes above 5400 ft. is found a third community, the sedge meadow, which is almost completely dominated by the Bigelow sedge, a rather broad-leaved species with a purplish fruit stalk. Both of these features may be recognizable in winter, since sedges are found in more exposed areas that do not collect a great deal of snow; though the plants may be covered by rime or groundwater ice, the dry leaves and stalks often protrude. In preparation for winter, sedges withdraw chlorophyll and other organic molecules into their root systems, allowing only skeletal brown leaves to take the full force of the weather. They develop a more extensive root system than other alpine plant communities, which provides a suitable anchor for the leafy sedges against high winds. The sedge meadow also includes some mosses and mountain sand-wort; downslope, this community may expand to include large clumps of rushes and low heath shrubs, and lower still is a heath–rush community, which includes three-forked rush, mountain cranberry, alpine bilberry, and three-toothed cinquefoil.

The fourth group, the rugged diapensia community, grows on rocky and windswept slopes and ridges at the limits of habitable terrain. Only the nonvascular lichens, which can withstand almost complete desiccation, exist under harsher conditions. Diapensia has thick, waxy leaves and grows in very tight cushionlike mats one inch or less in height, which help to hold what moisture may reach the thin, rocky soil on which these plants grow during the summer months. Completely exposed to winter weather, individual plants have only their neighbors to help them resist damage and uprooting. Members of this community include mountain cranberry, Lapland rosebay, alpine aza-lea, and bearberry willow. All have the ability to withstand intense cold without the insulation provided to more shel-tered communities by snow. Diapensia plants have under-gone freezing in liquid nitrogen at –210° C. and lived to produce seeds.

The Alpine Garden, Bigelow Lawn, and Monroe Flats (near Lakes of the Clouds) are the most popular locations for viewing the mountain wildflowers that bloom among the rocks each spring. In middle to late June the white diapensia, pink alpine laurel, and purple lapland rosebay bloom in bright patches on the slopes, along with many other less common or less showy plants. The most accessi-ble area is the Alpine Garden, which can be reached from the Mount Washington Auto Road or from the summit buildings where the Cog Railway stops, as well as by hiking up the mountain. The flowers are protected, as are the other plants in the White Mountain National Forest, and picking or otherwise damaging them is illegal. Preservation of these rare plants depends largely on the care exercised by hikers; be careful to remain on the trails in these areas, and step on rocks rather than vegetation, as damage is repaired very slowly in this severe climate. The habitat of the rarest of the plants, the dwarf cinquefoil, has been closed to all public entry to protect these tiny plants from accidental trampling.

Few animals and birds live in the alpine zone. L. C. Bliss lists nine animals that appear here, mostly small rodents such as mice, shrews, squirrels, woodchucks, porcupines, and chipmunks, and also snowshoe rabbits, but most of them are primarily visitors. Only two birds are known to nest above treeline, the slate-colored junco and the white-throated sparrow. However, other birds, such as ravens, hawks, and an occasional eagle, may be seen in the area. Insects are the predominant mobile life form here. One study lists 95 native species, including 61 beetles, although it is difficult to distinguish between those insects occurring naturally and the ones blown up on strong winds from the lowlands. Ten species of black spiders can be seen scurrying among the rocks. Of the fourteen species of moths and butterflies that appear here, three are endemics. The White Mountain butterfly, whose larvae feed on the local grasses, lives only above treeline in the White Mountains and can be seen fluttering about the sedge meadows, most frequently in early July. The White Mountain fritillary and White Mountain locust are also native species found only in this region.

The Presidential Range is, in fact, one of the finest places to study the ways in which plants and animals adapt to their environment. There is a wealth of understanding and knowledge available to those with the patience to study and observe the inhabitants of this unique area.

Bibliography

General Books

Burt, F. Allen. *The Story of Mount Washington*. University Press of New England (Dartmouth Publications), 1960.

Crawford, Lucy. *Lucy Crawford's History of the White Mountains*, edited by Stearns Morse. Appalachian Mountain Club, 1978.

Ford, Daniel. *The Country Northward: A Hiker's Journal*. Backcountry Publications, 1976.

Hill, Evan. *A Greener Earth*, photographs by David MacEachran. Society for the Protection of New Hampshire Forests, 1977.

Kidder, Glen M. *Railway to the Moon*. Privately published, 1969.

Kilbourne, Frederick W. *Chronicles of the White Mountains*. Heritage Books, 1978.

Oakes, William. *Scenery of the White Mountains*. New Hampshire Publishing Company, 1970.

Olson, W. Kent, and Brooks Atkinson. *New England's White Mountains: At Home in the Wild*, photographs by Philip H. Evans, Armory B. Lovins, and George DeWolfe. Appalachian Mountain Club, Friends of the Earth, and New York Graphic Society, 1978.

Randall, Peter. *Mount Washington: A Guide and Short History*. Down East Books, 1982.

Tanner, Ogden, et al. *New England Wilds*. Time-Life Books, 1974.

Tree, Christina. *How New England Happened: The Modern Traveler's Guide to New England's Historical Past*. Little, Brown and Company, 1976.

Getting Along in the Presidential Range

Allen, Dan. *Don't Die on the Mountain*. New Hampshire Chapter of Appalachian Mountain Club, 1972.

U.S. Forest Service (White Mountain National Forest). *Your Hike in the White Mountains*. Government Printing Office, 1976.

Various pamphlets and leaflets are also available from the White Mountain offices of the Forest Service and the Appalachian Mountain Club.

Hiking Guides

Appalachian Mountain Club. *AMC White Mountain Guide*, 24th edition, AMC, 1987.

Appalachian Trail Conference. *Appalachian Trail Guide—New Hampshire-Vermont*. ATC, 1983.

Doan, Daniel. *Fifty Hikes in the White Mountains: Hikes and Backpacking Trips in the High Peaks Region of New Hampshire*, 3rd edition. Backcountry Publications, 1986 (revised).

Doan, Daniel. *Fifty More Hikes in New Hampshire: Day Hikes and Backpacking Trips from the Coast to Coos County*, 2nd edition. Backcountry Publications, 1986 (revised).

Randolph Mountain Club. Randolph Paths, RMC, 1977.

Reifsnyder, William E. *High Huts of the White Mountains*. Appalachian Mountain Club, 1979.

There are also a number of hiking and backpacking guides to the East Coast and the United States as a whole that include chapters on the Presidential Range and its environs.

Maps

Appalachian Mountain Club. *Mount Washington Range.* AMC, 1983.

Appalachian Trail Conference. *Appalachian Trail Map No. 10.* ATC, 1968.

Preston, Philip. *Washington and Lafayette Trail Maps.* Waumbek Books, 1982.

Randolph Mountain Club. *Randolph Valley and the Northern Peaks.* RMC, 1979.

White Mountain National Forest. *White Mountain National Forest.* U.S. Forest Service, 1979.

The Presidential Range in Winter

Cole, Peter, and Rick Wilcox. *Shades of Blue: A Guide to Ice Climbing in New England.* Eastern Mountain Sports, 1976.

Ford, Sally, and Daniel Ford. *25 Ski Tours in the White Mountains: A Cross-Country Skier's Guide to New Hampshire's Backcountry Trails*, 2nd edition. Backcountry Publications, 1983.

Ski Touring Council. *Ski Touring Guide*, 15th edition. STC, 1978.

Tapley, Lance. *Ski Touring in New England and New York.* Stone Wall Press, 1977.

Ziegler, Katey (ed.). *Ski Touring Guide to New England*, 4th edition. Eastern Mountain Sports, 1979.

Nature Guides

Billings, Marland P., et al. *The Geology of the Mt. Washington Quadrangle,* N.H. Department of Resources and Economic Development, 1946 (revised 1979).

Bliss, L. C. *Alpine Zone of the Presidential Range*. Privately published, 1963.

Burk, C. John, and Marjorie Holland. *Stone Walls and Sugar Maples: An Ecology for Northeasterners*. Appalachian Mountain Club, 1979.

Harris, Stuart K., et al. *AMC Field Guide to Mountain Flowers of New England*. AMC, 1977.

Henderson, Donald M., et al. *The Geology of the Crawford Notch Quadrangle,* N.H. Department of Resources and Economic Development, 1977.

Jorgensen, Neil. *A Guide to New England's Landscape*. Glove Pequot Press, 1977.

Jorgensen, Neil. *Sierra Club Naturalist's Guide to Southern New England*. Sierra Club, 1978.

Marchand, Peter J. *North Woods: An Inside Look at the Nature of Forests in the Northeast*. AMC, 1987.

Steele, Frederic L. *At Timberline: A Nature Guide to the Mountains of the Northeast*. Appalachian Mountain Club, 1983.

Steele, Frederic L., and Albion R. Hodgdon. *Trees and Shrubs of Northern New England*. Society for the Protection of New Hampshire Forests, 1975.

Thompson, Betty Flanders. *The Changing Face of New England*. Houghton Mifflin Company, 1977.

Thompson, Will F. "The Shape of New England Mountains," *Appalachia* (12/60, 6/61, 12/61). Appalachian Mountain Club.

Periodicals

Appalachia, Appalachian Mountain Club
New Hampshire Profiles
Mount Washington Observatory Bulletin

Bibliographies

Brent, Allen H. *Bibliography of the White Mountains*. New Hampshire Publishing Company, 1972 (revised).

Wright, Walter W. "The White Mountains: An Annotated Bibliography, 1918–1947," *Appalachia* (12/48). Appalachian Mountain Club.

APPENDIX

Four Thousand Footers

The Four Thousand Footer Club was formed in 1957 to bring together hikers who had traveled to some of the less frequently visited sections of the White Mtns. In 1957, such peaks as Hancock, Owl's Head, and West Bond were trailless and practically never climbed. Other listed peaks with trails were seldom climbed, and the problem of over-use was unknown, except in the Presidentials and Franconias. Today the Four Thousand Footer Club is composed of active hikers whose travels in the mountains have made them familiar with many different sections of the White Mountain backcountry, and with the problems which threaten to degrade the mountain experience that we have all been privileged to enjoy. The Four Thousand Footer Committee hopes that this broadened experience of the varied beauties of our beloved peaks and forests will encourage our members to work for the preservation and wise use of wild country, so that it may be enjoyed and passed on to future generations undiminished.

The Four Thousand Footer Club recognizes three lists of peaks: the White Mountain Four Thousand Footers, the New England Four Thousand Footers, and the New England Hundred Highest Peaks. To qualify for membership, a hiker must climb on foot to and from each summit on the list. Applicants need not be AMC members, although the Committee strongly urges all hikers who make considerable use of the trails to contribute to their maintenance in some manner. Membership in the AMC is one of the most effective means of assisting these efforts.

If you are seriously interested in becoming a member of the Four Thousand Footer Club, please send a self-addressed, stamped envelope to the Four Thousand

Footer Committee, Appalachian Mountain Club, 5 Joy Street, Boston MA 02108, and details will be sent to you. After climbing each Four Thousand Footer, please record the date of the ascent, companions, if any, and other remarks.

Criteria for mountains on the official list are: (1) each peak must be 4000 ft. high, and (2) each peak must rise 200 ft. above the low point of its connecting ridge with a higher neighbor. The latter qualification eliminates such peaks as Clay, Franklin, North Carter, Guyot, Little Haystack, South Tripyramid, Lethe, Blue, and Jim. All 48 Four Thousand Footers are reached by well-defined trails, although the path to Owl's Head and some short spur trails to other summits are not officially maintained.

Following are the official lists of the Four Thousand Footers in NH, ME, and VT. Applicants for the White Mountain Four Thousand Footer Club must climb all 48 peaks in NH, while applicants for the New England Four Thousand Footer Club must climb the twelve peaks in ME and the five in VT as well. The New England Hundred Highest Club list includes a substantial number of peaks without trails, of which two are on private land where advance permission to enter is required. A copy of the full list and related information can be obtained by sending a self-addressed, stamped envelope to the Committee at the address above.

On the following lists, elevations have been obtained from the latest USGS maps, some of which are now metric, requiring conversion from meters to feet. Where no exact elevation is given on the map, the elevation has been estimated by adding half the contour interval to the highest contour shown on the map; elevations so obtained are marked on the list with an asterisk.

FOUR THOUSAND FOOTERS IN NEW HAMPSHIRE

	Mountain	Elevation		Date
		(feet)	(meters)	Climbed
1.	Washington	6288	1917	___
2.	Adams	5774	1760	___
3.	Jefferson	5712	1741	___
4.	Monroe	5384*	1641*	___
5.	Madison	5367	1636	___
6.	Lafayette	5260*	1603*	___
7.	Lincoln	5089	1551	___
8.	South Twin	4902	1494	___
9.	Carter Dome	4832	1473	___
10.	Moosilauke	4802	1464	___
11.	Eisenhower	4761	1451	___
12.	North Twin	4761	1451	___
13.	Bond	4698	1432	___
14.	Carrigain	4680	1426	___
15.	Middle Carter	4610*	1405*	___
16.	West Bond	4540*	1384*	___
17.	Garfield	4500*	1372*	___
18.	Liberty	4459	1359	___
19.	South Carter	4430*	1350*	___
20.	Wildcat	4422	1348	___
21.	Hancock	4403	1342	___
22.	South Kinsman	4358	1328	___
23.	Osceola	4340*	1323*	___
24.	Flume	4328	1319	___
25.	Field	4326	1319	___

	Mountain	Elevation		Date Climbed
		(feet)	(meters)	
26.	Pierce (Clinton)	4310	1314	___
27.	Willey	4302	1311	___
28.	North Kinsman	4293	1309	___
29.	South Hancock	4274	1303	___
30.	Bondcliff	4265	1300	___
31.	Zealand	4260*	1298*	___
32.	Cabot	4170*	1271*	___
33.	East Osceola	4156	1267	___
34.	North Tripyramid	4140	1262	___
35.	Middle Tripyramid	4110	1253	___
36.	Cannon	4100*	1250*	___
37.	Passaconaway	4060	1237	___
38.	Hale	4054	1236	___
39.	Jackson	4052	1235	___
40.	Moriah	4049	1234	___
41.	Tom	4047	1234	___
42.	Wildcat E	4041	1232	___
43.	Owl's Head	4025	1227	___
44.	Galehead	4024	1227	___
45.	Whiteface	4010*	1222*	___
46.	Waumbek	4006	1221	___
47.	Isolation	4005	1221	___
48.	Tecumseh	4003	1220	___

FOUR THOUSAND FOOTERS IN MAINE

Mountain	Elevation (feet)	(meters)	Date Climbed
1. Katahdin, Baxter Peak	5267	1605	___
2. Katahdin, Hamlin Peak	4751	1448	___
3. Sugarloaf	4250*	1295*	___
4. Old Speck	4180	1274	___
5. Crocker	4168	1270	___
6. Bigelow, West Peak	4150	1265	___
7. North Brother	4143	1263	___
8. Saddleback	4116	1255	___
9. Bigelow, Avery Peak	4088	1246	___
10. Abraham	4049	1234	___
11. Saddleback, the Horn	4023	1226	___
12. South Crocker	4010*	1222*	___

FOUR THOUSAND FOOTERS IN VERMONT

Mountain	Elevation (feet)	(meters)	Date Climbed
1. Mansfield	4393	1339	___
2. Killington	4235	1291	___
3. Camel's Hump	4083	1244	___
4. Ellen	4083	1244	___
5. Abraham	4006	1221	___

List of Trails

Note: Trails marked by an asterisk do not have a separate description, but are discussed or mentioned in groups or within other trails' descriptions.

Index

A

B

C

214

NOTES

NOTES

NOTES

NOTES